D1478374

Lay Sanctity, Medieval and Modern

Lay Sanctity, Medieval and Modern
A Search for Models

ANN W. ASTELL, EDITOR

University of Notre Dame Press
Notre Dame, Indiana

BX
1920
.L39
2000

Copyright 2000
University of Notre Dame Press
Notre Dame, IN 46556
All Rights Reserved
Manufactured in the United States of America

Library of Congress Cataloging-in-Publication Data

Lay sanctity, medieval and modern : a search for models / Ann
    W. Astell, editor.
        p. cm.
        Includes bibliographical references and index.
        ISBN 0-268-01330-6 (cloth : alk. paper)
        ISBN 0-268-01332-2 (paper : alk. paper)
        1. Laity—Catholic Church—History of doctrines.
        2. Laity—Religious life—History. 3. Christian saints—
        History.
    I. Astell, Ann W.
    BX1920.L39 2000   99-38114
    262' . 142'09—dc21

The paper used in this publication meets the minimum require-
ments of the American National Standard for Information
Sciences—Permanence of Paper for Printed Library Materials,
ANSI Z39.48–1984

For My Mother,
And All the Everyday Saints

Table of Contents

Acknowledgments

The first inspiration for this collection of essays came at a particular time, place, and occasion, when many of the contributors were gathered, in October 1992, at the International Schoenstatt Center in Wisconsin for an academic conference, entitled "Toward a Lay Spirituality for the Postmodern Era." The setting was conducive for genuine conversation among the participants. As we shared ideas, we realized that we could not speak meaningfully about lay spirituality without talking about lay sanctity and lay saints. We were troubled by the dearth of canonized lay persons. We knew, too, that we could not look ahead into "the postmodern era" (which is, in many ways, already upon us) without looking back with new eyes into the past, when the very words "laity" and "sanctity" were defined and redefined for us.

The first "thank you" must, therefore, go to the sponsors and organizers of that conference and to Father Joseph Kentenich (1885–1968), the founder of Schoenstatt, whose memory the conference honored. The second "thank you" goes to the contributors, whose enthusiasm has nourished mine, and whose patient work, waiting, revision, and untiring hope have made this collection in its present form a reality.

Working together has given us a keener awareness of our communion not only with each other but also with the saints in heaven whose lives and writings we have been studying, and who have interceded for us. I wish to acknowledge in particular Paul Parent, a saintly colleague of mine at Purdue University, who died on the Feast of All Saints in 1997. That night I entrusted the fate of *Lay Sanctity, Medieval and Modern* to his prayers. On the day of Paul's funeral, James Langford, the director of the University of Notre Dame Press, called to request a submission of the manuscript.

More "miracle" stories like this could be told. Here, however, I wish to thank James Langford, John McCudden, who copyedited the manuscript, and all the people at the press at Notre Dame for their commitment to this work and their belief in its importance. Without their vision and skill, this book simply would not be.

I want to acknowledge gratefully the anonymous readers of the manuscript, whose comments have affirmed its value, strengthened its cohesion, and caught occasional mistakes. Among its readers, however, Daniel Bornstein deserves my greatest gratitude. We have never met, but our correspondence on questions relating to historical sanctity has been enormously helpful to me. Indeed, from the first beginnings of this project, he has been my best advisor and teacher and the source of unflagging encouragement.

Another teacher of mine, Sherry Reames, deserves grateful mention here. Her writings on medieval saints' legends, especially on the *Legenda Aurea,* and her leadership in promoting hagiographic scholarship worldwide have been an inspiration to me. She and Thomas Head, another acknowledged leader in the field, were among those who participated in the 1992 conference and who have given me courage for this project.

Last but not least, I wish to thank all those special people in my life whose striving for simple, everyday sanctity has made tangible God's holiness and loving-kindness. To one of them, my mother, this collection is affectionately dedicated.

ANN W. ASTELL

Introduction

ANN W. ASTELL

> *The greatest in the Kingdom of Heaven are not the ministers, but the saints.*
>   Pope Paul VI

> *What we are looking for are saints of the ordinary.*
>   Peter Gumpel

> *The castaway cannot be made into a "saint."*
>   Michel de Certeau

Most previous studies that have conjoined the topics of "sanctity" and "laity" have explored them from the perspective of medieval popular religion, in order to define the cultural relationship of patronage between the saints and the laypeople who went on pilgrimage to saints' shrines.[1] They have, in short, been interested in the relationship of the laity *to* the saints, rather than in the laity's shifting historical understanding of themselves *as* saints, as people called to sanctity. Given the relative paucity of canonized commoners, the historical tendency to separate the "saints" from the "laity" as distinct groups and callings is not altogether without warrant.[2] In the wake of Catholic Action, Vatican Council II (1962–65) emphasized the universal call to holiness, but as Kenneth Woodward has shown, among the saints and *beati* officially recognized by the Catholic Church since 1588, "the one group which is clearly underrepresented is the laity."[3]

As the essays in this interdisciplinary collection suggest, the apparent binary opposition between the "saints" and the "laity" cannot simply be resolved by procedural reforms in the existing canonization process; rather, that process itself must be seen as but one part of a complex historical development. Looking back across two millennia of church history, we find that not only is the definition of "laity" multiple and shifting, depending on the contrastive term with which it is paired, but also the understanding of sanctity has undergone successive revision. Mapping the changing areas of overlap and intersection between these two spheres, which are never totally distinct, is the chief concern of this introduction.

The representation of laity among the saints was greatest during the age of martyrs in the early church. It remained relatively high during the patristic and medieval periods, when the functional and formative distinctions between the clergy and the laity were less pronounced than they became at the time of the Counter-Reformation. In those early periods, clergy and laity shared a numinous, quasi-monastic idea of sanctity, from which the criteria that came to be used in the canonization process derived. The twentieth-century church evinces a blurring of clerical and lay function and formation similar to that in premodern times, but its modernist inheritance has given the laity an ideal of "secular" sanctity that, by its very definition, diverges widely from the "religious" sanctity which has become normative in canonization. Whereas laymen and laywomen of the Middle Ages could aspire to sanctity by approximating the ascetical, world-renouncing lifestyle of the monks, present-day laity must excel in the this-worldly apostolate that is judged proper to them as laypersons. For such a secular sanctity, however, there are (and perhaps can be) few ecclesially recognized models.

The essays in *Lay Sanctity* focus on a series of specific historical personages and movements in order to address a set of recurring questions: What actually distinguishes the spirituality and the sanctity of the laity from that of the religious? To what extent must the laity orient themselves toward monastic ideals and practices in their pursuit of holiness? Is it really possible to become holy "in the world," or must one retreat from it? Does marital sex, the ownership of property, and involvement in politics impede sanctity, or at least the recognition of sanctity by the church, and if so, why? Is lay sanctity something inferior to religious sanctity? Why have so few lay saints been canonized, with the result that there are few canonically recognized models of lay sanctity?

The search for theoretical and personal models of lay sanctity takes two directions in this volume. Some of the contributors look at twentieth-century men and women who consciously aspired to holiness, whose lives have inspired others, but who have not yet been canonized, whereas other contributors look to the lay saints of the past. Not unlike many feminist scholars, who are unearthing the early writings of women in order to discover the "lost voices" of the "lost mothers" who can serve as models for women today, the latter contributors are engaged in a search for historical models of lay sanctity. This involves a revisioning of the lay saints of medieval times, who have frequently been represented to us as "religious" figures, but who in their own time were regarded as (at least relatively) lay, and who struggled to reconcile their lay status with their call to sanctity. Such a postmodern revisioning of saintly *legenda* asks a frankly anachronistic question: "To what extent can the lives of early lay saints be seen as an anterior 'response' to the imperatives of Vatican Council II? What can they, when viewed as laypeople, teach us?"

Feminist theory helps to explain not only the dialogic method but also the content of this collection, which gives prominence to women saints. Whereas men (even married men) can be admitted to the priesthood, women (even women in religious orders) are always canonically "lay." In relation to the male clergy, moreover, the faithful as a whole are regularly gendered as feminine.[4] The laity, in short, has a distinctly feminine face, and this holds true for the (male or female) lay saint.

At several different levels, then, this collection in its two directions puts the twentieth-century church in dialogue with its medieval "other," across the gap of the early modern period. Our medieval "other self" is both extraordinarily familiar and amazingly strange, and that recognition of sameness and difference is important to our understanding of ourselves. We must first know whence we have come, and who and what have shaped our definitions of "laity" and "sanctity," before we can see and decide where we are headed.

Let me begin this backward look by comparing and contrasting the views of two medieval contemporaries, Heloise, the abbess of the Paraclete (†1164), and St. Bernard of Clairvaux (†1153). Heloise's understanding reconciles lay status with the universal evangelical vocation to holiness in a way that looks backward to the patristic period, whereas Bernard's view crystallizes the new, medieval outlook, which effectively separates the two terms widely along a hierarchical, Platonic, and characteristically feudal axis. As we shall see, the Counter-Reformation in many ways maintained this Bernardine *scala,* even as it laid the foundations for a genuine lay asceticism at its lower rung. The modern separation of church and state tended to reinforce the notion of two different ways to holiness, but it also led the church to attach a greater importance to the this-worldly way of the laity. In the twentieth century, the church's renewed affirmation of both the lay apostolate and lay sanctity harkens back in striking ways to early Christianity and the ecclesial *memoria* evoked by Heloise. Precisely that "return," however, enables us to measure the degree to which our definitions of both "laity" and "sanctity" have changed and are changing.

Heloise's own status is notoriously problematic. When viewed as the lover, then the wife of Peter Abelard (†1142), and the mother of his son, Heloise is a laywoman who has been forcibly separated from her spouse. Seen from another perspective as a cloistered nun under the spiritual direction of a castrated and converted Abelard, who has in the meantime been ordained a priest, she is a vowed religious. The salutations of the personal letters between Heloise and Abelard highlight this problem as the two struggle to name themselves and each other properly.[5] In the so-called Letters of Direction, Heloise poses the question of status in more general terms when she as abbess writes to Abelard, asking him to teach her "how the order of nuns began and what authority there is for our profession."[6]

In framing the question, Heloise emphasizes that the Gospel precepts call all Christians to holiness and cautions against any prideful attempt "to go beyond" the Gospel and "be more than Christians" (p. 164) through the imposition of merely human rules. As a religious, Heloise resists the simple equation of ecclesiastical ranking, on the one hand, with degrees of holiness, on the other, and she does so in two directions, toward what is above (the clergy) and what is below (the laity). First, she observes that "the virtue of continence and also of abstinence makes us [nuns] the equals of the rulers of the Church themselves and of the clergy who are confirmed in holy orders." Second, she expresses the wish that she and her sisters "could equal religious laymen" in holiness. Calling to mind married biblical heroes like Abraham, David, and Job, Heloise cautions against underestimating the "religion of the laity." She calls upon the authority of St. John Chrysostom (†407), who in his seventh sermon on the Letter to the Hebrews reminds the laity that the biblical precepts apply to all Christians without exception:

> For [Paul] wrote these things not only for monks but for all who were in the cities, and the layman should not have greater freedom than the monk, apart from sleeping with his wife. He has permission for this, but not for other things; and in everything he must conduct himself like a monk. The Beatitudes too, which are the actual words of Christ, were not addressed to monks alone, otherwise the whole world must perish. (p. 164)

From this passage Heloise infers, first, that the holiness proper to the laity is quasi-monastic, and second, that "monastic perfection" consists in simply adding "the virtue of continence to the precepts of the Gospel"—a conclusion that Abelard subsequently challenges and corrects in a discussion of the three evangelical counsels enjoined upon religious: poverty, chastity, and obedience.

   In her emphasis on the biblical call addressed to all believers, Heloise recalls the situation of the early church, when the fundamental distinction was the external one, dividing the "people of God" (as a chosén λαός) from the pagans, rather than the internal division between the masses (λαϊκός) of believers and the clerical hierarchy, a functional division that profoundly altered the meaning of "laity" from the third century on.[7] Her focus on continence (rather than poverty and obedience) is similarly biblical and is drawn from the epistles of Paul, who in 1 Corinthians 7:1–40 delineates the *ordo* of consecrated virgins and widows in contradistinction to that of the married. Finally, in quoting Chrysostom's plea to the laity, in which he exhorts them to remember that they are called to sanctity even as the monks are, she introduces yet another conceptual pairing that harkens back to the post-Constantinian age.

   Whereas Christians of all kinds had met their deaths as martyrs during the Roman persecutions and thus achieved perfect conformity to Christ crucified, in a superficially Christianized society only the ascetics who, like St. Anthony of Egypt (†356), embraced mortifications tantamount to a living martyrdom, seemed to qualify for sanctity. When the arduous life of the desert hermits eventually gained a regular communal form in the West in the Benedictine monasteries, beginning in the sixth century, the laity who remained "in the world" outside of the cloister felt, as André Vauchez phrases it, professionally "disqualified, a priori, in the pursuit of sanctity" and "shifted to the monks the burden of mediation between heaven and earth without which, all contemporaries agreed, no society could survive."[8] This burden clearly weighs heavily upon Heloise, whose biblical (and philosophically Stoic) ideal of holiness extends to all Christians alike, and which, to the extent that it admits distinctions, finds the last to be first, and power perfected precisely in the "weakness" of the laity (p. 164).[9]

Abelard's great theological opponent, Bernard of Clairvaux, offers a view of the various ranks within the church that is strikingly different from that of Heloise. Referring to Luke 10:38–41, he pointedly associates the laity with Martha, the cloistered religious with Mary, to indicate that the *claustrales* have indeed chosen the "better part" and achieved a true conversion of heart through the radical renunciation of earthly desires and concerns.[10] In his allegorical interpretation of the reference to Noah, Daniel, and Job in Ezechiel 14:14, Bernard presents these Old Testament figures as types of the three respective social orders within the church: prelates, consecrated virgins and celibates, and married people.[11] These "tres ordines Ecclesiae" occupy ranked positions on a Platonic ladder, with the laity represented by Job at the bottom because of their total immersion in material things and secular pursuits. In Bernard's view, the vowed religious take spiritual precedence over the secular clergy because of their angelic detachment from possessions and power. In crossing the turbulent sea of life, Bernard says, the Daniel-like religious use a bridge high above the water; the prelates, following Noah, take a boat; and the Joban laity, the *plebs Domini*, wade and swim. Each group faces dangers, but the way of the laity, whom Bernard equates with the married (*ordo conjugatorum*), is especially perilous, long, hard, and beset with temptations—so much so that most laypersons perish on the journey and only a few pass safely through the waves of this world ("inter undas hujus saeculi [alias mundi]"). In contrast, Bernard avers, the monastic way is universally recognized as shorter, easier, and more secure than any other path to God.[12]

Bernard's tripartite social theory of the *praelati, continentes, et conjugati* repeats with a critical, parodic difference the familiar feudal division of Christendom into those who fight (*bellatores*), those who pray (*oratores*), and those who work (*laboratores*).[13] In both schemes the lay commoners at the foot of the body politic occupy the bottom rung of the social ladder, close to the land that they, typically poor and illiterate, work with their hands.[14] Bernard's model, however, answers to the constant struggle for temporal power between the secular and ecclesiastical leadership in medieval Christendom by conjoining the *bellatores* and *laboratores*. Bernard emphasizes the lay status of nobles and commoners alike as married people *(conjugati)* and distinguishes them not from each other but from the diocesan clergy and the religious, the two groups that feudal theory had lumped together as *oratores*. Dispensing temporal goods, the laity are irreducibly "in the world," tainted by it, and incapable of "leaving" it. Bernard's Platonism, in short, tends to distinguish sharply between matter and spirit, transitory and eternal things, and thus to oppose laymen to clerics and religious in an antithetical pairing. For Bernard, like Gratian, there are two kinds of Christians.[15]

This fundamental opposition, however, is further extended when Bernard suggestively subordinates the secular clergy *(praelati)* and the laity *(conjugati)* alike to the otherworldly ideal attained by the cloistered *continenti*, whose profession is prayer. Against the virtual (albeit strained and often contentious) identification of church and state during the Middle Ages—an identification symbolized in the quasi-sacerdotal anointing and sacramental coronation of kings— Bernard proclaimed a sanctity of radical withdrawal from the world into the "desert" of monastic enclosures; of the voluntary renunciation of earthly power, wealth, and pleasure; of an exceeding desire for, and actual angelic anticipation of, the contemplative bliss of heaven.

Rather than undermining the structures of feudalism, however, Bernard's ecstatic monasticism served to strengthen them by giving them, as it were, a visible soul, a substantial form, an other with which they could identify—most characteristically, perhaps, in the ritualized *desiderium* of courtly love; in the sacramental signs and asceticism of the "new chivalry"; and in Bernard's own charismatic creation: the Knights Templar and what Jean Leclercq has called the "Crusader mystique."[16] To a fascinated Europe, Bernard preached the Second Crusade (c. 1145) and issued a call to arms that sounded a new lay vocation. Through martial pilgrimage to the Holy Land, the penitential hardships of travel and warfare, and actual death on the battlefield, the layman—like the monk—could find a way to "leave the world" and enter the New Jerusalem.

Striking as the differences are between the views of Bernard and Heloise, they agree in pointing to the monk as the model for all holiness. Heloise seconds the dictum of Chrysostom that the layman "must conduct himself like a monk," and Bernard exhorts the Templars and crusaders, kings and commoners alike, to a monastic discipline. As Richard Kieckhefer and others have argued, beginning with the cult of St. Martin of Tours (†397), the preeminence of the monk as a saintly exemplar during the Middle Ages caused holiness itself to be generally defined in a way that valorized the contemplative life of prayer and study over the active life of works of mercy, virginity over marriage, extraordinary ascetical practices over the faithful fulfillment of duties, and "leaving the world" over temporal involvement.[17]

This monastic template had three important consequences. First, it encouraged the canonization of saintly monks and clerics whose lives directly conformed to this model. Second, it sometimes triggered what Vauchez has termed "serious disagreement"[18] between the hierarchy and the faithful, who spontaneously venerated as saints persons who were unlikely candidates (by monastic standards) for official recognition by the universal church. These controversies surrounded not only child saints like William of Norwich (†1144) and Simon of Trent (†1475), visionaries like St. Christina the Astonishing (†1224), and martyred heretics like Marguerite Porete (†1310) and St. Joan of Arc (†1431), but also simple friars like Marcolino of Forlì (†1397). Finally, as a third consequence, it gave a monastic coloring to both the self-image and the hagiographic reception of lay saints, so much so that, by the standards of contemporary theology, relatively few medieval saints are unequivocably "lay."

Lay Sanctity during the Middle Ages

As we have seen, the medieval monasteries were the heirs and spiritual descendants of the desert fathers and mothers of the fourth and fifth centuries—among the most famous of which were Paul the Simple (†339), Paul the Hermit (†342), Anthony of Egypt (†356), Joseph of Egypt (†394), Isidore of Alexandria (†404), Moses the Black (†405), Thalelaeus the Hermit (†450), and the legendary penitent Mary of Egypt (5th c.). From a purely functional perspective, these early hermits were "lay"—that is, very few of them were ordained priests, and they tended to offer a charismatic challenge to the secular clergy in its new alliance with civil authority. From an ascetical perspective, on the other hand, they were archetypally "religious" (and therefore nonlay) in their death to, and departure from, the "world." The hermitages of late antiquity thus gave birth to the monasteries. In the Middle Ages, however, the communal regularization of religious life in the monasteries tended to displace contemporary hermits and solitaries once again in the direction of the laity. St. Gerlac (†1170), for instance, a hermit in the Netherlands, refused to enter a religious order. The neighboring monks considered his vocation anomalous and tried to force the bishop to make him join them. Frustrated in their attempt, the monks grew embittered, calumniated Gerlac, and even refused him the sacraments as he lay dying. Although never officially canonized, Gerlac inspired local veneration among the people who claimed him as "their" saint.

If, in comparison with monks, hermits like Gerlac had a relatively lay status, the same can be said of the lay brothers who—like Bd. Franco of Grotti (†1291), a Carmelite; Bd. Thomas Corsini (†1345), a Servite; and Bd. James of Bitetto (†1485), a Franciscan—attended to the mundane affairs (cooking, gardening, cleaning) of the houses of their orders. Similarly, the Beguines of the Netherlands, inspired first by Bd. Mary of Oignies (†1213) and later by Bd. Gertrude of Delft (†1358), among others, were lay in comparison with the nuns of their times because, although professing chastity and obedience and living a form of communal life (albeit without solemn vows), they yet maintained private property, supported themselves, and placed considerable emphasis on active good works.[19]

Like the Lombard tertiaries of the Humiliati before them, Franciscan and Dominican tertiaries, beginning with Bd. Luchesio (†1260) and his wife, Bonadonna, strove to live the religious life while remaining in the world, but for many of them that entailed not only charitable works but also contemplative prayer, visions, and ascetical practices that rivaled the ecstasies and mortifications of the early ascetics. Among these medieval tertiaries were consecrated virgins like St. Rose of Viterbo (†1252) and St. Catherine of Siena

(†1380), who were relatively lay by medieval (that is, monastic) standards, but who appear religious to twentieth-century eyes—so much so that Vauchez points to them as evidence of the mendicant "monasticization of the laity."[20]

The strong tendency of medieval lay saints to "conduct themselves as monks" in their pursuit of holiness (as Chrysostom had advised the laity to do), albeit in adaptation to different settings and circumstances, led many married couples to virginal or continent marriages and/or to eventual separation, as the spouses left each other and the world to enter religious houses. The pattern of the virginal but happily married couple, engaged as brother and sister in good works—almsgiving, hospitality, nursing the sick in homes-turned-hospitals—emerges early in the lives of Sts. Julian and Basilissa (circa 300) and inspired imitation throughout the Middle Ages. The virginal marriages of St. Cunegund (†1033) to St. Henry of Bavaria, of Bd. Mary of Oignies (†1213) to her husband John, of St. Elzéar (†1323) to Bd. Delphine, of Bd. Joan Mary de Maillé (†1414) to Robert de Sillé, and later, that of St. Helen of Bologna (†1520), are outstanding examples.[21]

Other saints—Hedwig of Silesia (†1243) and Catherine of Genoa (†1510), for instance—severely limited or renounced altogether sexual relations within marriage after securing the hard-won consent of their spouses. A number of these holy wives—Margery Kempe (†1439) is perhaps the most famous example—suffered great inner turmoil over the loss of their virginity and sought to regain it through penitential practices. Indeed, medieval moral theologians attached such a negative valence to the conjugal act that St. Elizabeth (†1231) and Bd. Ludwig (†1227) of Thuringia stand out in the roster of officially recognized medieval saints as a rare example of a happily married couple, who combined outstanding charity to the poor and civil leadership, on the one hand, with marital affection and the rearing of children, on the other.[22]

Frequently a virtuous couple would agree to separate in order that one or both might pursue a monastic or eremitical life. This pattern first gained legendary expression in the fifth-century romance of Sts. Andronicus and Athanasia and then inspired imitation by such medieval saints as Bd. Santuccia (†1305), Bd. Maurice of Hungary (†1336), St. Conrad of Piacenza (†1351), Bd. James of Lodi (†1404), Bd. Mark of Montegallo (†1497), and St. Nicholas

von Flüe (†1487). The conduct of the many widowers and widows—
St. Angela of Foligno (†1309), Bd. Clare of Rimini (†1346), St.
Bridget of Sweden (†1373), and Bd. Helen of Udine (†1458), for
example—who, after the death of their spouses, devoted themselves
to extreme ascetical practices as solitaries and penitents or who
joined religious orders, may be considered a variation on this theme
of eremetical separation.

If the marked trajectory of the lives of these *conjugati* "away from
the world" ultimately limits their lay status and vocation, other lay
saints display a distinctly lay sanctity through their perseverance in
the lay state, the exemplary fulfillment of their duties, charitable
almsgiving and service to others, fervent prayer, and the patient endurance of trials. From the early Middle Ages on, as Vauchez notes,
"the perfect fulfillment of state duties" was a recognized way of
sanctity for "kings, queens, and more generally, those who wielded
power."[23] Rulers instrumental in the Christianization of their kingdoms and those outstanding for their almsgiving to the poor and
foundational support of religious houses were prime candidates for
the honors of the altar. In the later Middle Ages the "perfect ac-
complishment" of other callings began to be recognized as possible
ways of holiness, partly as a result of the increasing recognition of
the imitability of living saints and the need for patrons specific to
the various guilds and occupational groups. As Vauchez observes,
beginning in the twelfth and thirteenth centuries, a changing,
more complex society experienced "a need to diversify religious
experience."[24]

Among these saints of other callings, St. Homobonus of
Cremona (†1197) sets the pattern.[25] The first lay commoner to be
canonized (1199), Homobonus was a married man, a tailor outstanding for his honest business practices and almsgiving in the
midst of a Lombardy notorious for fraudulent greed. If merchants
sought in a special way to follow the example of Homobonus, commoners engaged in other occupations also had their exemplars,
among them, St. Dominic of the Causeway (†1109); St. Gualfardus
(†1127), a saddler; St. Isidore of Madrid (†1130), a husbandman;
St. Allucio of Tuscany (†1134), a shepherd and herdsman; St.
Theobald of Alba (†1150), a cobbler and porter; St. Bénezet the
Bridgebuilder (†1184); Bd. Novellone (†1280), a shoemaker; Bd.
Peter of Siena (†1289), a combmaker; Sts. Zita (†1278) and

Notburga (†1313), both of them household servants; and Bd. Bonavita (†1375), a blacksmith.

If active works and particular occupations distinguish these lay saints, sufferings distinguish others—not, however, the self-imposed mortifications of the ascetics and penitents, but rather the unasked for sufferings, patiently and redemptively endured by innocent victims. Included among these are five different kinds of "sufferers" or "cross-bearers":[26] the child saints, especially the reputed victims of ritual murder; the nonresistant victims of political persecution; the peacemaking matrons who, like Bd. Zdislava of Bohemia (†1252), St. Elizabeth of Portugal (†1336), Bd. Dorothy of Montau (†1394), and St. Rita of Cascia (†1457), heroically endured and helped to convert abusive husbands; the mother saints, who sorrowed and sacrificed for their children;[27] and those who, like the poor orphaned paralytic St. Fina of Tuscany (†1253) and the bedridden young mystic Bd. Lydwina of Schiedam (†1433), endured terrible diseases and deformity as a share in the cross of Christ.

Lay Sanctity and the Reformation

As the preceding roster of saints suggests, and as André Vauchez and Daniel Bornstein have argued convincingly, the church in the late Middle Ages had begun to accord greater prominence to lay saints, broadly defined as such.[28] Martin Luther (†1546), the Augustinian monk of Erfurt and Wittenberg, was less alone, therefore, than many have supposed, when he turned away from the monastery and "toward the world" in an effort to remind a Christendom in need of reform that sanctity is "a duty laid on every Christian living in the world," not the business of a few specialists.[29] The time of the Reformation saw a greater emphasis on the spiritual formation of the laity in Catholic and Protestant circles alike. In the Catholic Church, however, the education and formation of the laity was part of a two-tiered renewal that supported the development of the notion of two kinds of holiness—one secular and lay, the other clerical and religious. In general, only the latter was subject to canonization.

Whereas Protestant Christians rejected the need for mediation through priests and saints alike, the Catholic Church defended both. Indeed, the double nature of the Protestant challenge indirectly led to a clericalization of the cult of the saints. The Council of

Trent (1545–63) vigorously reaffirmed the veneration of the saints and their relics, on the one hand, and the functional distinction between the Catholic laity and hierarchy, on the other. In a related series of papal decrees, the process of canonization was reformed so that, in the words of Kenneth Woodward, "what was once a populist process" came to rest "largely in the hands of canon lawyers."[30] In 1588 Pope Sixtus V "created the Congregation of Rites and gave its officials responsibility for preparing papal canonizations."[31] Not long afterwards, during the pontificate of Urban VIII (1623–44), the papacy gained complete control over the process. In a final development, Prospero Lambertini, a canonist in the Congregation of Rites who later became Pope Benedict XIV, gave magisterial expression to "the Church's theory and practice of making saints" in his five-volume *De Servorum Dei beatificatione et Beatorum canonizatione* (1734–38).[32]

Even more important, perhaps, than these procedural changes, according to which candidates for sainthood were judged by clergymen and according to religious standards, were the broader developments in spiritual formation and spirituality. On July 15, 1563, the Council of Trent ordered the establishment of episcopal seminaries for the training of priests, a conciliar decree that was implemented by Pope Gregory VIII (1572–85) through the instrumentality of the Jesuits, who at that time, according to Dom Charles Poulet, "numbered no less than 5,000 religious, 110 houses, and 21 provinces."[33] A formative difference thus corroborated the functional distinction between the laity and the clergy.

At the same time, the spirituality of St. Ignatius of Loyola (†1556) fostered the idea of a specifically lay holiness to complement the holiness of priests and religious. As Robert E. McNally observes, "In the spiritual doctrine of Ignatius obedience to the Church is of prime importance."[34] In his emphasis on "enlightened orthodoxy," "absolute obedience," and service, Ignatius "broke ruthlessly with the monastic and mendicant tradition of the medieval Church."[35] Whereas the monastics had stressed virginity, and the mendicants poverty, Ignatius found the essence of holiness in obedience to Christ the King, an obedience that showed itself concretely in committed service to the church.

To such a holiness, the layperson within a hierarchical church could certainly aspire, and the Jesuits of the Catholic Reform devoted

themselves to the instruction of priests and laity alike. The formation given to the two groups varied, however. The Jesuits themselves
and the clergy under their spiritual direction made use of the
Ignatian *Spiritual Exercises,* which, according to McNally, "were never
intended to be a popular devotion. On the contrary, in their fullness they were most normally reserved to a select few, to men of special quality, influence, sanctity, education, and capability," to "men
of talent" who could be transformed into the "saints and leaders" of
the Catholic Reform.[36] By way of contrast, the formation of the laity
was usually based on only the first part of the *Exercises,* and it tended
to emphasize simple catechetical instruction, "morality, and imitation" over charism and mysticism.[37]

If the gap between asceticism and mysticism set the holiness of
the laity apart from that of priests and religious, it also distinguished
modern spirituality as a whole from medieval spirituality. Martin
Luther rejected the high mysticism of the medieval saints, and, as
Heiko Oberman has noted, "Protestant reference books and man-
uals of the late seventeenth and eighteenth century rarely lead to
genuine mysticism."[38] Similarly, in Catholic circles, there was a new
emphasis on asceticism. As Kees Waaijman has reminded us, "the
term *ascetical theology,* unknown to the Fathers in the Middle Ages,
emerged for the first time in the seventeenth century."[39] Spiritual
guidebooks, many of them authored by Jesuits, set forth practices
leading to the goal of Christian perfection—spiritual exercises that
were identified with a modernist "self-sanctification." "This ascetical
genre," according to Waaijman, "was to shape the entire development of the eighteenth and nineteenth centuries and to persist
right into the twentieth."[40]

The ascetical turn in the modern theory of spirituality had its first
beginnings in the practices of the Reformation. As Peter Burke has
shown, Catholic and Protestant reformers alike aimed at the reform
of popular culture in Europe, and that effort affected the laity in
negative and positive ways. In its negative manifestations, it entailed
"the triumph of Lent over Carnival," that is, the puritanical suppres-
sion of religious drama, liturgical parody, dancing, singing, and
many local customs associated with particular feast days. Leaders on
both sides were filled with a fear of irreverence that marks "a major
shift in religious sensibility," and they set out either to modify or to
destroy "the traditional familiarity with the sacred." The end result

was that "the separation between the sacred and the profane . . . became much sharper than it had been in the Middle Ages."[41]

In its positive manifestations, reform meant the religious education of the laity and their increased participation in church leadership. The Jesuits founded counter-reformist Marian sodalities for lay leaders, beginning in the sixteenth century (1567). Catholics and Protestants alike had their lay missionaries and martyrs, among whom St. Thomas More (†1535) is perhaps the most famous.[42] Both sides endeavored to reach the literate through translations of the Bible and the publication of catechisms and other forms of pious reading. In 1600, for instance, the Antwerp Jesuits published Thomas à Kempis's *Imitation of Christ* and thus gave new life among the laity to the *devotio moderna* popularized by Gerard Groote (1340–84) and the Brethren of the Common Life. Both emphasized Christian family life and the dignity of labor, which gave rise to the popular seventeenth-century Catholic cults of the Holy Family and St. Joseph and supported the 1622 canonization of St. Isidore the ploughman. Both sides explored new communal forms. In Catholic circles, St. Frances of Rome's 1440 foundation of a society of laywomen dedicated to God and the poor was followed by the foundations of other lay communities by Bd. Margaret of Ravenna (†1505), St. Angela Merici (†1540), St. Philip Neri (†1595), Bd. Hippolytus Galantini (†1619), Mary Ward (†1646), and Bd. Henry the Shoemaker (†1666).[43]

In the seventeenth century a puritanical Jansenism among Catholics (parallel to pietism among Protestants) was countered by saints like Vincent de Paul (†1660) and Francis de Sales (†1622), who exhorted the laity to charitable works and who served as spiritual directors to a group of remarkable women—happily married wives, devoted mothers, resourceful widows—many of whom became the foundresses of new women's communities. Among them were Sts. Barbara Acarie (†1618), Joan de Lestonnac (†1640), Jane Frances de Chantal (†1641), and Louisa de Marillac (†1660). For Madame de Charmoisy, de Sales wrote his *Introduction to the Devout Life* (1608), which may be regarded as a founding document for the redefinition of lay sanctity in modern times.

Like Ignatius of Loyola before him, de Sales found the essence of holiness in a loving attachment to the will of God, an attachment which must be displayed at all times and in every place, independent of sensible pleasure or displeasure, and even in the smallest matters ("chosettes"). Firm in his insistence that each state of life entailed its own way of practical holiness, de Sales advised the laity under his spiritual direction not to "conduct themselves like monks," but to devote themselves to the fulfillment of their everyday duties, to doing the ordinary things extraordinarily well. He distinguished between the "purely contemplative, monastic, and religious devotion" that cannot be exercised while "living under the pressure of worldly affairs," and the devotion "adapted to bring perfection to those living in the secular state," whether in the "regiment of soldiers, the mechanic's shop, the court of princes, or the home of married people."[44]

Lay Sanctity in the Modern Church

In principle, the Salesian understanding of all the different ways of holiness as various expressions of obedience to God's will moved beyond the late-medieval tendency to draw a correspondence between the three traditional states (lay, clerical, and religious), the three "lives" (active, mixed, and contemplative), and the three degrees of holiness (Do-Wel, Do-Bet and Do-Best). In practice, however, the church continued to regard the holiness of the laity as a lesser holiness that, because of its very ordinariness, could not and did not distinguish itself in canonized saints. The key criterion of obedience even in little things was, moreover, less easily brought to bear on the relatively irregular lives of laypersons than it was on the lives of religious—saints like the young Jesuit, St. John Berchmans (†1621), for example, who was outstanding for living in perfect conformity with his Rule.

The Salesian delineation of sacred and secular ways of holiness was, however, corroborated in the later modern period, especially in the aftermath of the American and French Revolutions, when decrees of religious toleration effectively separated the realms of church and state. This period, as Pope Pius XII observed, marks the decisive "origin of what is called the Catholic movements."[45] In the face of what Wolfhart Pannenberg has termed the desacralization of the public social order in the West, the Catholic Church, in particular, had to meet new spiritual and political challenges, which prompted a radical reconsideration of the role of the laity and of the importance of lay holiness.[46]

Whereas the medieval saint could choose to leave a "world" that was fundamentally Christian, and Christendom in turn found itself complemented and sustained by the "otherness" of the monastery, the modern Christian increasingly had no such "world" to leave. Indeed, from the eighteenth century on, the church found itself institutionally marginalized—to a degree that the monasteries within Christendom were not—by an autonomous world order newly independent and "come of age."[47] St. Bernard, as an oppositional voice, could sharply distinguish between the things of heaven and earth from within a sacramental Christian culture that pervasively joined them, but such an otherworldly spirituality could not satisfy the needs of the church in the new godless culture where religion was at best a private option.

Not surprisingly, therefore, the earliest papal documents on the lay apostolate date from the time of church/state separation, beginning with those issued by Popes Benedict XIV (1740–58) and Leo XII (1823–29) and leading to Pius X's *Il Fermo Proposito* (1905), the founding document of Catholic Action. As these early papal pronouncements make clear, however, the hierarchy tended at first to see the increased involvement of the laity in the service of the church as a sharing in the mission of the hierarchy rather than as the laity's fulfillment of their own distinct mission. The foreword to a 1961 collection of papal teachings on the subject is painfully careful to insist that the new emphasis in modern times on the apostolate of the laity does not "signify a reversal of the traditional system, nor an emancipation of the laity, as if the latter had at last come of age." Rather, the hierarchical appeals stem from "new needs": "the Church, now deprived of the natural support which she used to enjoy from Christian institutions, and handicapped in her apostolic activity by the dearth of priestly vocations, has been forced to ask for the help of all her children."[48] The documents of Vatican Council II, by way of contrast, emphasize the distinct, complementary vocations of the clergy and the laity.

A set of key terms—"Catholic Action," the "Action of Catholics," and the "apostolate of the laity"—which have been used to qualify the relationship of the Catholic layperson to the world, enable us to chart this apparent, gradual shift in the church's understanding of its own secularity. Much has been written about the primarily political focus of Catholic Action, its impact on Italian and South

American politics, its organizational testing of the extent of hierarchical control and lay autonomy, and its influence on the development of both papal social teaching and liberation theology.[49] The
other two terms, "Action of Catholics" and "apostolate of the laity,"
de-emphasize direct political involvement and party politics in particular to focus instead on complementary aspects of what recent
popes have called the *consecratio mundi*.[50]

If, as Pius XII admits, "It is certainly not easy to draw an exact line
of demarcation showing precisely where the true apostolate of the
laity begins,"[51] a brief look at the life of Antoine Frédéric Ozanam
(1813–53) indicates the three spheres of lay activity that have often
been called into prominence. A brilliant young French lawyer and lit-
erary scholar on the faculty of the Sorbonne, Ozanam has been
called "an exemplar of the lay apostolate in family, social and intellectual life."[52] Declared "venerable" by John Paul II in July 1993,
Ozanam was beatified by that same pope in the Cathedral of Notre
Dame during the World Youth Day held in Paris on August 22, 1997.
Ozanam's direct involvement in politics as a candidate for election
antedates Catholic Action. His 1833 foundation of a "conference of
charity" to promote practical work among the poor later became the
international Society of St. Vincent de Paul, an outstanding example
of what is often narrowly defined as "the Action of Catholics." His devotion to his wife and students, the living faith that animated his
prodigious scholarship, the charity that marked his intellectual ex-
changes with unbelievers and anti-Catholic colleagues—all evince the
leavenlike apostolate proper to the laity in their insertion into the
world (that is, the "apostolate of the laity" in its essential definition).

The question posed in 1951 by Pius XII whether or not the "ordinary performance of the duties of one's state by . . . millions of
conscientious and exemplary faithful" should be included in the
"lay apostolate" per se[53] gained an affirmative answer in the important theological reflections of Yves Congar and Karl Rahner on the
cosmological and eschatological dimensions of the Church[54] and
in the official documents of Vatican II (1962–65), which gave an
unprecedented formulation to an entire theology of the laity.
According to *Lumen Gentium,* all Christians are called to "the fullness of the Christian life and to the perfection of charity"; the laity
participate through baptism in the "priestly, prophetic, and kingly
functions of Christ"; and through baptism and confirmation Christ

himself has "commissioned" the laity to the lay apostolate whereby they "work for the sanctification of the world from within."[55]

Important as these theological formulations indubitably are, they need to be complemented by serious reflection on the spiritual formation necessary to prepare the laity for the recognition and then the fulfillment of their specific secular vocation. In general, as Rahner has warned, the recent emphasis on the participation of the laity in ecclesiastical ministries previously exercised by clerics (however great its immediate benefit) has distracted us from the more important and difficult task at hand: the work of spiritual formation. In Rahner's words, "Let us form laymen so that they can be Christians in the place where they are or should be—in the world. It is there that they must bear witness to Christ by their life. If they do this, then they are lay apostles."[56]

Lay Sanctity and the Postmodern Challenge

Unlike Chrysostom, who exhorted the laity of his time to "conduct themselves like monks," Pope Paul VI told his auditors at the Third World Congress of the Lay Apostolate in 1967, "You are not hermits who have withdrawn from the world in order to devote yourselves to God. It is in the world and in its activity that you must sanctify yourselves. The spirituality that should inspire you will, as a result, have its own characteristics."[57] The juxtaposition of quotes points to a paradigm shift in the church's understanding of lay sanctity, a shift which, in its profound implications for mystical and ascetical theology, has been compared to the rise of Neoplatonism in the third century.[58] If the laity are not to "conduct themselves as monks," what models of holiness are appropriate to them? What are the distinctive characteristics of their spirituality?

Historically speaking, the work of spiritual formation and the life-giving influence of particular spiritualities—e.g., Benedictine, Cistercian, Franciscan, Ignatian, and Carmelite—have been inextricably bound up with the exemplary lives and charisms of saints. The question of lay spiritual formation and lay apostolate, therefore, inevitably raises the more fundamental issue of lay sanctity and the model character of lay saints. Can the laity be "called to holiness" without being called to canonized sainthood? Given the dearth of canonized laity, where can we look to see examples of lay saints? What if popular sentiment recognizes the sanctity of laypersons—

Dorothy Day, for example—to whom the church is unlikely to give official recognition?

Unlike the medieval laity, who could aspire to sanctity by approximating a monastic lifestyle, modern laypersons are expected to strive for the secular holiness that is deemed proper to the lay apostolate. As Woodward and others have suggested, however, the criteria for canonization are often at odds with the church's current understanding of the layperson's calling. If the laity are to exercise a hidden apostolate, like leaven within the dough, transforming society and family life from within, then that very hiddenness and ordinariness preclude the extraordinary in its various forms—extreme penances, unusual charisms, physical miracle-working, mystical prayer, sexual renunciation, and voluntary poverty. The political involvement that is actually expected of the laity tends to exclude them from canonization, lest the church's recognition of them be put to partisan uses. Even if the layperson dies a martyr's death, unless the martyrdom is specifically "for the faith," rather than for the sake of justice or charity, for example, he or she cannot easily be admitted to the honors of the altar. The expectation that the life of the servant of God exhibit heroic virtue makes it, moreover, unlikely for penitents and children to be acknowledged as saints.

Some have suggested that the problem of the lay saint as a badly needed model for lay holiness could be solved, in part, by returning to earlier practices that distinguished between the "blesseds" and the "saints" and left the recognition of the former to the bishops.[59] Such a division, they say, would allow every diocese to honor outstanding Christians, to be assisted by their intercession, and to be inspired by their example. It would also serve to encourage a greater diversity among the *beati*. This proposal, however, also raises obvious objections. It would tend to perpetuate and solidify the modern, two-tiered understanding of holiness, according to which the laity can become "holy" without becoming "saints." It would also tend to separate the servants of God and the *beati* (as good examples of "heroic virtue") from the saints (as miracle-working intercessors), thus reinforcing the distance between the laity and the saints.[60] It would do nothing to change the papal process per se, which remains costly and time-consuming and which necessitates the sort of institutional support to which few laypersons can lay claim.

Since Vatican II, and especially during the pontificate of John Paul II (1978–), the church has recognized a remarkable number of saints and *beati,* but the intensified search for the lay saints whom Jesuit Peter Gumpel has called the "saints of the ordinary" has met with little success.[61] Excluding the laypersons included in groups of martyrs (of which there are many), only one layman, the physician Guiseppe Moscati (†1927) has been canonized between 1981 and 1993.[62] Among the twenty-nine open causes for canonization involving citizens of the United States, there are only two for laypeople, that of Bd. Kateri Tekakwitha (†1680), a Native American maiden, and Venerable Pierre Toussaint (†1853), a Haitian-born slave.[63] According to Gumpel, a member of the Congregation for the Causes of Saints, "part of the problem is . . . an incorrect idea of the church's notion of sainthood. . . . Rather than limiting its scope to prophets and stigmatics, the church in the post–Second Vatican Council era is looking for those who 'have done their duty constantly, joyfully. . . . person[s] who prayed, who [were] charitable to others' "[64] Few imitable laypersons, however, have inspired the requisite *fama sanctitatis*—a circumstance that awakens fear that the so-called "age of the laity" marks not only the triumph of what Bonhoeffer calls "cheap grace," but also the end of the "age of the saints."[65]

Weighing the potential cultural cost of the "passing of the saints," Jesuit theologian John A. Coleman doubts whether the existing formal canonization procedures can give us "the saints we need," and he worries with Kieckhefer about the trend toward a definition of sanctity that emphasizes the imitability of "hidden" and "little" saints like St. Thérèse of Lisieux (†1897) at the expense of the numinous and miraculous elements that have traditionally rendered sainthood "visible."[66] Indeed, Woodward has suggested that the effort to promote the causes of "ordinary saints" has actually impeded the speedy recognition of "extraordinary" saints, such as Padre Pio (†1968). Beatified by Pope John Paul II in 1999, Padre Pio was renowned already during his lifetime for his stigmata, charismatic gifts, and miracle-working, and he remains the popular center of a growing international cult. Not a "lay saint," Padre Pio is nevertheless a saint "for the people" in the classical sense, one whose remarkable gifts limit his imitability, even as they enhance his status as an intercessor.

We have, it seems, reached a point in which both "ordinary saints" (because of their hiddenness) and "extraordinary saints" (because of their inimitability) are a contradiction in terms. In a provocative essay on this topic, Coleman comments "on the absence of any vital ideal of sanctity in modern secular cultures" and asks a series of questions: "What kind of saint might be appropriate to modern, Western, secular societies?" "Where can we find [the necessary schools of sanctity] — equivalents of St. Anthony's desert or the medieval monastery—in the institutions of the modern West?" And finally, "Can there be saints—can there be hagiography—in an age of secularity?"

If Coleman is correct in his observation that "we have only vague ideas about what we might be striving for if we ourselves began to aspire to sainthood—a sainthood appropriate to our own age,"[67] then perhaps we can draw inspiration from the early Christian era, when the canon of saints included only martyrs. In the aftermath of the two world wars, Pope John Paul II has termed the twentieth century a new age of martyrs—a sentiment that resonates with the postmodern emphasis on "Auschwitz" as the symbol for what Edith Wyschogrod calls the "death event," the "normalization of death" in a global society where Auschwitz recurs and where life is increasingly "held cheap."[68]

Even as in the early church the recognition of sanctity in confessors and virgins took its bearings from the norm of martyrdom, so, too, the ideal of sanctity in the present age must be deconstructed and reconstructed from the perspective of Auschwitz.[69] In a pluralistic age in which the cross hangs heavily upon all alike—young and old, Christian and non-Christian, women and men, lay and clerical—perhaps the essence of holiness will be understood to be not chastity, poverty, or obedience, but rather the greatest of all gifts and virtues and the bond of their perfection, charity (1 Cor. 13). Perhaps new doctors and martyrs of charity will unfold a science of holiness that allows for what Barbara Newman terms a "mysticism of the mediated presence," for a contemplative knowledge of God in other human beings and in nature, for saintly marriages, for an asceticism of service to God in others, for works of social justice, for politics and peacemaking, and for moral miracles.[70]

As one symbol of this association of Auschwitz with a new ideal of sanctity, we need only point to the informal foundation in 1944 of a

Schoenstatt secular institute for married couples, now worldwide in its membership. Its first members were political prisoners at that time in the Nazi concentration camp at Dachau, along with Schoenstatt's founder, Father Joseph Kentenich (1885–1968) and Bd. Karl Leisner (1915–45). A martyr of the camp, young Karl Leisner aspired, in union with the members of his Schoenstatt group, to be, like and for Christ, a "victor in chains" *(victor in vinculis)*.[71]

As Peter Brown has eloquently demonstrated, the holy men and women in patristic times—unlike the Christocentric medieval saints who focused in their *imitatio Christi* on particular aspects of Christ's historical life (his prayer, his poverty, his virginity, his preaching, his works of charity, his suffering)—were simply Christ-bearers who endeavored to bring Christ himself, the *whole* Christ, to a world that had no knowledge of him. That *repraesentatio Christi* meant "making Christ present by one's own life in one's own age and region" as an *alter Christus;* it had a profoundly "revelatory quality" that allowed people the experience of a "double-vision," of actually seeing and encountering Christ in a beloved human being to whom one was attached, as a disciple to a teacher, a child to a father. Such saints were not just "good examples" (in the sense of Enlightenment pedagogy) or "patrons" (in the familiar sense of the medieval helpers), but organic intermediaries in whose human nearness Christ was uniquely present in a way that he had never been present on earth before.[72]

The Search for Models

Perhaps in the contemporary absence of ideas about sanctity and indeed about God himself, we are beginning to witness such a representational lay sanctity that will bring Christ to us in a myriad of new ways, new places, new faces. In this volume the search for new faces, for models of lay sanctity, looks both backwards and forwards and often into unexpected places that test the limits of our understanding of lay and saintly status. The arrangement of essays reflects a basic juxtaposition of medieval and twentieth-century paradigms of lay sanctity, while attempting to put the two in dialogue. That juxtaposition calls silent attention to the pivotal changes that occurred during the early modern period in the aftermath of the Reformation and Counter-Reformation.

Six of the contributing scholars—Mary Skinner, Kristine Utterback, Mary Walsh Meany, Karen Scott, Peter Pellegrin, and

Patricia Healy Wasyliw—seek to recover models for lay sanctity in early saints who have been represented to us as "religious" but who in their own time were regarded as (at least relatively) "lay," despite their appropriation of aspects of monasticism. Skinner argues that the quasi-monastic ascetical practices of the laity, the leadership in church affairs that was exercised by laypersons and clergy alike, and the existence of married priests worked together to keep the church as a whole relatively egalitarian, and the definition of the various estates within the church fairly fluid, until the Gregorian reforms of the eleventh century. She discovers in the lives of Carolingian lay saints patterns of conversion, self-sacrifice, service, and communal membership that have a model character for present-day laity.

Kristine Utterback calls attention to the popular practice of pilgrimage in the Middle Ages, a predominately lay practice of travel to distant holy places that complemented, and stood as an alternative for, the monastic commitment to enclosure and *stabilitas loci*. For saints like Birgitta of Sweden, taking the pilgrim's path was a way of combining action with contemplation. Drawing upon extant accounts by late-medieval pilgrims, Utterback argues that pilgrimage was for many laity a genuine way of holiness that led (in the terms of anthropologist Victor Turner) through a threefold process of separation, liminality, and aggregation. It frequently resulted in changed lives and aimed at both an earthly and a heavenly homecoming.

Mary Walsh Meany, Karen Scott, and Peter Pellegrin examine the lives of three women whose status as "saints" involved a complex personal and social negotiation of their lay status that simultaneously denied and affirmed it. Meany reflects on Bd. Angela of Foligno's problematic reaction to the sudden death of her husband and children as an event that set her free in her pursuit of a Christocentric and eucharistic sanctity. That pursuit, however, led Angela in the end to affirm some distinctly lay values. She remained uncloistered as a Franciscan tertiary, engaged in corporal works of mercy, assumed leadership in her local community as a spiritual mother, and saw in the Eucharist a sign of, and a means for, the *consecratio mundi* to which Vatican II has subsequently called the laity.

Scott highlights an ambivalence not only in St. Catherine of Siena's view of herself, but also in her biographer's representation of her uncloistered apostolate and charismatic opposition to clerical figures. As Scott insists, however, Catherine saw her authoritative mission as a laywoman in being an "angel" to the "shepherds," correcting and guiding even kings and popes in her letters of advice. Pellegrin shows that Margery Kempe, like Angela of Foligno, found her marital status to be a hindrance to her pursuit of holiness. She insisted, therefore, on conjugal continence and symbolic virginity, but her experiences as wife, mother, entrepreneur, and pilgrim undeniably continued to color and condition her experience of God, making her a model for a cataphatic mysticism suitable for laypersons even today.

Patricia Healy Wasyliw analyzes the late-medieval cults of child saints, virtually all of whom were (by definition) lay and the objects of popular devotion. Their original, spontaneous appeal as innocent (often political) victims was significantly affected, she argues, by the clericalization of the canonization process, which required child saints to exhibit precociously the "heroic virtues" of adulthood. Her historical survey raises the question not only of the appropriateness of the criteria currently used in the evaluation of child saints, but also of the meaning of child martyrdom in the present age of child abuse, abortion, genocide, and widespread political oppression.

Whereas the essays dealing with the medieval period all affirm—albeit to different degrees—the dominance of the monastic ideal in the self-awareness of lay saints and their evaluation by others, the five studies addressing twentieth-century figures (none of whom have yet been canonized) strongly suggest the emergence not only of new spiritualities but also of new, secular ideals of lay sanctity. Janet Ruffing's treatment of Elizabeth Leseur discovers in her spirituality a remarkable set of qualities, some of them traditionally Salesian, but others evincing an original, radically hidden heroism and self-effacement uniquely appropriate to contemporary laypersons. My study of Gertraud von Bullion focuses on the particular problem of discerning and answering a vocation to the lay apostolate within the historical context of the foundation of laywomen's communities in Schoenstatt. Astrid O'Brien traces in the writings of Jacques and Raissa Maritain the effort to seek Christian perfection and, in particular, to understand and practice a form of contemplation suitable for married life and secular professions. Patricia M. Vinje probes the political mysticism of Dorothy Day, whose works of mercy not only continue, but also creatively alter, the characteristically lay emphasis on the active life by placing it within a revolutionary, eschatological context. Finally, Donald W. Mitchell examines the "collective spirituality" of Chiara Lubich and the Focolare as a new "unitive way" with a communal, ecumenical, and interfaith emphasis.

An essay comparing and contrasting the "ways" of these "saints"—Elizabeth Leseur, Gertraud von Bullion, Jacques and Raissa Maritain, Dorothy Day, and Chiara Lubich—would no doubt afford interesting (albeit preliminary and limited) insights into contemporary spiritualities as schools of holiness. What they share most obviously, however, is the sense that they are lay not only incidentally (by default, as it were) but also by vocation, and thus in their cosmological commitment and in their whole asceticism. Unlike the monks of old, these saints characteristically move "toward" the world, not "away" from it, in order to render God "present" precisely there, in the desert places of a secularized society where the God who has suffered abandonment is experientially "absent," silent and hidden.

No doubt many postmodern saints, like the self-emptying God they love and serve, will go unrecognized. In an age of mass communication and shifting forms of hagiography (novelistic, journalistic, cinematic), others will receive recognition in forms other than canonization. Some will be canonized. But one thing is certain: the lay saint appears, if at all, "in the world." Coleman's words sound the prophecy that gives hope to our search: "In the desert places of modern life, where one does not expect God, just there the saint emerges."[73]

Lay Sanctity and Church Reform in Early Medieval France

MARY S. SKINNER

> *All the faithful of Christ of whatever rank or status are called to the*
> *fullness of the Christian life and to the perfection of charity.*
>   Vatican II: *Lumen Gentium*

Before 1050 the laity shared power with clergy and monasteries in governing church and society. Protestant Europe largely returned to this pre-Gregorian model of shared lay-clerical governance, but did away with the monasteries and eroded the prestige attached to sanctity. The call for reform issued by Vatican II has led to renewed discussion among Protestants and Catholics of the equality-in-baptism and "priesthood" of all believers, but has cast into doubt the credentials of many of the saints of old, thus raising two fundamental questions addressed in this essay: To what extent does the pre-Gregorian church offer a model of lay leadership for us today? And if lay leaders and reformers of the early medieval church were often saints, do medieval ideals of sanctity have any relevance for Christianity today?

Early Christian Asceticism: Root of Lay Sanctity

The first laypeople were, in fact, the disciples: those fishermen, tax collectors, and women who surrounded Jesus and whom the Jewish priests termed untutored laity (Acts 4:13). The first house churches were led by women like the dye-merchant Lydia (Acts 16:1–15) or later the courageous young Roman martyr, Perpetua, both of whom were converted with their entire households.[1] The apocryphal Acts also disclose Christian women inspired to evangelical celibacy by itinerant prophetic teachers like Paul of Tarsus.[2] Bishops, deacons, and priests were in place in the second century but were still competing for authority with wandering lay prophets, teachers, and confessors (i.e., near-martyrs). Lay women and men were still teaching, preaching, administering sacraments, leading worship, and appointing and deposing clergy for several more centuries, although not always without controversy.[3]

Early Christian writers like Tertullian, Cyprian, and Augustine affirmed the dignity and priesthood of the laity. Confessors upheld a rigorous morality in the face of persecution and demanded a say from their bishops on how and when the lapsed, who had performed pagan rituals rather than accept martyrdom, might be accepted back into the Christian community. Christians formed corporations on the model of the Roman *collegia* for agape or funeral meals, the study of Scripture, mutual discipline, and support and charity toward those in need.[4] Their assemblies became increasingly visible, and when Christianity became the imperial religion, they were supplemented by public liturgies in which the laity played a prominent part.

Elisabeth Schüssler Fiorenza traces the "patriarchalism" of the church and the consequent diminishment of the laity, especially women, to a very early date. Jacques Fontaine also maintains that "the condescending and negative view of the laity is ancient," the result of an aristocratic elitism based on a dualist, Platonic worldview.[5] Equality among Christians quickly broke down, Fontaine argues, when martyrs and ascetics were ranked above the ordinary laity in holiness, and clerics were, from the reforms of Constantine, granted the privileges of a separate order. Furthermore, the oligarchical structures of Germanic society reinforced the Roman hierarchical views inherited by new Christians.[6] As Peter Brown and Philip Rousseau have shown, early Christianity not only had great attraction for the poor and dispossessed, but many of its converts were a new elite, who as bishops and lay aristocrats, were soon directing both church and empire and who imprinted their social prejudices on the Church.[7] The consequent tendency toward hierarchy, however, did not mean that the laity lost all leadership roles in the established Christian church. On the contrary, lay ascetics and saints were to retain authority and prestige all through the early medieval period. All levels of society participated in the emerging cults of the saints and in pilgrimages to their holy places at home and abroad.[8]

From the fourth century, saintly lay ascetics like Macrina, sister of Bishop Gregory of Nyssa, lived religious lives with relatives, friends, and former slaves in their own homes, using their wealth to care for the poor.[9] Peter Brown contends that ascetics demonstrated their sanctity by disengaging not only from their aristocratic families but also from Roman society, by entirely refusing sex and marriage, children, and civic responsibilities.[10] I see asceticism, especially for women, rather as a rallying point which enabled Christians to attain reputations for sanctity within society by creating egalitarian communities, often including relatives; these transformed families engaged in evangelical and social action.[11]

The lay ascetic lived in a group, or with a spouse or ascetic partner. Some, like Anthony, took to the desert, but most, especially women, remained local urban leaders. They sought frequent prayer (even married couples kept midnight vigils) and gathered for celebrations of the Eucharist, at first simply at home and later in long public liturgies. Christians were urged to fast twice a week and to eat very little during Lent, thus saving money to assist the poor, prisoners, and the sick.[12]

Astounding to us is their preoccupation with celibacy. Married couples suspended sexual relations not only in Lent, but often completely after children were born. Widows and widowers often refused to marry a second time, heeding what they saw as the teaching of Jesus and Paul to lead a celibate life for the Kingdom of God. Second-century Syrian catechumens may have made baptismal vows of celibacy. Communities resulting from this rigorous asceticism were known as "sons and daughters of the Covenant." By the fourth century, young men and women were brought up by ascetic relatives to lives of perpetual virginity. Celibacy did not, of course, guarantee sanctity, but it was increasingly seen as a sign and foundation of it.[13]

John Cassian, a Westerner who sojourned among ascetics in the East, has traced the formation of monastic communities to the cooling of the ascetic zeal of ordinary laypeople.[14] The transition from ascetic lay households to separate monastic communities was very gradual, however, and the boundaries long remained fluid. Ascetics often became bishops in the West and championed the cults of saints that inspired people to imitate earlier ascetics and martyrs.[15] One fourth-century couple, Melania and Pinianus, spent years touring the Christian world, distributing their great wealth to the poor, and founding new religious communities.[16] Rules of life, like that of

Caesarius of Arles and Benedict, modeled on the family, offered organized monastic life by the sixth century, but hermit groups, couples in spiritual marriages, and informal ascetic communities of men and women continued to flourish in and near the towns. Wandering lay missionaries, on ascetic pilgrimages with family and friends, converted non-Christian populations. In short, as W. H. C. Frend expresses it, "In this period . . . the laity played an astonishingly active part in the intellectual and moral life of the Church."[17] Lay Christians still believed that they could live in family groups, engage in secular work, guide the mission of the church, and live holy lives.

The Carolingian Background

It is difficult for us today even to imagine the church before the clericalizing Gregorian reforms of the late eleventh century. The Carolingian church (ca 800–1000) was not caught in the grip of the laity, as portrayed in the leading *l'histoire de l'église* of my graduate school days,[18] but was governed rather by a balance of lay, clerical, and monastic institutions. Lay aristocrats, especially the Germanic monarchs, had long influenced affairs of the church, and in them "the 'royal priesthood' of the whole people of God had its representative[s]," with the result that "the layman could never be completely ignored."[19] Canons, abbots, abbesses, and especially bishops had great influence in both ecclesiastical and secular affairs; however, boundaries between clergy, religious, and laity were still quite blurred, and we must not imagine a church dominated and governed by clergy as a separate order.[20] Priests and bishops were mostly married and also firmly enmeshed in their extended families. Few monks and not all canons were priests. Thus monasteries and colleges of secular canons were quasi-lay institutions.

In the Roman imperial model, which Charlemagne adopted, the emperor and his administrators, both lay and clerical, called church synods, attended by clergy and laity alike, that formulated theology, defined heresy, and enforced ecclesiastical discipline. Royal officials, whose successors became independent lords, also taxed and judged both clergy and laity, owned churches, and founded (and appointed the superiors of) religious communities, occasionally becoming lay abbots themselves.[21]

The era was one of great violence in which warring nobles and impoverished refugees, not to speak of Viking invaders, frequently robbed, looted, and pillaged those without protectors. Most buildings were of wood, and the secret weapon of invading armies was fire, which wreaked horrible devastation on civilian populations.[22] The tenth century, however, was actually more peaceful and prosperous than has previously been thought.[23] Even amid the ravages of civil war, many were trying to protect the vulnerable, settle disputes, and create cultural oases where people could survive and prosper. Laity often cooperated with clergy and monasteries to promote peace and justice. Ninth-century kings, like Louis the Pious, and counts, like Gerald of Aurillac, had reputations for sanctity, were praised for their clemency, and attempted to mitigate the violence of the time.[24]

As Gerhard Ladner once proposed, monasticism was a movement on the cutting edge of Christianity, attempting to draw the faithful back to the early Gospel ideals.[25] Monastic ideals and rules exerted tremendous influence on lay society throughout the medieval period. The early stages of the "Peace of God" in France can particularly be seen as a movement that carried monastic values into secular life in the late tenth and early eleventh centuries.[26]

Carolingian political treatises, chronicles, and saints' lives, imbued with monastic ideals, set forth the Christian life as it ought to be lived by different groups. Emperor Louis the Pious, who championed Benedict of Aniane's monastic reforms, was reported to have seen himself as abbot of the realm.[27] Monastic ideals are recommended for the laity in a variety of Carolingian sources.[28] The influence of monastic ideals on lay Christian spirituality continued in the west Frankish kingdom.[29] Some ninth- and numerous tenth- and eleventh-century charters further illustrate monastic ideals in action.[30] Despite political crises, violence, and corruption, lay and clerical members of leading families frequently cooperated in founding monasteries, promoting peace, enforcing justice, and protecting the poor.[31] They also produced more than the occasional saint, but many of these local lives have yet even to be translated.[32]

When ecclesiastical and secular authority devolved from the emperor to hereditary counts and their brother bishops whose ancestors had served the emperor, these new lords promoted monasteries for a variety of reasons. They wished the monks and nuns to pray for their relatives who had died.[33] They built monasteries as they built castles, as part of a strategy of consolidating their principalities, dominating the countryside, and maintaining peace. Sometimes they wished to acquire monastic lands with which to reward their *fideles*.[34] Monasteries were highly valued for the services they provided; they cared for the poor, the sick, and travelers; they provided libraries and schools, as well as monastic vocations for lay sons and daughters. New towns sprouted around them, fostering the local economy.[35] Monastic communities structured the religious life of their neighbors with liturgies, processions, and feasts of the saints. A powerful abbey might dominate the local politics and economy. Religious houses often challenged the authority of the counts or bishops who built them, and attempted to win immunity from local jurisdictions by appeals to king or pope. The abbey of Redon (one of the few which has ninth-century documentation) undermined village autonomy in becoming the first powerful lordship in Brittany.[36] Aristocratic lay strategies can be viewed positively as promoting peace and stability and the interests of the church, rather than a greedy grabbing of land and power.[37]

Carolingian writings and charters show how laypeople were influenced by monastic spirituality and experienced individual or corporate conversion to lives of prayer, asceticism, and service. Their piety overflowed in efforts to keep the peace and protect and provide for the poor. The historical record, in short, shows a striving on the part of many Carolingian laypeople toward ideals of sanctity preserved in monastic tradition and practice. This quasi-monastic asceticism of the laity helped to unite clergy, religious, and laity, and to keep the early medieval church remarkably cohesive.

John Navone, writing of Christian spirituality today but drawing from this long tradition, has distinguished four stages of the spiritual journey based on the Paschal mystery of Christ: (1) *metanoia* (or conversion); (2) *kenosis* (or asceticism and self-sacrifice); (3) *diakonia* (or service); and (4) *koinonia* (or community).[38] From the accounts that we have, these phases seem to also fit the lives of lay Christians of the pre-Gregorian Latin church.[39] I envision this process, however, as circular rather than linear. Medieval Christians did not advance to sanctity alone but were nurtured in their various Christian communities and returned to serve them. Lay men and women of the so-called "dark age" have been underestimated as faithful proponents of ecclesiastical and social reform, for both charters and narrative sources depict laypeople supporting ecclesiastical reform and monastic values.

Metanoia or Conversion of Life

There are many examples of conversions in which individuals abruptly changed direction in their lives through penance or a quest for holiness. They became hermits, pilgrims, regular canons, or joined or founded monastic communities. Some notable group conversions occurred in the Peace of God movement or in response to popular preachers who were sometimes held suspect by the church. Following conversion, laypeople often took on an apostolic or quasi-monastic lifestyle of prayer, fasting, celibacy, and service. Personal conversions described in the sources may be patterned on biblical examples or earlier hagiography. Thus, conversion stories of aspiring saints must be examined with some suspicion, but there are often specific details that lend them credibility.

Benedict of Aniane, son of a Carolingian count of Gothic descent, who had been a soldier and cupbearer to Kings Pepin and Charlemagne experienced a religious conversion which he kept secret for three years. As his biographer, Ardo, describes it, "He began to blaze with heavenly love to abandon this flaming world with all its exertions."[40] Although Ardo borrowed this phrase from Guthlac's "Life of St. Felix," he placed it within a vivid description of Benedict's specific situation that rings true. Benedict's conversion had been triggered by nearly perishing in an attempt to rescue his brother from drowning in a river. After it, Benedict seemed somewhat at a loss as to how to best live out a religious life and wondered "whether to assume the habit of a pilgrim, or perhaps attach himself to someone to take care of men's sheep and cattle without pay, or even to engage in the shoemaker's craft in some city and spend on poor folk whatever profit he might be able to gain."[41] These options show the variety of ways the radical Christian life was lived in the late eighth century, often in small semi-eremitic groups; any of these choices would have required great humility for a count's son. In the end, he discovered and adopted the Benedictine Rule, which he spent his life propagating.[42]

Odo of Cluny wrote the biography of a ninth-century count, St. Gerald of Aurillac, as an inspiration for laypeople of the early tenth century. Like Benedict and Odo, Gerald had military talents and training and also excelled in learning. On inheriting his father's county, Gerald divided his time between prayer, study, and administration. When still a youth, he experienced conversion through an instance of passionate attraction to one of his serfs. He at first demanded that her father present her to him one night, while at the same time halfheartedly praying that he might be delivered from temptation. Through divine grace, he later believed, at the critical moment she no longer appeared beautiful to him and, his ardor cooled, he rode hastily away. Gerald learned from this experience not only to resist lust, but more important not to abuse his power over his poor dependents: "But now that you know by experience what a man may be by himself and by the grace of God, do not scorn to have compassion on the weakness of your supplicants."[43]

Gerald freed the serf, arranged for her marriage, and considered that the cataracts he suffered from for more than a year were divine punishment. Later he even refused a suitable marriage and chose to live a celibate life, lamenting even nocturnal emissions. He would have become a monk had he not thought his secular responsibilities essential to those who depended on him for protection, but finally he founded a monastery on his family lands.[44]

As a young man in military service to Count William of Aquitaine, Gerald's biographer, the future abbot Odo of Cluny, experienced his conversion when spending Christmas with the canons of St Martin. He wrote: "Impatient youth that I was, I sprang into the midst of them and joined them in singing the praises of the King who had been born."[45] He was then plagued with migraine headaches until he discovered that his father had dedicated him as an infant to St. Martin. He joined the community by accepting a prebend, but rather than live as a secular canon with private property, he took up a life of poverty in a small cell in imitation of St. Martin and later joined the reformed monastery of Baume.[46]

As a young monk when travelling on business, Odo once stopped to see family friends and was confronted by a young woman who begged him to help her enter religious life. Since her parents were away, and he probably should not have been visiting anyway, Odo was very anxious about his abbot's reaction to his returning with a woman in tow. But the girl, who had been enthralled by his conversation that evening, was not to be dissuaded:

The whole evening this girl pondered most deeply on his way of life. Then full of compunction she went secretly to him by a back way, and prostrate at his feet told him she was condemned soon to be given in marriage, begging that for the sake of God, whose servant he professed to be, he might liberate her that same night. . . . overcome by the love of God and the sobs of the girl, he at length consented to take her away.[47]

Many charters hint enigmatically at similar conversion experiences. When Archbishop Teotolo of Tours and Abbot Odo of Cluny founded the monastery of St. Julien in 942, much religious fervor was generated, and two scions of the city, Erkembald and Fulculf, gave up their wealth and entered the new monastery.[48] About 990 Emma, the wife of William of Aquitaine and sister of Count Odo of Tours, founded the monastery of Bourgueil, appointing her relative Gauzbert as abbot. When he also became abbot of Marmoutier and St. Julien, they launched a local monastic reform. Their charter for Bourgueil stressed the duty and the authority of the count(ess) to carry on the work of the apostles in guiding the ship of church and opposing all those inclined to evil who might undermine ecclesiastical foundations. Emma was apparently exiled to the castle of Chinon by her husband at the time, but he later ratified her foundation.[49]

About 1000, Hervé of Tours wanted to become a monk, but his family objected, and the king made him treasurer of St. Martin, which could be held by a layperson. Hervé at first lived as a canon, but then established a cell on an island in the Loire where he could retreat with other reformed canons to live a more monastic life. (He was undoubtedly influenced by the examples of St. Martin and Abbot Odo. St. Côme later became a priory of the monastery of Marmoutier.)[50] Hervé also supported a group of women struggling to live an informal religious life at the basilica of St. Martin. Lamenting that a former convent for women at Tours had been destroyed, he founded for them a new monastery called Beaumont.[51]

In 1028, Alan of Brittany founded St. Georges, Rennes, for his sister who, perhaps like Hervé's women devotees at St. Martin's, had been living an informal religious life and along with several friends wanted to become a nun. Alan's love for his sister moved him to provide her and her companions an appropriate place to serve God and St. George by living the Benedictine Rule.[52] At about the same time, Count Geoffrey Martel of Anjou and his wife Agnes founded the monastery of Trinity, Beaulieu, on the spot where they had been deeply shaken when three fragments of a comet had fallen, striking terror into their hearts. In the years around 1000, apocalyptic fears and hopes abounded, triggering many conversion experiences. Geoffrey also founded a chapter of canons at his castle of Loches on his return from one of several pilgrimages to Jerusalem.[53]

There were many benefits for laypeople in founding a monastery, sometimes even gaining control of lands and swaying abbatial elections of the new abbey. Nonetheless, many gifts seem to have followed on personal conversions, especially the gift of oneself. Hints of conversion stories in the charters often mark the first step toward gradually more intentional religious lives, for many women and men were only able to enter monastic life after their children were grown.[54]

Kenosis and *Diakonia*: Peace and Justice for the Poor

Following a conversion experience, many Christians sought lives of simplicity, poverty, and community. They often divested themselves of power and wealth in a kind of self-emptying or *kenosis,* gradually using up their resources in the service of others. They took the advice of an ancient baptismal formula in Philippians 2:1-8 that holds Jesus Christ up as the model for any serious Christian:

> Out of humility of mind everyone should give preference to others, everyone pursuing not selfish interests, but those of others. Make your own the mind of Christ Jesus,
>
> > Who being in the form of God
> > did not count equality with God
> > something to be grasped.
> > But he emptied himself,
> > taking the form of a slave,
> > becoming as human beings are;
> > and being in every way like a human being,
> > he was humbler yet,
> > even accepting death, death on a cross.[55]

Feudal lords have often been accused of exploitation and occasional wholesale slaughter of the people in their charge, and the sources seem sometimes to be covering up oppression on the part of kings, counts, and clerical leaders.[56] Protection of the poor was, nonetheless, an important seigneurial responsibility and a key element of the Peace of God movement. Giving alms was also the duty of all Christians, who were urged to seek out and alleviate the needs of the poor. Monasteries in these centuries have been credited with extensive poor relief by one authority (although accused of only token assistance by another).[57]

Laypeople of all social ranks became involved in the actions known as the Peace of God. The peace movement commenced in the late tenth century when bishops called a series of councils attended by knights, clerics, and people who then swore on sacred relics not to disturb the peace. The peace councils formed the background of the day-to-day adjudication of disputes among laity and clerics over the control of church and secular properties. As peace and justice were better maintained, the violence subsided for which lay and clerical lords were frequently responsible. Occasionally, however, even a peace "army," as that at Bourges in 1028 led by a bishop, ran amok, killing innocent civilians.[58]

Radical ideas of peace-keeping and wealth-sharing, as marks of the Christian life and the only hope of the poor, can be found in the early Carolingian moral literature. Bishop Jonas of Orleans' "Treatise on the Laity," must have been widely known.[59] Paraphrasing Augustine, Jonas calls on those in power to adopt the apostolic life: "For in them [the apostles] the brotherhood of Christ was stronger than blood. . . . And so they were not afraid of going hungry: on the contrary, their fear was that others might go hungry."[60] Jonas urged the king to recognize his human fallibility and thus be willing to share his wealth and power and be guided by others. He should "be slow to punish," and then only for the common good, and "swift to pardon," that others might see their errors and amend. Rulers should never indulge private enmities, but live disciplined lives and work to spread the kingdom of God.[61] These admonitions were similar to those for the abbot in the Benedictine Rule. It would seem that Louis the Pious generally listened to Jonas's advice.[62]

Louis had granted the west Frankish kingdom to Charles the Bald, his younger son by his second wife, Judith. This led to devastating rebellions on the part of his older sons Pepin, Louis, and Lothair. At this time of civil strife, William, the young son of the Frankish countess Dhouda, was held at the court of Charles the

Bald as a guarantee of the loyalty of William's father, Bernard of Septimania, to Charles. Dhuoda's manual, Carol Neel argues, was meant to instruct not only her son, William, but also the princes who were destroying the kingdom with their fratricidal wars. If they would honor their father's division, unjust as they might think it, the essential peace of the realm would be maintained. William's father, Bernard of Septimania, was, however, deeply implicated in political intrigue, and when he was executed by Charles the Bald, William tried to avenge his death and was himself killed.[63] In this case the nobles involved proved deaf to both Jonas's warning and Dhuoda's motherly advice, and the demands of the Germanic blood feud once more prevailed over Christian ideals of peace and brotherhood.

Nonetheless, Dhuoda must be credited with setting a Christian regimen for her son and other young princes "that might have strained a monk."[64] The whole manual is permeated with monastic spirituality.[65] William was to immerse himself in the Scriptures and Psalms and personally to pray for those of his relatives who had died. He was to divide his time between study, prayer, and work and especially to avoid anger and violence.[66] Dhuoda's own poetry captures succinctly William's duties to the poor and powerless:

> Help widows and orphans often,
> And be generous to pilgrims with food and drink.
> Prepare lodgings for them and extend your hand with
> Clothing for the naked.
> Be a strong and fair judge in legal matters.
> Never take a bribe from anyone,
> Nor oppress anyone.
> For he who has been your benefactor
>   Will repay you.[67]

A Carolingian layman who embodied these values (according to his biographer, Abbot Odo of Cluny) was the late-ninth-century Count Gerald of Aurillac, whose conversion has already been described. His dependents complained, however, that his excessive generosity was a weakness that was goading his enemies to despoil him. When forced to fight, Gerald ordered his soldiers to reverse their spears. Nonetheless, the count's reputation for sanctity and invincibility effectively cowered his enemies: "He therefore exerted himself to repress the insolence of the violent, taking care in the first place to promise peace and most easy reconciliation of his enemies. And sometimes indeed he soothed them and reduced them to peace."[68]

In penance for nearly raping his serf, Gerald began to seek out and care for the poor.[69] He became known for sparing thieves and protecting runaway serfs. Almost every chapter of the first book of his life stresses his concern for the needy of his society and his efforts to promote peace.[70] His home was a veritable monastery where the poor person was received as if Christ:

> Chairs for the poor were always placed in his presence, and at intervals meals were put in front of them, that he might see for himself what and how much food was given to them. Nor was he limited to receiving a certain number. . . . No one was ever turned away from his door without alms being given.[71]

There are other Carolingian laity who, like Gerald, poured themselves out for the poor. Young Wala, cousin of Charlemagne, acted as a diplomat for Louis the Pious and later became abbot of Corbie. While still a lay advocate, he sought to defend a widow who had been defrauded of her property by an unjust judge. The entire court was against him, as several were implicated in a plot to do away with the widow, in which some of the would-be assassins had been killed. After fasting and pleading with God for justice, Wala presented his case and apparently threatened a "trial by ordeal," when with groaning and tears the judge admitted his guilt.[72]

The charters reinforce the narrative sources in demanding that Christians show concern for the maintenance of peace and the plight of the poor. In an early charter for the province of Touraine (about 900), Count Robert, lay abbot of St. Martin, rebuilt the hospice of St. Clement to receive the poor and sick. There were a number of such hospices in Tours in the tenth century, for many came to the basilica of St. Martin to seek a cure.[73] A century later, King Robert granted the abbey of Marmoutier a priory, including income for the feeding of paupers.[74] Around 1030, Fulk Nerra, count of Anjou, and his wife, Hildegarde, gave an alod and taxes to the abbey of Ronçeray for the nourishment of the poor.[75] Free, but relatively poor, peasants often gave all that they had to the local monastery. For example, before his death in 994, a miller named Letaldus gave his mill to St. Julien of Tours in an elaborate ceremony in the parish church.[76] Thus rich and poor alike seemed ready "to give all to the poor and follow Christ" (Cf. Luke 18:22).

Restoring *Koinonia*: Seedbed of Sanctity

Western France was far more peaceful in the tenth than in the early eleventh century. The wars over Touraine, which pitted Counts Fulk and Geoffrey of Anjou against Counts Odo and Tetbald of Blois, raged intermittently for two generations. There were many complaints about the depredations of the castellans of the new Angevin castles of Montbazon and Mirebeau on the lands and against the people of the monasteries of Cormery and Bourgueil.[77] In an invasion of Tours in the 990s, Fulk Nerra violated the cloister of St. Martin, pursuing a fugitive on his horse; in response, the monks performed a ritual whereby they humiliated the relics of the offended saint by literally lowering them to the ground, pronounced maledictions against the peace-breaker, and suspended all religious services until he agreed to do penance. These were the methods by which the church might restore ruptured community relations.[78] At about the same time, Hardouin, a knight whose family held the castle of Roche near Marmoutier, invaded the cloister there with his men and killed a cleric named Sulio. In repentance he gave the abbey an island in the Loire.[79] Thus, violence was contained and recompense exacted either by ecclesiastical sanctions, such as excommunication and interdict, or by legal prosecution.

Violence erupted again just prior to 1044, when Geoffrey Martel of Anjou conquered Touraine.[80] André, Geoffrey's knight, was forced to compensate Marmoutier for damage he did to their lands in the war but was granted the lands of a defeated citizen of Tours to enable him to pay up.[81] Bouchard of Isle and his nephews drove out the monks of Tavant and burned the monastery during the wars, but later made restitution.[82] Such acts of violence were increasingly recorded in the charters after 1000. Their very notation, however, usually meant that the perpetrators had been brought to justice, as had Wala's unjust judge, compensation exacted, and community restored.

Equally visible in the charters of these years was the voluntary restoration to monasteries of admittedly usurped church properties. Having acquired by heredity or conquest churches, tithes, or other ecclesiastical goods, many landowners began turning these over to monasteries. Restoration of church property was another part of the reform program of the peace councils and a means of drawing the community back together.[83] The very lords, like the count of Anjou and his men, who would seize the churches and monastic lands of their enemies to consolidate their political power, were also very active in protecting and endowing "their" churches. The balance, overall, seems to have favored restoration over lay usurpation of ecclesiastical properties. As one reviewer recently put it: "In the eleventh century, in much of France, when the sound and fury of the peace movement had passed, seigneurial fortresses were the places of peace."[84]

The Gospels and the Benedictine Rule were the main inspiration of Carolingian biography and works of moral guidance. Even when they did not live up to them, people seem to have been aware of the demands of the Christian life. They learned about them in the communities in which they were raised: the family, the village, and the church or monastery of the local saint. The monasteries and churches rewrote the lives and celebrated the festivals of their local saints. Indeed, as Thomas Head has argued, the monasteries "functioned as communities of interpretation" for the laity, who "attended monastic liturgies" in great numbers and who heard from the monks the "stories about the 'fathers' of the diocese."[85]

At St. Riquier in Picardy, on Palm Sunday, the monks went out to escort the people into Mass. A special cross, one of three, was erected in the church on Good Friday for the veneration of the laity. Similarly, as Susan Rabe relates, "On Easter itself, the monks celebrated a special procession, mass and office. The townspeople (*populus*) attended the mass at the church of the Holy Saviour and participated in communion with the brothers. The common worship of the entire community of believers was paramount."[86] It cannot any longer be argued that the people did not understand the liturgy or the lives of the saints (since they were explained to them in the vernacular) or that they did not fully participate in the liturgical life of the church (given the many examples that are emerging from regional studies). The local saints, in fact, competed for the loyalty and affection of their people. These communities of the saints-of-old were the seedbeds in which new saints were nurtured.

Many saints' lives indicate that it was the family of origin that encouraged the career of an aspiring lay saint. Parents with a reputation

for piety had premonitions or dreams about their offspring and ensured they would be properly prepared for religious life. St. Leoba's
mother, for example, had dreamed she was carrying a church bell
in her womb which rang merrily when she gave birth: "The nurse
said to her, 'We shall yet see a daughter from your womb and it is
your duty to consecrate her straightway to God.' . . . And when the
child had grown up her mother consecrated her and handed her
over to Mother Tetta to be taught the sacred sciences."[87] As described earlier, St. Odo of Cluny had been promised to St. Martin as
an infant by his father.[88]

Of course, some parents opposed their children's aspirations to
religious life, as did the relatives of Hervé of Tours described
above,[89] but the positive encouragement of religious aspirations by
family and community is more typical of this hagiography. Parental
approval of a young person's decision is a strong component of
most entry charters. Indeed, the extent of parental initiative in charters of entry to monasteries has led some scholars to propose that
children, especially girls, were placed in them against their will. I
would see this rather as indicative of family support, financial and
otherwise, of aspiring vocations.[90]

When young people were established in some recognized form
of holy or religious life, they rarely forgot the family that had nurtured them. For example, a canon named Vivien appeared before
his fellow canons of St. Martin, offering to give them the chapel of
St. George, which belonged to his family. There were strings attached, however. The canons must promise to keep up the annual
feast-day pilgrimage to the chapel and appoint any qualified member of Vivien's family as chaplain. Vivien wanted to assist his canonical community, but not at the expense of his family and their close
relationship with St. George and his chapel.[91] Aristocratic families
were more and more uncomfortable with owning churches out-
right, perhaps, but wanted to barter their churches so as to gain a
closer association with the saint.[92] As Lester Little has shown, a gift-
exchange economy was still in force which bound people to their
patron saint and local monastery by reciprocal gift-giving.[93]

Besides their familial ties, these medieval Christians had great loyalty to fellow villagers, which was sometimes in conflict with their
equally fervent attachment to local saints and their monks. One example is the story of Letaldus's mill, which was presented above. The

local villagers had observed Letaldus grant his mill to the abbey of St. Julien in a solemn ceremony. After his death the monks were morally obliged to look out for his family. When his wife and children died in poverty, the people challenged the abbey, demanding justice. The provost argued that the monks had provided a pig, ample *modii* of rye and wheat, and funerals and memorial masses for all; nevertheless, they felt obliged to justify themselves to the people.[94]

The people held the monks accountable for mediating correctly to them the lives of "their" saints. Richard Landes has recently described a revival of the "apostolic life" in Aquitaine in the early eleventh century. The monks of St. Martial had developed an elaborate liturgy and history for their saint, promoting him from martyr and confessor to cousin of St. Peter and companion of Jesus and the apostles. Popular enthusiasm showed the great interest there in reviving the life and ideals of the early church. At the critical moment before the saint's new apostolic liturgy was to become official, however, a visiting Lombard preacher discredited the apostolicity of St. Martial, and the movement collapsed. Landes argues, on the one hand, for an incident of popular iconoclasm in which a number of people were trampled to death in the church by those who turned away from the discredited saint. On the other hand, the monastic chronicler, Adhemar de Chabannes, who had been promoting the cult, imputes the deaths to the crowds beseeching the saint.[95] At any rate, the importance of the local saint and his or her cult in the life of the people, as well as the mediating function of the monks, is amply illustrated.

The inspiring figure of a local saint provided a powerful source of unity among his or her devotees, clerical and lay. Odo of Cluny expressed well the unity of people with their saint in a poem dedicated to St. Martin at the consecration of St. Julien's Abbey in 942: "Thronging from all directions / Enthusiastic people of all languages and races celebrate him, / Vying with each other to rush to his tomb. / Martin is highly deserving of such honor." The poem goes on to praise Martin as "our mediator with the Lord," who "restore[s] peace here."[96]

That peace had multiple dimensions and affected many circles. A life of St. Dagobert (thought to be tenth-century) describes a peaceful and ordered village under the united rule of a king, as the monks of Stenay near Verdun liked to envision it:

> The priestly order sang hymns to God the All-Powerful at the pre-
> scribed times; militant, the priests dedicated themselves to their
> king with repeated service. The order of farmers cultivated the
> land with an unalloyed joy, blessing him who had brought peace
> to their parish and who satisfied their hunger with abundance of
> wheat. The young men of the nobility, following the ancient cus-
> tom, besported themselves in due season, hunting with dogs and
> birds. They did not fail for all that to perform the actions pre-
> scribed by the Lord, giving alms to the poor, supporting those in
> difficulty, aiding widows and orphans, clothing the naked, taking
> in even beggars without a roof over their heads, visiting the sick
> and burying the dead.[97]

As this passage clearly envisions, each group within society had its
own proper functions and responsibilities. The primary practical responsibility for an ordered Christian society lay, however, not with
the monasteries, but with the local nobility, who had the means to
maintain peace and care for the poor.

M. D. Chenu asserts that laypeople, as well as monks and canons,
led the evangelical movements that swept Europe in the eleventh
and twelfth centuries:

> The new role of the laity was the logical outcome of the revolu-
> tion in progress. Since the evangelical awakening took place not
> by a revision of existing institutions but by a return to the Gospel
> that bypassed these institutions, one could predict what its dy-
> namics would be: witness to the faith, fraternal love, poverty, the
> beatitudes—all these were to operate more spontaneously and
> sooner among laymen than among clerics, who were bound
> within an institutional framework.[98]

The earliest hallmark of this awakening, according to Chenu, was a
desire to live the apostolic life, by which was meant a common life
as recorded in Acts 4:32 and Luke 10:1–12.[99] Such a lifestyle gave lay
people an advantage over monks and clerics who seemed to live too
well, and perhaps also some authority to preach.

The people were still a force to be reckoned with in the church of
the tenth and eleventh centuries. They might for a time support an
episcopal "peace army" that resorted to violence or a monastery that
was promoting dubious apostolic claims for its saint. Ultimately, however, they judged each by the Gospel message, for the Carolingian

renaissance had done its work well in instilling monastic and early Christian values. The seeds of apostolic poverty were bearing fruit, and the powerful were judged, whether bishops, counts, or prosperous Benedictine monks, according to the piety of their lives, their promotion of peace, and their concern for the poor, in accord with the evangelical dictum: "By their fruits, you will know them" (Matt. 12:33). Although today we might shy away from the concept of sanctity, we can still relate to the Gospel ideals of these Christians of the first millennium and admire their striving to realize them.

A Call to Active Devotion
Pilgrimages to Jerusalem in the Late Middle Ages
KRISTINE T. UTTERBACK

> *The Church, "like a pilgrim in a foreign land, presses forward amid*
> *the persecutions of the world and the consolations of God," an-*
> *nouncing the cross and death of the Lord until He comes.*
> Vatican II: *Lumen Gentium*

If laypeople of the late Middle Ages wanted to express their piety or religious fervor, what possibilities did they have? Then as now, the business of life kept most people occupied. They lived an active life rather than a contemplative one, and lay expressions of piety and devotion generally reflected this *vita activa*. Many pious individuals chose to make pilgrimages. Such a journey gave the pilgrim the chance to show devotion publicly and in a fashion accepted by society. In and of itself pilgrimage conferred grace and pardon, and many shrines offered indulgences as a further benefit. Pilgrimage, in short, was not merely a way for the laity to honor and to encounter the Holy, but also a means for them to become holy themselves. It taught them to see all of life as a pilgrimage path to heaven, and it afforded them an alternative, mobile, this-worldly way of holiness that was comparable in its arduous demands to the static, otherworldly way of monastic enclosure.[1]

Pilgrims might travel a short distance to a neighborhood shrine, a greater distance of a few days' travel, or thousands of miles to Santiago de Compostela, to Rome, or to Jerusalem, that quintessential pilgrimage destination, the *omphalos* or navel of the world.[2] While any pilgrimage had merit in the medieval scheme of salvation, nothing could compare with a journey to Jerusalem. As a result, despite or perhaps because of the journey's great hardships, Christian men and women flocked to Jerusalem and the surrounding area throughout the Middle Ages. How better to join with Christ than to walk where he had walked and participate in his sufferings?

The phenomenon of pilgrimage seems to have attracted people almost since time began, and its popularity has heightened in recent years. (One need only think of the hundreds of thousands who have traveled to Marian apparition sites, such as Lourdes, Fatima, and Medjugorie.) Indeed, the universality of pilgrimages allows us to view the phenomenon as an archetype, to borrow C. G. Jung's phrase, because it demonstrates a constantly repeated pattern in human experience.Calling pilgrimage "archetypal," however, does not explain the particular experiences of medieval pilgrims, which always varied, despite the constancy of the outward form. As Jean and Wallace Clift remind us, "In principle, [an archetype] can be named and has an invariable nucleus of meaning—but always only in principle, never as regards its concrete manifestation."[3]

Understood archetypally, "pilgrimage is a journey, a commemoration, a search for something, perhaps something the pilgrim cannot express in words, perhaps even something the pilgrim does not fully perceive. Pilgrimages are connected with the spirit, but it is difficult to say precisely how."[4] Richard R. Niebuhr suggests that the mysterious connection to the spirit is as intimate as the link between body and soul:

> Pilgrims are persons in motion—passing through territories not their own—seeking something we might call completion, or perhaps the word clarity will do as well, a goal to which only the spirit's compass points the way. . . . We mortals make passages— on foot, on horseback, in a boat or raft. . . . These physical passings through apertures can print themselves deeply into us, not in our physical senses alone, but in our spiritual sense as well, so that what we apprehend outwardly becomes part of the lasting geography of our souls.[5]

The accounts left to us by modern and medieval pilgrims alike indicate a link between spiritual and physical geography, such as Niebuhr describes, not only in their motives for going on pilgrimage, but also in the actual process of their journey and in its lasting effects. Modern people relate that their pilgrimages were motivated by the desire to go to see the place where something momentous had happened, to draw near to something sacred, to achieve pardon, to ask for a miracle, to give thanks, to express love for God, to answer a sense of inner call, or to honor a vow made in extreme circumstances.[6] Medieval pilgrims list similar reasons. Margery Kempe (†1439) tells us of her sense of inner call: "Soon after, this creature was moved in her soul to go and visit certain places for spiritual health." And later: "This creature, when our Lord had forgiven her her sin (as has been written before), had a desire to see those places where he was born, and where he suffered his Passion and where he died, together with other holy places where he was during his life, and also after his resurrection."[7]

Margery's choice to go on pilgrimage, especially to Jerusalem, must be understood within the larger context of late medieval piety—indeed, as an outward expression of her prayer life. During the fourteenth and fifteenth centuries, popular religious writings placed great emphasis on meditation as a form of spiritual exercise. In these meditations, the reader was encouraged to "be present" in imagination in the Gospel scenes, to picture Christ's humanity and his active doings in and around Jerusalem, to feel Christ's sufferings along each step of his Passion, and to imitate his holy life through the practice of virtues. People who prayed in this meditative way were naturally encouraged to feed their imaginations and their memories with actual pilgrimage to the Holy Land, and thus to combine the active with the contemplative life. As Friar Felix Fabri pointed out, the Virgin Mary was the ideal pilgrim and thus the model for all pilgrims, precisely because of the perfect balance of action and contemplation in her life.[8]

The express motives given for pilgrimage by Margery and other medieval pilgrims differ significantly from those attributed to them by many scholars, who view pilgrimage simply as a means of escape from drudgery and oppression and fail to take seriously the spiritual or religious element of pilgrimage. The standard work on medieval pilgrimage, Jonathan Sumption's *Pilgrimage: An Image of Mediaeval Religion,* exemplifies this "escapist" view. It stresses that "the world which the mediaeval pilgrim left behind him was a small and exclusive community. The geographic and social facts of life made it oppressive and isolated and, except in the vicinity of major towns and trunk roads, the chief qualities of human life were its monotonous regularity and the rule of overpowering conventions," especially those of parish life.[9]

From Sumption's mid-twentieth-century, individualistic perspective, medieval life seems the epitome of monotony and oppression, but from the viewpoint of a person raised in a communal environment, village and parish also offered support and comfort and provided a measure of security in an uncertain world. If medieval pilgrims had primarily wanted to escape from the tedium of their monotonous existence, why did they leave with the intention of returning? The very fact of leaving and returning points to the archetypal meaning of pilgrimage as a means, especially for the laity, of religious and spiritual growth.[10]

Pilgrimage in the late Middle Ages was clearly a holistic process that we may understand, in the terms of anthropologist Victor Turner, as having three phases: separation, liminality, and aggregation.[11] We can see these three phases, to different degrees, in the surviving accounts of late medieval pilgrims to Jerusalem. The separation phase includes the activities from the beginning of the preparation for the journey until boarding the ship for the Holy Land. The liminal phase includes the travel to the Holy Land and the time spent visiting the holy sites. During this liminal phase the group of pilgrims who board ship and travel together forms a natural and necessary sort of *communitas* for the individual members.[12] The aggregation phase begins when the pilgrims return to their ship(s) for the voyage home and ends when they have completed their reentry activities at the end of their pilgrimage journey.

Only a minuscule percentage of Jerusalem pilgrims left any account at all of their journeys and experiences. Of these, clerics have left the most extensive reports. Dominican Friar Felix Fabri's accounts of his journeys to Jerusalem in 1490 and 1494, for instance, run to hundreds of printed pages.[13] Similarly, his Milanese Dominican brother, Pietro Casola, left a detailed account of his pilgrimage to the Holy Land in 1491.[14]

While these clerical writings provide information about the trip to, and experiences in, Jerusalem for clerics and laity alike, clergy formed a minority of the travelers. Casola describes running short of supplies on the return journey and mentions that the captain had over four hundred people to provide for.[15] Although Casola does not number the crew members, we may be sure that the vast majority of these people were lay pilgrims. Two other travelers who left accounts of the same voyage, the Germans Bemmelberg and Parsberg, mention that the passenger list included twenty-four monks and twenty women.[16]

Clerical accounts are useful for the study of pilgrimages, but we cannot assume that the laity experienced or understood their pilgrimages in exactly the same way as the clergy did, given their different backgrounds and expectations. Fortunately some accounts by lay men and women do survive, including Book 7 of the *Revelations* of Saint Birgitta of Sweden, written during her trip to Jerusalem in 1373, the year before she died; the *Holy Jerusalem Voyage* of Ogier VIII, who traveled to the Holy Land in 1395; and *The Book of Margery Kempe,* which tells the story of Margery's trip to Jerusalem in 1413.

These lay accounts, however, also present difficulties. Birgitta and Margery wrote devotional literature, not pilgrimage histories. In their works we can see the "something" that they experienced, but the pilgrimage itself often serves as a backdrop to their devotions. Ogier's work is typical of many pilgrimage itineraries, describing the sights and recounting the stories (probably those he had heard from his guides) about the famous places in the Holy Land. It lacks, however, the detail and chatty narratives provided by such writers as Friar Felix and Casola, as well as the piety and visions of Birgitta and Margery, and it seems lifeless by comparison. Using a variety of accounts with care, we can nonetheless glean considerable information about the meaning of pilgrimage to Jerusalem for late medieval laypeople.

If we use Turner's categories to analyze our pilgrims' experiences, the separation phase involves preparing for pilgrimage and leaving home. A trip to the Holy Land, as recounted by such travelers as Birgitta of Sweden, Ogier d'Anglure, Margery Kempe, or Pietro Casola, typically required between one and two years to complete and required substantial planning and preparation.[17] Those making this pilgrimage would have been self-selecting to a large degree, mainly limited to those of great means, like Ogier, or great piety, like Margery.

The prospective pilgrim needed to prepare both spiritually and temporally. The dangers of travel magnified the uncertainty of daily life, and one wanted to be prepared for one's end, in case that end came while on the road or at the shrine itself. Several authors recount the death of a fellow pilgrim, so this was far from an uncommon experience. According to Margery, God had told her that no one who traveled on her ship would die on the journey, a revelation which had convinced her companions to change their passages to the galley she had booked.[18]

How did one commit oneself to a pilgrimage to Jerusalem? Often the prospective pilgrim had made a vow at a time of great devotion or when facing death, perhaps because of illness or due to a storm at sea or an impending battle. Canon law distinguished two types of pilgrimage: necessary and voluntary. Necessary pilgrimages included those prescribed as penance, either by civil or by ecclesiastical authorities. The editor of Ogier's *Voyage* suggests that he made his pilgrimage after having received a royal pardon for a serious sexual offense in 1391.[19] Voluntary pilgrimages, on the other hand, proceeded from a vow which committed a person to a certain action, in this case to visit Jerusalem.[20] Pietro Casola describes such a vow:

> a great longing always remained with me to visit those holy places beyond the sea, although in my youth I was unable to satisfy it, being continually hindered by some cause or other. Since, however, the most high God by His Grace, freed me in my old age from every impediment and provided me with all I needed, it seemed good to me to renew the determination to go on this holy voyage. And in order that I should have no opportunity of becoming lukewarm any more, I bound myself by a vow, two years ago, to go at all costs, although I was then between sixty and seventy years of age.[21]

By taking a formal vow, the pilgrim gave herself or himself certain rights and protections as well as obligations. Pilgrims formed a special class, and laws attempted to enable the successful completion of their vows. All pilgrims came under the protection of the church for the duration of their pilgrimage. Thus all judicial matters pertaining to pilgrims were to be considered by ecclesiastical courts, not secular ones. Clerical and lay pilgrims alike could also have contact with the excommunicates and persons under interdict who were fellow-travelers making a necessary pilgrimage.[22]

Before leaving, one needed to put one's affairs in order. The time needed to do so could easily account for the four years that elapsed before a nobleman like Ogier left for Jerusalem. Casola tells us that two years passed between his vow and his departure. Prospective pilgrims were encouraged to make a will, in order to provide for one's family if one did not return. Noble pilgrims or landholders needed to provide for the lands and people they were leaving during their absence, while clerics needed to obtain permission from their superiors.

Pilgrims also needed to settle their debts before they left on their travels, for both temporal and spiritual reasons. Thus when Margery Kempe planned to visit Jerusalem, she asked the parish priest of Lynn to announce from the pulpit on her behalf that any man or woman who claimed any debt against her or her husband should come and speak with her before she left, and she, with God's help, would settle anything due to such persons, so that they would hold themselves content.[23]

Many pilgrims received a formal blessing before they left on their journey, ritually setting themselves apart for their coming experience. The Sarum Missal provided such a service of blessing for pilgrims, with psalms, a responsory, and collects, which were said while the pilgrims lay prostrate before the altar. Then they arose, the priest blessed their scrips or pouches, and placed one around each pilgrim's neck. Then he blessed the staffs, and delivered one to each pilgrim as well. Then followed a Mass for Travelers. After the Mass, the priest said prayers over the pilgrims, once again prostrate before the altar, "whether they shall be traveling to Jerusalem, or to the threshold of St. James, or on any other pilgrimage. Then shall the pilgrims be commissioned, and so depart in the name of the Lord."[24]

The liminal portion of the journey looms largest in the written accounts, as the pilgrims tell us about their voyages to the Holy Land and their experiences there. In this phase the pilgrims have left their familiar surroundings and have entered into *communitas* with fellow pilgrims as they travel together to Jerusalem. Many pilgrims actually embarked for Jerusalem from Venice. The Venetians built a sizable and regulated industry transporting pilgrims to and from the Holy Land, and securing passage and provisions there took a good deal of attention. Pietro Casola spent days going through the markets in Venice, partly for pleasure, but also to acquire necessary goods for his trip.[25]

The search for supplies caused ongoing problems, especially for those with little money, or even for those with foreign currency. Shipboard travel exacerbated the situation, since once on the ship, travelers were required to have everything they would use during their voyage. Ships did stop periodically along the coast, but sometimes passengers could not buy additional provisions. Apparently passage on a ship did not necessarily include linens and food service. Margery Kempe's traveling companions bought containers for wine and bedding for themselves, but not for Margery, and she was forced to obtain her own provisions. Apparently they hoped to be rid of her for the rest of their journey, but she outsmarted them. Despite their dislike of her, when she claimed that the Lord had told her not to sail in the ship they had booked but had assigned her to a galley instead, her fellow-travelers sold their containers of wine and booked passage on Margery's galley.[26]

The trip to Jerusalem was long, difficult, expensive, and dangerous. After the fall of Acre in 1291, the pilgrims traveled to land not held by Christians but controlled by Muslims. All the travelers discussed here journeyed by sea from Venice. Pietro Casola's trip took about six weeks; he boarded his ship near Venice on June 4 and anchored off the coast of Jaffa on July 17.[27] Casola had originally agreed to pay forty-five gold ducats to the *patrono* of the pilgrim galley, but he later paid sixty Venetian ducats. His fare included passage and care by land and sea, as far as the River Jordan, if Casola wished to travel there, and a place at the *patrono*'s table.[28] Many pilgrims paid less and received less as well. Venetian statutes of 1440 indicated that *patroni* should not charge pilgrims more than fifty ducats for passage money and expenses.[29] Probably the statutes were not scrupulously enforced, since Casola paid sixty ducats, but this amount may have provided services for his journey beyond those covered by the statutes.

Most travelers describe fierce storms at sea. Casola's ship was menaced by pirates as well.[30] Many pilgrims suffered from seasickness.[31] By his own admission, Casola fared better than many pilgrims, probably owing to his clerical status and wealth, but he still suffered many hardships. Ogier describes the lack of "necessities" on the return voyage: "We had been three days and more without drinking any wine, and also all of our food had been exhausted for the past four days, nor did the steward have any victuals with which he could help us, except a very little water which stank and a little rancid biscuit full of weevils."[32] Even rank and wealth could not always assure a pilgrim's comfort.

Pilgrims sometimes died on their pilgrimage to the Holy Land. Casola describes the death of a Datian pilgrim: "It was said that he had fallen ill at Candia through eating unripe grapes. The truth is that hardly enough money was found on him to bury him. With the permission of the Custodian of Jaffa, who represents there the Governor of Jerusalem, he was carried on land and buried in a cave on the seashore."[33] Those pilgrims who died while staying at hospitals of the Order of St. John could be buried in the order's cemeteries, and rules governed the burial of the dead, according to twelfth-century statutes.[34] Ogier also lost one of his three companions on the trip home. Simon of Saarbruch, a man of stout constitution and good health, contracted a fever on Cyprus. After several attacks, the fever broke, and he thought himself cured, but he suffered a relapse and died a few days later. He was buried in the Church of Saint Francis in the Franciscan monastery of Nicosia.[35]

As pilgrims approached the Holy Land, they needed to make peace with one another, as Margery demonstrated when she and her shipmates were approaching the port. There, despite their mistreatment of her, which included locking up her bedclothes and the theft of one of her sheets by a priest, Margery sought the pardon of her companions: "I pray you, sirs, be in charity with me, for I am in charity with you, and forgive me if I have annoyed you along the way. And if any of you have in any way trespassed against me, God forgive you for it, as I do."[36] One could hardly expect to receive the merits of even such an arduous pilgrimage as one to Jerusalem if one was not in love and charity with one's neighbors.

Once in the Holy Land, the pilgrims often described harassment and maltreatment by Saracen officials and guides. Muslims held the Holy Land, and they curtailed the movements of pilgrims. They also levied high tolls at the entrances to holy places, providing themselves with steady income.[37] When Birgitta prepared to enter Jerusalem itself, she paid 72 dirhems (4 florins) entry fee.[38] Pietro Casola describes staying several days on shipboard at Jaffa, awaiting permission first to land and go to Jerusalem, then to see many of the holy places.[39] Ogier writes similarly about leaving Castle David for nearby Jerusalem: "Shortly after, we left there all afoot, and by leave of the sultan's lieutenant entered the holy city of Jerusalem."[40]

In Jerusalem itself, Christians could not wander freely or visit whatever places they wished. Ogier reports that they were only allowed to see "the holy Temple of God and Solomon" from a distance, "for as soon as the Saracens see a Christian coming up this street leading to the holy temple, they shout at him and make him turn back and jabber that he must not come there to see the holy temple."[41] Conditions improved somewhat for pilgrims at the beginning of the fourteenth century, when King Robert d'Anjou and his wife Sancha of Sicily bought the region around the ruined temple. They presented it to the Holy See on condition that the Franciscans should serve as its custodians for all time. Pope Clement VI confirmed the donation in a bull of November 21, 1342.[42]

Franciscans led guided tours, sometimes hustling the pilgrims from place to place. Those with limited time could go on a one-day tour, which included twenty-two stops. The tour group assembled before dawn at the Church of the Holy Sepulchre and struck out on the Via Dolorosa, following the stations of the cross in reverse order. They went to the Rich Man's house, some thirty yards south of the Via Dolorosa, where the dogs had licked the sores of Lazarus. Next they visited two stations of the cross, one where Simon of Cyrene took the cross, and the second where Mary met Jesus with the cross. A slender arch spanned the street at the site of Pilate's palace, where Christ appeared before the multitude. Fourteenth-century tradition held that the two stones inserted in the arch came from Pilate's Seat of Judgment (pp. 52–54).

Leaving Pilate's palace, they passed the site of Herod's palace, then went eastward to the Church of St. Anne, the traditional childhood home of the Virgin Mary and her parents, Anne and Joachim. Although St. Birgitta could not visit it in 1371, fifteenth-century pilgrims sometimes could enter the crypt which preserved the dwelling through a special side entrance, using a small window in the lower part of the church wall (p. 54).

Next the Christians visited the Pool of Bethesda, near the Church of St. Anne, where they could climb down steep steps and glimpse a stretch of water in dark underground cellar-like pits (pp. 54–56). Continuing eastward they passed through the Sheep Gate or St. Stephen's Gate, near where St. Stephen had been martyred. They then turned south and followed the wall to the Golden Gate. Fourteenth-century pilgrimage accounts held that the gate was impossible to open since Christ had ridden through it on an ass on

Palm Sunday, but the iron rivets from the huge cyprus doors offered themselves as prized relics and souvenirs for pilgrims (p. 56).

After leaving the city, the tour visited the Valley of Josaphat and crossed Cedron Brook where, according to the legend of the Holy Cross, the stock of Jesus' cross had once formed part of a foot-bridge. Across the stream, at the foot of the Mount of Olives, lay the Church of the Tomb of the Virgin Mary. Through the mediation of Queen Joanna of Naples, the Franciscans had received permission from the Sultan of Egypt to celebrate Mass there (pp. 56, 61).

They moved on to the Cave of Gethsemane on the slope of the mountain just above the Church of the Virgin, where tradition held that Christ retired to pray with his disciples before he was taken before Pilate. In the fourteenth century a Latin inscription was added on the wall above the spot where Christ knelt and prayed, which in translation reads: "This is where the Holy King sweated blood while he prayed, saying, 'Father, if Thou be willing, remove this cup from me'" (p. 61). Near the cave lay the Garden of Gethsemane, flourishing with olive trees and flowers. From the Mount of Olives the Virgin Mary ascended to heaven, an event witnessed by the Apostle Thomas alone. Another small chapel there, marking the spot where Jesus wept over Jerusalem, had been in ruins since the beginning of the fourteenth century (p. 62). The most important site to visit was the ruins of the Eleona, erected by Constantine's mother, Helena, in memory of Christ's ascension. Tradition held that Christ had taught the disciples the Pater Noster at the destroyed Pater Church, and that the apostles had met there to compose the Apostles' Creed in the cave (p. 62).

Following the same road down the Mount of Olives, the pilgrims turned left and passed stonework hewn from the cliff and known as the graves of the prophets, of Absalom, and of Zacharias. Then they followed the Cedron Valley along the slope below the city wall to the pool of Siloam. Nearby on the slope of Mount Zion lay the shrine of St. Peter Gallicante, where tradition held that Peter had denied Christ three times. By the fourteenth and fifteenth centuries, only the ruins of an early Christian church remained there (pp. 66–68). Most of the sites on Mount Zion were ruins by the fourteenth century, including the place where Christ had instituted the Eucharist and washed the feet of the apostles. Only the Chapel of the Holy Ghost, the Cenacle, had escaped destruction (p. 68). The final two

sites were the house of the high priest Caiphas and the cathedral of
the Armenian patriarchate, consecrated to the apostle St. James the
Greater (p. 70).

The Franciscan tour ended at the Holy Sepulchre, the ultimate
goal of the entire pilgrimage. Since their day had been so long, some
pilgrims waited until the next day before leaving the site. Others, by
special arrangement with the Muslim watchmen, remained all
night at vigil in the church (p. 75). Casola describes spending such
a vigil there, hearing Masses and praying.[43] Margery Kempe also
spent the night in the Church of the Holy Sepulchre, in company
with other pilgrims: "They were let in on the one day at evensong
time, and remained until evensong time on the next day."[44]

Not everyone sped around Jerusalem so quickly on the one-day
tour. Birgitta remained in the Holy Land for four months, almost
entirely in Jerusalem itself, and she lodged at the pilgrims' hostel
one block from the Holy Sepulchre. She received one of her revelations on Good Friday, the day after she reached Jerusalem, as she
prayed that day at the Holy Sepulchre.[45] During her lengthy stay,
she must have spent much time in prayer and meditation at many
of the holy places and traversed the Via Dolorosa regularly.

Margery Kempe spent three weeks in Jerusalem, enjoying visions
and wailing and crying at the places of the Passion. Unlike many
others recounting their pilgrimages, she does not complain about
being mistreated by the Franciscans or the Muslims, only by her fellow Englishmen. She reports that "the friars of the Church of the
Holy Sepulchre were very welcoming to her and gave her many
great relics, wanting her to remain among them if she had wished,
because of the belief they had in her."[46] Similarly, she praises the
Muslims, who, she says, "made much of her and conveyed and es-
corted her about the country wherever she wanted to go."[47] In particular, a handsome Saracen gentleman helped her up Mount
Quarentyne when her companions refused to assist her. She "put a
groat into his hand, making signs to him to take her up the mountain. And quickly the Saracen took her under his arm and led her
up the high mountain where our Lord fasted forty days."[48] In fact,
Margery reports that "she found all people good and gentle to her,
except her own countrymen."[49]

With the visit to the Holy Sepulchre, the pilgrims had officially
completed their pilgrimages and fulfilled their vows, whether or not

they started for home immediately. When they did, they entered the last phase of their pilgrimage, aggregation, returning and arriving home and reintegrating into their former society. With his typical asperity, Ogier d'Anglure offers only a brief report: "The following Thursday, the twenty-second day of June and two days before the feast of Saint John the Baptist, in the year of grace of Our Lord 1396, we were back for dinner in Anglure."[50] Pietro Casola, however, describes an elaborate ritual action of welcoming that symbolically marks his return to his former life and effectively reintegrates him into his community:

> On Friday, the 14th of November, by the grace of the Most High and Excellent God, I reached Milan and entered the city by the Porta Orientale, in pilgrim's dress and alone, although many of my friends had come to meet me at an early hour.
>
> I first visited the principal church and thanked Our Lady for the notable help vouchsafed to me in the many perils I had passed through on this voyage, both by sea and by land. Then I went to see our Most Reverend Lord the Archbishop, who, as I said before, had given me the cross and bestowed his blessing upon me. He received me in his chapel most graciously, and did and said over me all that is laid down in the Pontifical to be done to a pilgrim when he returns to the fatherland. Thus with his blessing I went home, and was very joyfully welcomed by my friends.[51]

The blessing for the returning pilgrim clearly mirrors that for the outgoing one and incorporates the journey to the earthly Jerusalem into the larger salvific pattern, whereby the soul proceeds from God into the world and returns to him in heaven, the eternal fatherland. The lay pilgrim Ogier, too, evidently understood this, for he closes his pilgrimage account with the following benediction: "May the grace of Our Lord Jesus Christ be the guard of all Christians who are making, will make, and have made this holy voyage, and bring us all to Paradise. Amen."[52]

With the end of the journey and the aggregation phase, the pilgrim had completed the pilgrimage as a physical and spiritual exercise. What followed after resuming one's life marked the real importance of that spiritual experience. Perhaps the former pilgrim could not ever describe how the voyage to Jerusalem had changed him or her. Margery Kempe certainly came back from Jerusalem fortified for her future life. She had received the assurance of God's love for her and the righteousness of her actions. Birgitta learned in one of her visions in the Holy Land that her wayward son Charles had found pardon, that her prayers had caused the devil to forget the charges against him, and that he had died penitent.[53] This revelation consoled her, and Birgitta herself died peacefully less than a year after she returned to Rome from Jerusalem.

The lay saint Birgitta of Sweden may perhaps serve as the chief exemplar for medieval pilgrimage to the Holy Land. She certainly had desired to go to Jerusalem for years. As early as 1341, when she returned from a pilgrimage to Santiago de Compostela with her husband, a prophetic vision had shown her visiting both Rome and Jerusalem. About thirty years elapsed, however, before this prophecy came true for her Jerusalem pilgrimage. When the call actually came, she hesitated. Nearly seventy and frail from her ascetical life, she found the prospect daunting, but Jesus himself allayed her fears in another vision: "Why dost thou plead thy age? I am the creator of life. I am able to weaken or strengthen life as I please. I shall be with thee, I shall choose thy path and lead thee from Rome and back and provide thee with all that is necessary, even with more than thou has ever had before."[54] Thus filled with Jesus' assurance and obedient to his call, Birgitta set off to Jerusalem. In this way her contemplative life had eventually led her to accept the call to the very active devotion of the arduous pilgrimage to Jerusalem, a pilgrimage she shared with thousands of other late medieval pilgrims, most of whom were lay.

Judging by the extant accounts, the motives that originally moved these pilgrims to go on pilgrimage found fulfillment. Margery Kempe sought to give thanks for the grace of her conversion, to find spiritual healing, to be confirmed in her unusual vocation, and her *Book* bears witness to the reception of these graces. Pietro Casola was able to fulfill his vow and the longing of his youth. The pilgrims also found the pardon they were seeking, whether for themselves (as in Ogier's case) or for another (as in Birgitta's). Thus coming in contact with the physical geography of the Holy Land— the place where Jesus had lived, died, and risen from the dead— truly may be said to have shaped what Niebuhr calls "the lasting geography of [their] souls."[55]

Angela of Foligno:
A Eucharistic Model of Lay Sanctity
MARY WALSH MEANY

> *The ministry of word and sacrament . . . has been entrusted in a*
> *special way to the clergy. However, lay people have their own im-*
> *portant part to play in this ministry too.*
>   Vatican II: On the Apostolate of the Laity

Angela of Foligno (†1309) was a married laywoman who became a
visionary, a Franciscan tertiary, and a spiritual director whose circle
of disciples included Ubertino of Casale, a leader of the spiritual
Franciscan movement.[1] At first sight, she seems to be anything but
a model of lay sanctity, because her own spiritual life, in the sense
both of her identity and worldview and of her active presence in the
world, required separation from her family and from other elements that we ordinarily recognize as belonging to lay Christian
life.[2] She is wrongly but not altogether surprisingly depicted in visual art as a religious.[3] The encomiastic epilogue to her *Book*, moreover, displays a distinct ambivalence about Angela's lay status. On
the one hand, it uses the topos of the unlettered woman chosen by
God to bear a prophetic message to the hierarchy who have been
corrupted by worldly wisdom and power; on the other, it implies
that Angela became holy to the extent that she ceased to live as a laywoman. According to the epilogue, God in His wisdom "raised up a
woman of lay estate, who was bound to worldly obligations, a husband and sons, possessions and wealth," but who "broke these
worldly bonds and ascended to the peaks of gospel perfection."[4]

  A closer look at Angela's life and writings, however, reveals her
to be (as the Prologue to her *Book* indicates) an exemplum for all
those "who are truly faithful," especially God's "people," the laity
(pp. 123–24). Angela's personal encounter with the God-Man in the
Eucharist, her experience of the church as community in her circle

of disciples, and her deliberate embrace of poverty all serve to high-light basic liturgical and sacramental conditions of lay sanctity within the Catholic tradition. They illumine what Lawrence Cunningham has called "the ultimate meaning of being a believer."[5] They even shed light on what to our eyes are apparent shadows in Angela's portrait of lay sanctity: her asceticism and her renunciation of fa-milial ties.

Angela's pursuit of evangelical poverty—indeed, her entire way of receiving the Divinity, of being open to the Other, of entering into the life of grace—is marked by the influence of Saint Francis of Assisi, who encountered the Divine in a historical person, the God-Man Jesus Christ, and in the Eucharist. In his "First Admonition" Francis presents Incarnation and Eucharist as two kenotic acts of humility:

> See, daily [the Son of God] humbles himself as when He came down from the royal throne into the womb of the Virgin; daily He comes to us in a humble form; daily He comes down from the bosom of the Father upon the altar in the hands of the priest. And as he appeared to the holy apostles in true flesh, so now He reveals Himself to us in the sacred bread. . . . And in this way the Lord is always with His faithful.[6]

Francis's "Second Version of the Letter to All the Faithful" simi-larly focuses on the Eucharist and likens the reception of the host by the laity to Mary's conception of Christ within her womb. To be Christ's mother, Francis insists, means to carry him "in our heart and body through love . . . , [and to] give birth to Him through His holy manner of working," that is, by making him present in the world.[7]

Standing among "the faithful" as a follower of Francis and a "mother" of Christ, Angela bears witness both to the abiding pres-ence of the eucharistic Christ and to the constitutive importance of the laity in the institutional life of the church. Through the clergy, the church nourishes Angela's spiritual life with the Eucharist, and she in turn gives life to the church through her original spirituality, which is Christocentric, kenotic, and sacramental. Angela encoun-ters the poor Christ in the Eucharist; her imitation of Christ, there-fore, is a struggle for poverty understood as a self-emptying. Thus in her eucharistic piety she brings together two fundamentally important themes in thirteenth-century Christianity: a spirituality shaped by devotion to the God-Man and a morality inspired by the rejection of property and power.[8]

Franciscan in its general features, and first inspired by devotion to Francis, Angela's own spirituality combines an attachment to the incarnate God-Man with an intense eucharistic receptivity that extends into a remarkable vision of, and service to, the members of Christ's body. Whereas her encounters with the poor, naked Christ take place, first of all, in the extraordinary experiences recorded in the "steps" of her spiritual journey, they continue in an ongoing fashion in the context of the Eucharist.

Angela was born to well-to-do parents around 1250, married young, and had several children. The "Memorial" of her *Book* indicates that in 1285 she went to confession in tears and began to live a converted, penitential life (pp. 124–25). She accuses her youthful self of luxury, of hypocrisy, of having lived what Paul LaChance describes as "a loose and unconscious life."[9] Writing of her luxuriousness, Angela refers to three elements of life in the world which are familiar to a contemporary American woman: enjoyment of food and drink and sexual pleasure, enjoyment of comfortable surroundings and nice clothes, enjoyment of family love.

It is not entirely clear, however, what Angela means when she decribes herself as "a great sinner" (pp. 219–21). One interpretation is that she was guilty of adultery, but it may be that she accuses herself of failing to live a life of poverty. From Angela's own point of view, poverty was certainly of central importance in her struggle to be a good Christian. This attitude of hers was shaped, on the one hand, by her longing to desire only Christ, to be free to be his beloved; on the other hand, by her realization of the importance of poverty, by her understanding that the God-Man is the poor, naked, crucified Christ.

Moved by this essential Franciscan insight, she found it necessary to dislocate herself from the complex self-presentation we call respectability, from the web of associations and responsibilities which make up the life of a good daughter, wife, and mother. After her initial conversion, she detached herself from material goods, putting "aside [her] best garments, fine food, and fancy headdress" (p. 126), and she prayed to God for the death of her mother, her husband, and her sons, whom she perceived to be "great obstacle[s]" on her path to perfection. She reports that when all her family members did, in fact, die, she took "great consolation" in that occurrence and thanked God for having heard her prayer (p. 126).

Angela's statement shocks us. That Angela lived exactly as she did, however, does not mean that we are to live exactly as she did. The imperative is not to reenact the narrative, but to be at the disposal of the Other *as she was*. "Blessed" Angela was a "saint" such as Cunningham describes: "a person so grasped by a religious vision that it becomes central to his or her life in a way that radically changes the person and leads others to glimpse the value of that vision."[10]

Angela's eucharistic vision transformed her life so powerfully that even today her story (to echo Edith Wyschogrod) "can sweep us up by its narrative force."[11] Faithful to the Gospel, Angela accepted the mission to make Christ present in the world in ways that resonate for twentieth-century laypersons who, like Angela, are and remain receptive to Jesus Christ precisely in a eucharistic context.

The eucharistic tenor of Angela's whole spirituality clearly reflects her self-awareness as a layperson and a woman. As Caroline Walker Bynum has observed in her important study of late medieval food asceticism, "The pattern of [eucharistic] miracles, like the pattern of canonizations, underlines the dichotomy: men are priests, whose act of God shimmers with unearthly power; women are recipients, whose act of eating is dignified with the reassurance that the food they take is really God."[12] According to Bynum, the religious practices of women like Angela elevated the "role of vessel, of recipient . . . to a new significance." The tendency of "male theologians to equate priest with church" (on the grounds of hierarchical office and headship) was countered and complemented by a charismatic tendency on the part of women to image the church as a mother "pregnant with salvation," and to use the members of their own bodies as a means of identification with the Body of Christ.[13] This identification is carried forward through abstinence, reception of the Eucharist, and distribution of food to the poor.

As Bynum argues, Angela's long fasts from human food during the preliminary steps of her spiritual journey nourished her physical and spiritual craving for the divine food of the Eucharist as a positive replacement for the worldly sustenance she had denied herself. Only after the crisis of her conversion did Angela overcome this dichotomy through a deeper understanding of the Eucharist as an avenue into Christ's infinite love for her, a love revealed through his physical body, broken on the cross, and mediated through the eucharistic host. Angela then expressed and extended her eucharistic experience in charitable works, especially feeding the poor.[14]

While medieval women are famous for their corporal works of mercy, Angela seems to have undertaken not only this traditional ministry but also a different, spiritual ministry: she became both a nursing mother for the poor through almsgiving and a teaching mother to her disciples through admonition and instruction. Brother Arnaldo's "Memorial" of her revelations is so striking (and the questions about his editorial role are so interesting) that the twentieth-century reader may forget that Angela devoted herself not to cultivating her own experience, not to her self, but to instructing her disciples, so that they would grow into responsible roles in the church.

This pedagogical dimension of Angela's ministry is, as we shall see, as profoundly eucharistic as her almsgiving. According to Angela, apostolic action is "the sign and measure of love" (p. 290). In her "Instructions," she directs her disciples to the Eucharist as the source of their vitality: "All the saints . . . can and do . . . find joy in this mystery because of the good and the benefits this sacrament procures for the holy souls of the militant church" (p. 297). If they are to make Christ present in the world, she insists, Christ must first be present to them through their reception of the Eucharist. Indeed, in the mystical experience of Angela, the Eucharist is inseparable from the church as the body of Christ. In the "sacrament of the altar," she finds herself in the presence not only of Christ but also of the faithful, for, as the eucharistic Christ himself told her, "Wherever I am, the faithful are also with me" (p. 217).

Angela's entire spiritual development may be said to lead her to this eucharistic vision. Not only does Angela's experience of the body of Christ—historical, sacramental, and ecclesial—form an organic whole, but also her very understanding of personal and communal holiness as a series of "transformations" (and even "transubstantiations") centers radically on the effective grace of the Eucharist, in which she discovers and receives the God-Man, present in his body, blood, soul, and divinity. In the Eucharist Angela finds the true mirror for her own human nature, divinized through

grace; from the Eucharist she derives her fundamental understanding of her self, her mission, and her relationship to others.

In the compilation known as *The Book of Blessed Angela of Foligno*—
which comprises the "Memorial" that Angela dictated to Brother
Arnaldo, as well as the so-called "Instructions"—Angela describes
her journey to God as a sequence of thirty steps, but also as three re-
current, but progressive, transformations: "Sometimes the soul is
transformed into God's will; sometimes it is transformed with God;
and sometimes it is transformed within God and God within the
soul" (p. 222).[15] These three transformations correspond to three
important turning points in Angela's life.

Angela's first transformation, which "occurs when the soul strives
to imitate the works of the suffering God-Man because God's will
has been and is being manifested in them" (p. 222), develops
through the first nineteen penitential steps on her way after her initial conversion in 1285. It marks her turning away from sin, her
movement away from her familial location, and her embrace of her
desire for Christ, the suffering and lovable God-Man. According to
Angela's own testimony, her conversion meant "beginning to look
at the cross" (p. 125) and discovering in it "the Book of Life." On
the basis of personal experience, therefore, she counsels her disciples to practice "gazing on the cross in continual prayer" (p. 268),
until the soul finally "distances itself from the weighty cares of the
world," rises above itself, and "is transformed into the God-Man."

This second transformation, "when the soul is united with God,
feels deeply the consolations of God's presence, and can express
these with words and thoughts" (p. 222), coincides with the twentieth step on Angela's spiritual way. In 1291 Angela made a pilgrimage
from Foligno to Assisi, the twentieth step in her spiritual journey; as
she approached Assisi she came to a crossroads, literally and figura-
tively. (The image of the crossroads is, of course, a pervasive ancient
and modern symbol which refers, among other possibilities, to a con-
vergence of possibilities and to a moment of decision.) As she approached the crossroads, Angela was praying to St. Francis of Assisi
that he ask God to give her the grace of poverty. At the crossroads,
God spoke to her with an unprecedented intimacy:

> He began to say: "My daughter, my dear and sweet daughter, my
> delight, my temple, my beloved daughter, love me, because you
> are very much loved by me; much more than you could ever love

me." Very often, he also said: "My daughter and my sweet spouse."
And he further added: I love you so much more than any other
woman in the valley of Spoleto. I have found a place to rest in
you; now in turn place yourself and find your own rest in me."
(pp. 139–40)

The language of indwelling transforms Angela's hunger and emptiness into a "temple" where Christ lives, and he in turn becomes a
resting place for Angela. He identifies himself to Angela first in
terms of his historical passion and the eucharistic sacrifice: "I am the
one who was crucified for you. I have known hunger and thirst for
you; and I shed my blood for you, I have loved you so much" (p. 140).
Then, flooding her senses with "joy and sweetness," God tells her, "I
am the Holy Spirit who enters into your deepest self" (p. 141).

The transforming experiences of God's personal love for her
that Angela enjoyed during this pilgrimage to Assisi had two immediate effects on her eucharistic devotion. First, as Bynum has noted,
it overcame the dichotomy between human food and divine food.
On the way home to Foligno, Angela remembers that God had said
to her as she approached Assisi: "Your whole life, your eating, drinking, sleeping, and all that you do are pleasing to me" (p. 142).
Angela understands that God loves her at all times and in all things.
Thus, even her "eating and drinking," the ordinary food and drink
that sustain her mortal existence, assume a eucharistic quality as a
memorial of God's constant, loving presence and concern.

Second, after the pilgrimage to Assisi, Angela strongly associates
the humanity of Christ with the Eucharist. Her visions join together
the body of Christ raised on the cross with the consecrated host elevated during the sacrifice of the Mass, and her theological reflection begins to assimilate the paschal events of Holy Thursday, Good
Friday, and Easter. Upon her return to Foligno, Angela "was medi-
tating on the great suffering which Christ endured on the cross"
(p. 145) and stretched out her arms in a cruciform position. Suddenly she had a vision of Christ's throat and arms that filled her with
"a new joy, different from the others" that she had known. In her
attempt to describe the beauty of the vision, she refers to similar
eucharistic experiences:

I do not know how to compare the clarity and brightness of that
vision with anything or any color in the world except, perhaps,

the clarity and brightness of Christ's body, which I sometimes see
at the elevation of the host. (p. 145)

The transfigured body of Christ that Angela sees in visions of the
host takes various forms. Sometimes the "body" appears in the form
of light, as a pure radiance that "surpasses the splendor of the sun"
(p. 146). At other times Angela beholds in the host "two most splen-
did eyes, and these are so large that it seems only the edges of the
host remain visible" (p. 147). On another occasion, she saw "the
Christ Child in the host" as the priest raised it, and she became "very
upset because the priest put down the host on the altar too quickly"
(p. 147). All these visions, she says, filled her with "great and ineffa-
ble joy."

Extraordinary visions like these were not, however, essential to
Angela's eucharistic devotion. In an interesting exchange, Angela
tells her scribe about an experience she had one day during Mass at
the moment of the elevation of the body of Christ.[16] She relates that
Mary had spoken to her, "making [her] understand that her Son
was at that moment already on the altar": "[This] filled my soul with
such great joy that I cannot find words for it." When the scribe asks
Angela if her joy had been inspired by an actual vision of Christ,
"something similar to what she was accustomed to seeing on other
occasions," she replies "no," but insists that "she truly felt Christ in
her soul." Her "extreme delight" was such, in fact, that all the members in her body "[felt] a disjointing." She goes on to say that she actually hears her "bones cracking . . .when they are thus disjointed."
This experience recurs, moreover, whenever her "soul . . .knows
that God is truly present," but especially when she stands or kneels
in the eucharistic presence: "I hear this disjointing more when the
body of Christ is elevated. It is especially then that my hands suffer
this disjointing and are opened" (pp. 157–58).

This description of Angela's experience contributes a great deal
to our understanding of her as a model for lay sanctity. Most basi-
cally, it locates her relationship to Christ in the ordinary eucharistic
context available to other lay Christians. The image of the disjointed and open hands directs our attention, moreover, to a ges-
ture of openhanded giving and kenotic suffering on the part of
both Angela and Christ. The "disjointing" Angela feels in her limbs
not only brings her own body into contact with Christ's body; it also
opens her soul to an encounter with Christ's soul and divinity, pre-

sent in the host.[17] Brother Arnaldo, Angela's "brother scribe" and confessor, relates that "at each communion, Christ's faithful one used to receive a special grace," and that Angela desired "to receive communion daily" in the firm belief "that receiving communion purifies, sanctifies, consoles, and preserves the soul" (p. 209). The reception of communion gave Angela "an indescribable feeling of God's presence" and inspired her soul's desire "to give itself totally to Christ because it saw that Christ gave himself totally to us" (p. 174). Every communion reminded Angela of God's words: "Beloved, the All Good is within you, and you have come to receive the All Good" (p. 186).

What seems to be significant here is that for Angela the eucharistic experience is not only an encounter with Jesus Christ, but also an experience of his body that draws her into Christ's own soul and thus into the indwelling Trinity. In receiving the triune God, "the All Good," into her own body, Angela comes to recognize God's omnipresence in the universe: "This whole world is pregnant with God!" (p. 170). The host thus becomes a doorway for her into the realization that Christ is not only present in the sacrament but also ubiquitous in creation. Paradoxically, the belief in Christ's special, real presence in the host—which she receives into the limited space of her own body—deepens and enlarges her understanding of God's abiding, universal presence in her and in all things:

> And close to the moment of the elevation of the body of Christ, he said: "Behold, the divine power is now present on the altar. I am within you. You can now receive me because you have already done so. Receive communion, therefore, with the blessing of God the Father, the Son, and the Holy Spirit. I who am worthy make you worthy." (p. 170)

The eucharistic reminder of abiding presence ("I am within you"), the naming of the persons of the Trinity, and the language of charismatic empowerment evoke the apostolic blessing of Christ with which the Gospels conclude (Matthew 28:16–20; Luke 24:44–53; Acts 1:6–9). This Trinitarian blessing and communion filled Angela with such "great joy and . . . indescribable sweetness" that the memory of it sustained her throughout her life and inspired her apostolic work.

Bynum has rightly characterized Angela's almsgiving—especially in the distribution of food to the poor—as an extension of her reception of the Eucharist. In feeding and caring for the sick, Angela, like many Italian tertiaries, found a means to come into loving, physical contact with human bodies that served "as a substitute for Jesus' own."[18] One Holy Thursday, for instance, when Angela visited the hospital, she and her companions first distributed alms and then "washed the feet of the women and the hands of the men, and especially those of one of the lepers which were festering and in an advanced stage of decomposition" (p. 163). Afterwards they "drank the very water with which [they] had washed him," and Angela recalls, "We tasted its sweetness, and it was as if we had received Holy Communion."

Satisfying the needs of the sick and poor also enabled Angela to bring the body of Christ indirectly to others. On one occasion, as Angela was praying a meal prayer, she remembered Christ's Last Supper with his disciples and asked his blessing over her food. In reply she received the answer: "Almighty God always blesses whatever you eat and drink for as long as you live in this world" (p. 156). In addition, Christ bestowed a sacramental power on the alms that Angela received and distributed to the hungry "so that whomever we share[d] them with—such is the power already contained in this blessing—[would] benefit from them according to the measure of their disposition." Those in mortal sin who ate Angela's bread would, for instance, be moved inwardly to penitence.

As Paul LaChance observes, because Angela's prayer before eating and distributing alms makes the food holy and a medium of actual grace, it "seems to arrogate . . . a kind of priestly role" for her.[19] Like most of the female mystics, however, Angela claims priesthood (to use Bynum's phrase) "only by analogy."[20] Even in this incident, Angela describes herself as the recipient of Christ's blessing, not as a consecrator in her own right. Hers is thus neither an "aping of the clergy nor open rebellion against clerical prerogative."[21] Despite Angela's strong eucharistic orientation, she never places herself, even in vision, in the official role of a priest. Rather, in keeping with her Franciscan legacy, she affirms that "the priest ought to and does pronounce" the words of consecration (p. 296), and is the normal mediator of the Eucharist.[22]

On the other hand, Angela insists that Christ himself can and does act directly in her soul, even in a sacramental sense, without clerical mediation. When, for instance, the friars grumbled about Angela's too frequent reception of the sacrament of the sick and refused to anoint her on her sick bed, she received this mystical assurance from Christ: "I with all my priests will anoint you; you will indeed be anointed" (p. 276). Similarly, when Angela in her last illness before her death desired greatly to receive communion and grew very sad "because there was no one available to bring [her] the most sacred body of Christ" (p. 312), she had a vision of angels who led her to a heavenly altar where Jesus himself awaited her in the host, and the angels told her, "Prepare yourself to receive the one who has espoused you with the ring of his love."

These incidents—and indeed Angela's life as a whole—make her an outstanding example of what Bynum calls a "charismatic model, a lay model" for holiness, which stands as an alternative, a complement, and a powerful corrective to the clerical model of office:

> Women's devotion to . . . the eucharistic elements was . . . an endowing of their role as "nonpriests" with a new spiritual importance. . . . Women's eucharistic devotion was the devotion of . . . those who are lay rather than clergy, those whose closeness to God and whose authorization to serve others come through intimacy and direct inspiration rather through office or worldly power.[23]

Furthermore, Angela's ability to attract a wide circle of male disciples, to be a "holy mother" to many spiritual "sons," supports Bynum's thesis that "clerics . . . actively sought, in holy women, both a standard of piety and a window open to the divine," and found in lay mystics like Angela "a reversal and a critique of exactly those things about which [they] felt greatest ambivalence": "wealth, power, and office."[24]

In Angela's case, it seems appropriate to say that her understanding of her responsibility to make the Gospel present in the world is colored by her years as wife and mother. Angela was not a recluse who was visited by those seeking her advice, like Julian of Norwich was. She was a laywoman living in the world, and it is in that context that she was given her mission. As she assumes responsibility for directing the spiritual progress of others, she acts in roles which were fitting for a laywoman: she is God's spouse and a mother to the friars. She is responsible for directing and feeding others, but her authority to do so comes from her location in her spouse's

network; she is his delegate. In this case Christ is the spouse, and
her relationship with him is the source of her authority. To put this
another way, Angela's role is to influence rather than to command
others to live a life of openness to Christ, as a mother might influence rather than command her sons.

Angela herself explicitly associates what she calls "the third transformation" with the "wisdom, maturity, depth, discernment, and enlightenment" that knows how to "regulate the love of God and
neighbor" (p. 222) and thus with her ability to be a spiritual mother
to her sons. The third transformation, as we have seen, occurs
through "a most perfect union" whereby the soul "is transformed
within God and God within the soul."[25] What has been insufficiently
noticed and understood is the eucharistic significance of this transformation, which virtually refashions Angela into a host for others,
and thus makes her a bond of unity for the reformist Franciscan
community at Foligno.

The third transformation, in which the soul "feels and tastes
God's presence in such a sublime way that it is beyond words and
conception," describes the grace granted to Angela in her
apophatic, trinitarian vision of God in darkness, the so-called "seventh supplemental step" on her way.[26] This last, highest transformation serves to reveal the pervasive eucharistic character of the
whole of Angela's religious experience. The Eucharist is not less,
but more, important to Angela as she moves through her progressive transformations. As Paul LaChance points out, Angela's ultimate experience of the Divinity "is not the abstract transcendental
notion of metaphysics but the Trinitarian God, who in his love has
introduced Angela into intimate communion with the Three
Persons."[27] This transforming, trinitarian communion characteristically takes place for Angela in sacramental communion.

The Book of Blessed Angela gives two vivid accounts of this third
form of transformation. In the "Memorial" Angela records an experience of the divine abyss, a vision of the Trinity in darkness,
which can be sustained only briefly: "When I am in that darkness, I
do not remember anything about anything human, or the God-
Man, or anything that has a form. Nevertheless, I see all and I see
nothing" (p. 205). As she enters and exits that divine darkness, she
encounters the God-Man, who supports her and who tells her: "You
are I and I am you":

When I am in the God-Man, my soul is alive. And I am in the God-Man much more than in the other vision of seeing God in darkness. The soul is alive in that vision concerning the God-Man. The vision in darkness, however, draws me so much more that there is no comparison. On the other hand, I am in the God-Man almost continually. (p. 205)

A second account of this transforming experience, which appears in the "Instructions," qualifies the oscillation that Angela describes in her encounter with the uncreated God, on the one hand, and the Incarnate Son, on the other, as a "double state" in which Angela is "both totally absorbed in the experience of the sweetness of God and also crucified as a result of the vision of Christ crucified . . . filled with joy and sorrow, sated with myrrh and honey, quasi-deified and crucified" (p. 246). As Angela's redactor observes, through this bipolar mystical experience "the blessed and glorious Jesus, by an invisible act, had fittingly bestowed upon her soul, in a perfect manner, the double state of his own life" (p. 246).

The redactor goes on to characterize this "double state" as deriving from "an ongoing process," "a process of continual transformation in God and in his most infinite light and . . . into feeling the pain of the Crucified" (p. 247). Angela, he reports, believes that this double "state . . . will be hers forever," and she experiences it as "a continual state of being plunged into the fathomless depths of God and of being transformed into the Crucified" (p. 247).

This "total transformation into God" (p. 261) makes Angela, as it were, into a consecrated host. Her new, twofold nature reflects not only the double nature of the God-Man but also the double nature of the Eucharist, which retains the appearance of bread after it has been transubstantiated into the body of Christ, who is present in the host in his divinity and humanity. The vivid descriptions of Angela's personal mystical experience translate somewhat awkwardly, perhaps, into the technical, scholastic language delineating the "lesser reality" and the "greater reality" of the Eucharist (p. 295), but the parallel is unmistakeable and derives from the prominent role eucharistic devotion plays in Angela's spirituality.[28] Receiving the host repeatedly and focusing on it in visionary prayer, Angela eventually becomes identified with it so profoundly that it becomes her very self. She allows herself to be consecrated, to become food for God and others. The same "mystery so new, wonderful, unheard of, unique, perfect, full of love, and precious" (p. 296) whereby "supreme divine goodness and supreme human charity" (p. 295) unite in the consecrated host effectively transforms Angela "into God": "You are I and I am you" (p. 205).

Having become a host, Angela becomes a source of nourishment and a uniting center for the members of her spiritual family.[29] One with God, she enters into a transforming union with her Franciscan sons. To one of them she addresses the very words that the God-Man has spoken to her: "It seems to me that I am no longer myself but you. This makes me say to myself: 'I wonder to whom I am writing, since I am you and you are me'" (pp. 271–72). In one of Angela's visions (part of the seventh supplemental step), "a multitude of the sons of this holy mother" appear, and she sees "the blessed and sorrowful Jesus" taking them tenderly into the wound at his side to nourish them with his blood (p. 246; cf. p. 283).[30] In them she sees a mirror image and an extension of her own eucharistic transformation:

> My sons seem to be so transformed in God that it is as if I see nothing but God in them, both in his glorified and suffering state, as if God had totally *transubstantiated* and absorbed them into the unfathomable depths of his life. (p. 249; emphasis mine)

Through the Eucharist, Angela comes into, and remains in, vital contact with the body of Christ that is the church, the communion of saints. Jesus, speaking to Angela from the host, tells her: "Wherever I am, the faithful are also with me" (p. 217). Later Angela offers the following confident instruction on the subject: "The angels and the saints do indeed find, see, feel, and taste a new joy and sweetness in [the host]. Furthermore, they not only stand in its presence, but are also within it, in Christ, the infinite good, the cause of their blessedness" (p. 297).

According to Angela, the same communion that unites the saints with Christ as head of the mystical body also unites them "with his members, the just and the faithful" (p. 297). As a living host, Angela herself mediates between the head of the church and its members, between the clergy and the laity. Her own favorite designation, however—"Christ's faithful one"—places her principally among the *fideles,* the holy laity, the saints who are themselves consecrated to Christ and transformed by him through the reception of the Eucharist. As we have seen, Angela prizes the Eucharist as a privileged regular moment of encounter with the God-Man that is necessary for all Christians. This makes her Francis's daughter, as well as one of those who (in the words of Vauchez) "asked more of the Church: mystics who desired frequent communion."[31]

Angela's experience of the Divinity in the Eucharist was an experience which was radically Christocentric. The eucharistic experience shaped her understanding of her responsibility, her mission to make Christ present in the world, even as it shaped her image of the church as institution and communion of saints. These are themes which resonate not only in the medieval *Book of Blessed Angela*, but also in post–Vatican II Catholicism, lights which illuminate the Catholic tradition for contemporary Catholics. Indeed, Angela's way of holiness helps us to understand the eucharistic tenor of the *consecratio mundi* to which Vatican II has called the laity of today.

Hagiographies often describe women as though they had turned their lives to God from infancy with a decisive self-consciousness that precluded any other choice. Angela, however, became aware of the demands of God's presence in her life, of her vocation to be God's lover, when she was already an adult who had been a wife and mother. She was not called to consecrated religious life as virgin. Although she served God as a widow, she began to follow Christ as a wife and mother and daughter. She came to know the God-Man first in a series of special visionary experiences, but she continued to know him through her reception of the Eucharist. In the piety she communicated to her spiritual sons, she stressed the central importance of the Eucharist. She did not urge them to seek special revelations, but to participate in the liturgical celebration of the Eucharist. Perhaps most significant, she did not emphasize their priestly power to consecrate the sacred elements. Instead, she spoke to them (as she speaks to us) about the nourishment they would receive from the sacramental presence, about the "good and the benefits this sacrament procures for the holy souls of the militant church" (p. 297).

Catherine of Siena and Lay Sanctity in Fourteenth-Century Italy

KAREN SCOTT

> *We intend to accord St. Catherine of Siena the title of Doctor of the Church.*
> Pope Paul VI: On the Layman's Sphere of Action

> *The true apostle seeks out opportunities for preaching Christ.*
> Vatican II: On the Apostolate of the Laity

The title of a 1986 conference on medieval preaching, *Dal pulpito alla navata* ("From the pulpit to the nave"), reflects a rather common view of the place of the laity in the medieval Italian church.[1] On the part of many ecclesiastical historians, such language has implied that the creative energy and real initiative in the medieval church lay with the bishops and the specially trained priests whom they commissioned to preach to illiterate and only superficially Christianized masses.[2] Following a similar model of how the church functioned, but one which they have deplored instead of celebrated, many secular historians have portrayed the laity as people herded like sheep into the enormous naves of thirteenth- and fourteenth-century mendicant churches and subjected to clerical indoctrination from the pulpit.[3] Whether they see the medieval laity as ignorant people in need of instruction or as a class oppressed by the ecclesiastical hierarchy, both interpretations imply that lay people had only two choices in relation to the church: they could either accept and passively absorb the preachers' formulation of Christian beliefs, morality, and spirituality, or they could reject that formulation and become heretics.

Such a model of the way the church functioned can be used to explain the fact that ordinary laypeople were not often canonized in the Middle Ages.[4] The status of saint was bestowed on certain ecclesiastical leaders—holy bishops, founders of religious orders—and on secular rulers who protected the church, but spiritual perfection seemed mainly the prerogative of those special individuals who had renounced the world and truly sought God by taking the three monastic vows and living as solitary hermits or in religious communities. How could simple laypeople, generally so ignorant of spiritual matters and immersed in the world through family and work, have been able to "compete" with the professionally religious in the church's canonization process?

Though this hierarchical model remains useful, historians have begun to debate these generalizations about lay spirituality and sanctity in the Middle Ages. For example, it has been argued that the Italian communes of the high and late Middle Ages produced a relatively high number of lay saints. While some of these saints enjoyed only a limited local cult, others were officially canonized by the church. More lay women with mystical gifts were canonized in the later Middle Ages than before. The cult of lay saints in Italy would seem to reflect a greater acceptance of lay participation in religious and political affairs there than elsewhere.[5]

Moreover, work on lay confraternities shows that by the fourteenth century men were participating in confraternities in large numbers to do penance for their sins, to sing hymns, to give alms, to gain a sense of community, to forge alliances, and this with minimal control by the clergy.[6] There is also abundant evidence that late medieval laywomen throughout Europe sought God and spiritual perfection through ascetic practices which were much more austere than those recommended by the preachers.[7] There were many ways for laypeople to establish their own religious identity and to contribute to the church without incurring the charge of heresy.

It is in part against this background of the relative acceptance of lay autonomy and participation in religious affairs in late medieval Italy that the career and thought of St. Catherine of Siena (1347–80) can be understood and explained. Like all medieval women, Catherine was a layperson in the sense that she was excluded from belonging to the clergy because of her sex. The fact that this uneducated, functionally illiterate woman of the artisan class who became a lay Dominican tertiary was canonized in 1461 by Pope Pius II is an important example of how positively the late medieval church could view lay sanctity. Although Catherine of Siena's life was certainly unusual, even for Italy, it would be impossible to explain the extent of her involvement in the affairs of the world and the church without positing her contemporaries' acceptance of a certain role in society for lay holy women.

Catherine's holiness took on a variety of forms, all associated with her lay status. After seeking God in solitude at home through rigorous ascetic practices and mystical prayer, Catherine became known in her native Siena for her charitable activities on behalf of the poor and the sick and for her spiritual direction of lay and religious people. In the last five years of her life, between 1375 and 1380, Catherine's mystical gifts continued to develop, but her activities took on a more political and ecclesiastical character. Following a model which could be called "From the pulpit to the nave and back to the pulpit," she preached to popes and clergy what they had preached to her. In the very act of teaching, edifying, cajoling, and berating the churchmen of her day by word and by letter, she implied that the laity have an essential role to play in ecclesiastical reform and in the spiritual conversion of the clergy. She encouraged other laypeople to take an active part in church affairs as well.

In 1376 Catherine and her group of disciples and friends traveled from Florence to Avignon to convince Pope Gregory XI to make peace with a league of Italian cities and to return the seat of his government to Rome. With papal approval she preached peace and salvation in the Sienese countryside in 1377. In 1378 she spent several months trying to persuade the Florentines to end their war with the papacy. By 1379 she had finished dictating the theological masterpiece which she called her *Libro* or Book, and which later editors entitled *Il Dialogo della divina provvidenza (The Dialogue of Divine Providence)*.[8] By then she had also sent the majority of her 382 letters to prominent rulers, prelates, and ordinary laypeople, clerics, and religious.[9] In 1379 Pope Urban VI called on Catherine to help end the Great Western Schism which had just begun. When she died in Rome in April 1380 she was Italy's most famous holy woman, known certainly for her fasts and her visions, but also for her active desire to effect political and ecclesiastical reform.

It was her lay status in the church that made Catherine's career possible. She was not a holy nun speaking out to the hierarchy, as she has sometimes been described, for late medieval nuns did not speak out publicly or travel.[10] At the same time, she was not quite an ordinary laywoman, either. As her former disciple and confessor Raymond of Capua explained in the *Legenda Major*, his hagiographical account of her life written some years after her death, Catherine had taken a private vow of virginity as a child and she was firmly intent on seeking a spiritual life.[11] Moreover, she was a Dominican *soror de poenitentia,* a "sister of penance." In fourteenth-century Italian she was called a *mantellata*—a woman who wore the Dominican mantle or black cape—or a *vestita di San Domenico*—a laywoman wearing the white and black colors of the Order of St. Dominic.[12] As these vernacular names indicate, the clothing which these groups of laywomen wore seems to have been essential to the way their status was perceived. Raymond made his story about Catherine's being clothed in the *mantellata* habit a prominent part of his *Legenda,* but significantly he included no account of a ceremony of vows or promises. He explained that the habit was important to Catherine as an external sign that would protect her virginity in the city and induce her family to cease trying to find her a suitable husband. He made a great point of the symbolism of the white and black colors she was clothed in, as signs of her conversion to penance and the spiritual life.[13]

On a more official level of Catherine's canon-law status, Raymond made it very clear that Catherine was neither a "religious" nun living in an enclosed community under the discipline of the three monastic vows, nor a "secular" married woman. Rather, Raymond stated, "these sisters avoid every enclosure *[clausura]*"; they each "live in their own homes"; and "the holy virgin did not take the three principal religious vows, because this state does not include them."[14] He had little to say about what this state did include, however, and his tentative account of its origins betrays his ignorance of its history. Besides stating that an unofficial rule (not including the three vows) existed for the sisters and that all of them were widows except Catherine, he indicated only in passing that the sisters met at the local Dominican church to pray, to receive new members, or to discuss the moral status of the community.[15]

For Raymond of Capua, the main function of the *mantellate* was to do penance and to pray, and they did this in an ecclesiastical status that appears ambiguous, somewhere between lay and religious. Catherine lived her private vow of virginity, but she did so in the solitude of her home, not by taking public vows or living in a religious community. Not restricted in her movements to the enclosed space of a monastic house, she moved around her city of Siena and eventually over much of southern France and northern Italy. For Raymond, though, Catherine always remained a mystic who sought union with God above all else. In the last years of her life her spirituality focused less on withdrawal from the world than on embracing the world to bring it to God.

It is then a lay, or nearly lay, woman who set out to reform the church and preached to the clergy and to the people by spoken word, letters, and example. The letters and treatises which Catherine dictated provide interesting evidence for her view of herself as a lay preacher, for her understanding of the church as a community of believers that gives great dignity to the laity, and for her concern to stimulate other laypeople's active involvement in church reform. Out of the corpus of her writings there emerges a very positive appraisal of a lay spirituality for men and women, involving both apostolate and contemplation in the world. Such a positive view of the laity surely evolved out of Catherine's own experience as a committed lay Christian, and it helps explain her self-confidence as a lay apostle.

One of Catherine's most eloquent expressions of her important role as a layperson in the church is the account of a vision which she sent to her confessor, Raymond of Capua, in early April 1376, right before she set off to Avignon to speak with Pope Gregory XI:

> As the fire of holy desire grew within me as I gazed, I saw the Christian people and the Infidels entering into the side of Christ crucified. And I passed in their midst by desire and affection of love, and I entered with them into sweet Christ Jesus, accompanied by my father St. Dominic and John the especially beloved, along with all my [spiritual] children. And then he [Christ] gave me the cross and put it on my shoulder and the olive branch in my hand, as if he wanted, and so he said, that I carry it to the one people and the other. And he said to me: "Tell them, 'I announce to you a great joy.'" Then my soul was even more filled. It was drowned in the divine essence, together with those true tasters [the Saints], by union and affection of love.[16]

Catherine's vision reflects an understanding of her dignity as a laywoman in the church. When Christ grants her the symbols of her mission, the olive branch and the cross, she implies that God wanted her to contribute to the spiritual well-being of her immediate circle and to the peace and salvation of all Christians and infidels. Most important, the vision suggested or confirmed to Catherine that the most appropriate means for her to bring peace and salvation to all of humanity was to travel and to speak. Rather than sit in a cell, pray, do penance, and at most communicate with people orally or by letter, Catherine recalled that she was told to *carry* the olive branch and the cross *to* the Christian peoples and the infidels. Throughout her travels she was to preach to the people she would meet, what she called "announcing a great joy." The message which Catherine was asked to communicate here repeats the angels' words announcing the birth of Jesus to the shepherds (Luke 2:8–14). As an angel of peace and messenger of good news, Catherine's mission was to preach to all people of good will, and in particular to the shepherds of the church, that is to the pope and his bishops.

Informing Catherine's perception of herself as an angel called to speak to the shepherds is a view of the church that differs considerably from the model of the clergy in the pulpit speaking down to the laity in the nave. When Catherine saw herself as an angel sent by God to preach the Good News to the shepherds, she implied that, though laypeople are not shepherds, people like herself can serve the useful purpose of reminding the clergy of their duties and interpreting events for them in the light of essential Christian beliefs. Roles within the church are different, but the ecclesiastical hierarchy needs the active participation of the laity, especially in the form of prophetic preaching.

During the last five years of her life, Catherine's writings and activities gave ample testimony to this view of the laity's high responsibilities. In the *Dialogue of Divine Providence,* dictated between 1377 and 1378, she stated that all Christians, including laypeople like herself, must actively walk on the Bridge of Christ crucified toward the same very high spiritual goal, which is union with God the Father. Along their walk on the Bridge, all pilgrims need to stop at local sacramental "taverns" *(bottighe)* run by the clergy to quench their thirst with the blood of Christ and regain strength for the journey.[17] Although for Catherine there was a clear difference in roles between laity and clergy—priests serve the sacraments and the people receive them—she also emphasized the laity's important role. She described the church as a vineyard planted by God and now tended by all the baptized. Far from depending exclusively on the clergy for salvation, laypeople in her view have a responsibility both to cultivate their own vineyards and to care for those of their neighbors.[18]

In particular, God tells Catherine in the *Dialogue,* all lay Christians have an active role to play in world salvation. They must help the clergy tend the souls in the "mystical body" of the church:

> See that I have set you all *[tutti v'o messi]* to be workers [in your vineyards]. And now I invite you all *[v'invito]* anew, for the world is in trouble due to the multiplication of thorns which have so suffocated the seed that they do not want to make any fruit of grace. So I want you all to be *[siate]* true workers so that with much solicitude you all help *[aitiate]* tend souls in the mystical body of the holy Church. I elect you all *[v'eleggo]* to do this because I want to be merciful to the world for which you Catherine *[tu]* pray to Me so much.[19]

God's—and Catherine's—message is that the church cannot afford to do without the contribution of the laity. The passage sets up a church with two parts, the clergy and the laity, and addresses them both: *voi tutti* or *voi,* "all of you," that is, the entirety of the Christian community, to whom God is speaking here. The language Catherine uses for the laity implies a strong and active role. If they have all been "elected" by God to "work" with "solicitude" and "help" the clergy do their "work" of tending souls, it is because the world is in great need and nothing less than people's eternal salvation is at stake. The clergy alone is unable to respond to the world's need and serve God's desire to be merciful to all, and so priests should accept help with humility. Accustomed to a passive role, the laity need to hear God's exhortation to offer their help and take on a more active role.

An even clearer expression of Catherine's idea of the church as a community of different roles organized in a spirit of reciprocity and mutuality comes in a statement in the *Dialogue* about God's providential pedagogy to instill charity. God the Father explains to her that there is a reason why society and the church are made up of different parts and why people have different skills: it is so that they would realize their need for each other, would be obliged to practice love and humility, and thus would learn how to live in true community. God tells Catherine:

> So that you use charity with each other in your actions and feelings . . . I provided not to give every person the capacity to know how to do all the things that are necessary for human life. One has one thing, while another has another thing, so that the one has reason because of need to have recourse to the other. So you see the artisan has recourse to the agricultural laborer, and the laborer, to the artisan. The one needs the other, for he does not know how to do what the other does. In the same way, the cleric and the religious needs the lay person, and the lay person needs the religious. The one cannot manage without the other. And so it is with every other thing. Could I not have given everyone everything? Yes, but I wanted in My providence that they be humbled one to the other, constrained to practice charity together in their actions and sentiments.[20]

Catherine's large correspondence reflects in a practical way this idea expressed in a more abstract form in the *Dialogue,* that the church is made up of different kinds of people who ought to rely humbly and lovingly on each other in order to work as effectively as possible to spread the Gospel. She sent about half of her letters to laypeople, and half to the professional religious, and she presented their roles as both different and essentially the same. The differences Catherine mentioned were the obvious ones for the fourteenth-century church. Laypeople, she usually wrote, ought to obey God's commandments and partake regularly of the sacraments, while religious should live the counsels of perfection. Nuns should observe silence and cloister, while the clergy should speak out assertively against sin and lead pure lives in accord with their calling to the sacramental ministry. Catherine saw prominent lay men and women as people with a moral obligation to support the needs of the poor, especially the clergy and the religious, with their wealth and political influence. All Christians should respect the shepherds of the church and obey their religious superiors.[21]

Although Catherine distinguished among the roles of laity, religious, clergy, and prelates, she did not adopt a simple one-way hierarchical model in which the clergy mediates God and the holy to a passive, ignorant laity, in which people who take vows are automatically more pure and closer to God than married people, in which there are varying clearly defined degrees of spiritual expectations for these different kinds of people. Rather, a close reading of her entire correspondence shows that she set the same, and I should say, extremely demanding spiritual standard for all Christians. Catherine's passionate focus was the highest common denominator, the essential Christian message valid for all regardless of special roles in the church.

In her view, all must seek the same God, walk on the same "path" or "Bridge" of Christ crucified, and dedicate their lives to the same "honor of God and the salvation of souls." All need to understand doctrine, especially the nature of God, Christ's central mediation of salvation on the cross, and the church's function, which is to communicate Christ's saving blood to all people. All must cultivate the same virtues in the garden of their souls, especially humility, patience, and the love of God and neighbor. Moreover, because all Christians are sinners, all need to become aware of their failings and to beg for the same divine mercy. As Catherine put it with the imagery she used so often, it is necessary to "enter into the cell of self-knowledge," where one can perceive that "creatures, as creatures, are nothing and that our being is entirely from God." To be saved, all need to "drown" in the blood of Christ, to plunge into "the sea of God's immeasurable love" for them, and to keep moving on the path to God, aided by prayer and the sacraments.

Because of the essential sameness of all Christians' spiritual journeys, some of the differences that one might expect to find among the various church roles become less meaningful. In particular, Catherine taught that no one should focus on God alone, even contemplative hermits and nuns; and that no one should focus on the love of neighbor alone, even the laity and secular clergy. The social dimension of spirituality is essential for all Christians, because all men and women are called to "bear fruit" and "give birth to spiritual children," that is, to develop as apostles in some way. By the same token, no one should be content with a socially based spirituality alone. The laity and the clergy should aspire to the same degree of mystical union with God as the contemplative religious do. To ensure a proper balance between the love of God and neighbor, all need to be freed from excessive attachment to earthly cares and the false self, or as Catherine put it, all need to learn how to "love self for God, neighbor for God, and God for God."

It is precisely because different kinds of Christians are traveling on the same journey toward God, in Catherine's view, that they all have something legitimate to offer the church. Catherine's correspondence shows that this basic assumption of hers was essential to the way she chose to participate in two significant series of events, the War of the Eight Saints and the Great Schism. First, the series of peacemaking letters she sent to Pope Gregory XI and to the lay governments of Tuscany between 1375 and 1378 to help end the War of the Eight Saints is a dramatic example of Catherine's evenhanded respect for the integrity of both the clergy and the laity (as well as her evenhanded view that both shared some blame for the war). She tried to mediate the conflict by reminding each side that the other had some justified grievances and arguments in its favor.

When Catherine wrote to the Florentine government in 1376 to press for reconciliation with Gregory XI and the church hierarchy, she emphasized the terrible spiritual consequences of the papal interdict imposed on the city. She pointed out that the Florentines should become "obedient sons" in order for the people to have access to the blood of Christ in the sacraments.[22] The laity, she argued, cannot be saved without the clergy's service. Even more significantly, though, Catherine also wrote the pope a series of stern rebukes. In a masterpiece of blunt diplomacy, she stated that despite the objective evil of the Florentines' position (equivalent to killing Christ) Gregory should listen to their point of view, recognize the papacy's faults in causing the war, and agree to make peace. He should realize that the church-run governments in some of the papal states had been acting most unjustly (like incarnate demons) and that the Florentines had no choice but to fight back:

> I am certain and know that they [the Florentines] all feel that they have done wrong [in fighting the Pope's forces]; and though they have no excuse for evil doing, still, because of the great suffering and the unjust, iniquitous things they have had to bear from the bad shepherds and governors [Church prelates], they thought that they could not do otherwise. In smelling the stench in the lives of many rectors, who you know are incarnate demons, they came to such a very bad fear that they acted like Pilate who killed Christ in order not to lose his power. And these ones [the

Florentines] have done the same, they have persecuted you in order not to lose their position. So mercy, father, is what I ask you for them. . . ; and give peace back to us wretched children who have offended you.[23]

In the short run, Catherine's efforts to help end the war did not succeed, perhaps because neither side was willing or able to understand the other's position, perhaps because they did not share her ideal view that prelates need both to speak to the laity and to listen to the laity, and that laypeople need both to speak to the prelates and to listen to the prelates, even when they disagree on important questions. When a peace agreement was finally reached in the summer of 1378 with Catherine's continued mediation, the protagonists had changed. It took a new pope, Urban VI, who needed to end the war because his election was already being questioned, and a new Florentine government, which was more amenable to Guelph politics and the sacramental needs of the populace, to overcome the impasse.

Catherine's correspondence regarding the Great Schism between the autumn of 1378 and her death in April 1380 provides a second illustration of her vision of the church as a community of interdependent Christians, in which the clergy, the religious, and the laity all have important responsibilities. Two popes disputed the see of St. Peter, and Catherine did all she could to persuade the various parties that the Italian pope, Urban VI, was the legitimate vicar of Christ. She wrote letters to Urban himself, both to encourage him to persevere and to reprove him for his rather great nastiness. She wrote letters to cardinals and bishops, begging them to support Urban. She wrote letters to the governments of Italian city-states, to the king of France, the queen of Naples, and other secular rulers, requesting loyalty to the pope. She wrote letters to nuns and monks, informing them of the course of events and requesting their prayers for church unity. In one famous case, she even asked a hermit to leave his beloved solitude to come to Rome and help Urban more directly (Letter 328). She wrote letters to her male friends in Sienese lay confraternities, asking them to pray and to intervene and influence her city's policies. She wrote her Dominican tertiary friends, asking them to pray for peace. She wrote a letter to three laywomen in Naples, informing them of events in Rome, asking them to follow Urban's lead, to announce the truth about his being the true pope, and to pray for Church unity (Letter 356). Persuaded that the church needed all of its members to be informed and to take action to resolve the crisis, Catherine relied equally on lay-people, religious, and prelates.

The period of Catherine's most active involvement in church af-fairs and most intensive sending of letters, between 1375 and 1380, was characterized by a state of flux, crisis, and disarray in the church. Popes were changing residences, waging wars, fighting other popes. There was a constant demand for ecclesiastical reform. Catherine's message, that the church needs the contribution of everyone, including the laity, including women, to help communi-cate the Gospel message and survive, was surely needed and timely, and it seems to have been well-received in her day. Her self-confident activity as a female apostle and theologian would not have been pos-sible without the assumption of ordinary people, as well as ecclesi-astical and secular rulers, that the laity had an essential role to play in the church.

However, it would be a mistake to assume that Catherine's par-ticular kind of lay holiness was not controversial. Within fifteen years of her death, when Raymond of Capua, her former confessor and disciple, finished composing the *Legenda Major,* he expressed a relatively cautious evaluation of her lay activity. Although he was careful to state in unequivocal terms that Catherine's ecclesiastical status did not include taking vows or living under enclosure, and al-though he did discuss Catherine's apostolic activities in Siena, Avignon, Florence, and Rome, his narrative deemphasizes her lay status in a number of important ways. In telling stories about Catherine's cutting off her own hair and covering her head with a veil to avoid marriage, or about her taking a vow of virginity, or ex-periencing in a vision her mystical marriage with Christ, Raymond highlighted the parallels between these events and female monas-tic rituals. He did not draw attention to the private nature of these three religious commitments, which in fact were not ecclesiastically sanctioned, but rather he stressed the mystical character of her ex-periences to give them a very special legitimacy.[24] Throughout the *Legenda,* Raymond consistently called Catherine a "holy virgin," em-phasizing that she lived her life as if she had taken the three monas-tic vows, and he set her apart from "ordinary" people by stating that God's mystical gifts to her far outshone those given to other saints.[25]

Finally, and this is most important, Raymond's account of Catherine's life reflects a certain uneasiness about her apostolic activities that is not present in her own writings. Although he tells an important story about her call to leave the solitude of her cell and begin a new life of service and apostolate in the world, and although he provides an important theoretical justification for the sanctity of her active life, the context for this story is clearly polemical.[26] He seems to be on the defensive, and he implies that what he is saying is radical and quite controversial. Whereas Catherine wrote about the role of the laity in church reform as an obvious, divinely sanctioned reality, he felt the need to respond to objections about the sanctity of the lay female apostolate. Moreover, the actual information which Raymond supplied about Catherine's apostolic activities is very small, and he hid what little he did say in the midst of stories highlighting her mystical gifts. For example, Catherine's main claim to historical fame, that she traveled to Avignon and brought the pope back to Rome, is based on a parenthetical aside which Raymond set within a story about her power to prophesy the future. Raymond attributes Catherine's ability to convert sinners and exhort churchmen successfully not to her ordinary words and example, as she did, but to an extraordinary intervention of God's supernatural power.[27] As a result, although the *Legenda Major* presents a discreet defense of the lay apostolate, Raymond's portrait of Catherine actually emphasizes her extraordinary and charismatic character and champions an almost monastic and contemplative model of sanctity.

Just how successful Raymond was in deemphasizing Catherine's lay status and involvement in public affairs is evident in the development of early modern iconography based on his hagiographical masterpiece. While the earliest visual representations of Catherine show her dressed in the late-medieval lay tertiary's habit—white tunic and veil, black cape—in the fifteenth and sixteenth centuries the iconography evolved significantly to give her the semblance of a nun. Artists added scapular, rosary, and black veil, and they represented her almost exclusively in moments of visionary trance.[28] Her lay status, her travels, her peacemaking work, and her own strong words of advice or reproof to clerics were forgotten. Her stance on the importance of the laity in the church was not noted. She was cited as a model of ascetic virtue and mystical gifts to female contemplative communities. At a time when the early modern "pulpit" was asserting itself, it was becoming much more difficult to see any value in Catherine's lowly lay status and in her assertive involvement as a laywoman in late-medieval church affairs. Perhaps it will be the responsibility of another era to reevaluate the significance of St. Catherine's lay contribution to the church and to learn new lessons from it.

"I wold þow wer closyd in a hows of ston"
Sexuality and Lay Sanctity in *The Book of Margery Kempe*
PETER PELLEGRIN

> *In his itinerant ministry Jesus was accompanied not only by the Twelve but also by a group of women: "Mary, surnamed the Magdalene, from whom seven demons had gone out, Joanna the wife of Herod's steward Chuza, Susanna, and several others who provided for them out of their own resources" (Luke 8:2–3).*
> Vatican Declaration on the Question of the Admission of Women to the Ministerial Priesthood, October 15, 1976

As Aviad Kleinberg has reminded us, "The fate of Margery Kempe (1373–1439) demonstrates the community's power to determine a legitimate claim to sainthood and the variety of responses to the same phenomena."[1] According to Kempe's own testimony, the hostility provoked by her "roarings" in church marked only a part of her trials. A provocative figure, Kempe inspired sharply divided opinion among her neighbors in Lynn, her fellow-pilgrims, and the local clergy—some of them affirming her claim to God's special favor, others denouncing her as a heretic or impostor:

> For summe seyd it was a wikkyd spiryt vexid hir; sum seyd it was a sekenes; sum seyd sche had dronkyn to mech wyn; sum bannyd hir; sum wisshed sche had ben in þe hauyn; sum wolde sche had ben in þe se in a bottumles boyt; and so ich man as hym thowte. Oþer gostly men louyd hir & fauowrd hir þe mor.[2]

The Book of Margery Kempe, which records the story of her visions, locutions, travels, trials, and persecutions, has inspired a similar division of opinion among her twentieth-century readers, some of whom accept her as an authentic (albeit unusual) mystic, while others reject her as a troublemaking hysteric. Some things, however, are certain: Margery Kempe aspired to holiness; she did so as

91

a married laywoman living in the world; and her personal struggle to pursue sanctity as she understood it put her not only in personal crisis but also in frequent conflict with those around her. Her *Book* lays bare the obstacles she faced as she attempted, in her own original way, to reconcile her lay status and mundane circumstances with her religious ideals. Twentieth-century lay Catholics, faced with the same challenge, can learn much from Kempe's experience, from her successes and failures, and, above all, from her struggle to imitate Christ.

The *Book* of Margery Kempe allows her to teach us. Discovered in 1934, it proved to be somewhat of a disappointment—if not an embarrassment—to students of mysticism. Scholars had held preconceived notions of her book, based on a 1501 publication by Wynken de Worde, which gave a distorted view of Kempe by featuring only excerpts of a contemplative nature.[3] De Worde's disservice to scholars was compounded in 1521 when Henry Pepwell reprinted the original de Worde publication, adding the term "anchoress" to the title. Based on the excerpts and the term "anchoress," scholars had understandably come to view Margery's *Book* as similar in tone and content to Julian of Norwich's *Revelations of Divine Love*. The discovery of Kempe's lost book forced a radical reevaluation of Kempe, whose married status, secular calling, and religious experience did not fit into the traditional paradigm of English mysticism. Freudian scholars explained Kempe as a prime example of clinical hysteria.[4] One scholar even described reading the *Book* as "painful."[5] Later scholarship either accepted de facto that she was not a mystic or relegated her experience to what they considered a lower, cataphatic form of mysticism.

Cataphatic mysticism, also known as "positive" mysticism, emphasizes the physical and the self, using "imagery and analogy to approximate and approach God, seeing the Incarnation as the type and the legitimation of such symbolizing, the means through which God descends, and reciprocally the means of mystical ascent to God."[6] A form of *imitatio Christi*, cataphatic mysticism relies extensively on physical manifestations such as visions, locutions, tears, and pain—all of which are evident in Margery's religious experience. By contrast, apophatic or negative mysticism, to which *The Cloud of Unknowing* gives classic expression, requires not only the negation of self-consciousness and world-consciousness, but also the transcendence of imaginative representations of God in the attainment of a "wholly Other" mystical union.

As Bernard McGinn observes, the foundation for this distinction between the cataphatic and the apophatic can be found in Platonic writings, which express both "world-affirming views in which material reality and erotic relations are used as integral parts of the ascension process . . . and more negative views, where discipline of and flight from the body as the soul's prison give a more pessimistic, almost dualistic tone to the ascetical program."[7] Every kind of mysticism involves "an immediate consciousness of the presence of God," but cataphatic mystics tend to experience the Divine Lover's presence and absence in succession, as a coming and going, whereas for apophatic mystics "presence and absence are more paradoxically and dialectically simultaneous."[8]

Scholars generally evaluate the apophatic over the cataphatic, the negative over the positive, as the "higher form" of mysticism, to the detriment of lay mystics like Margery. For example, F. C. Happold, in *Mysticism: A Study and Anthology,*[9] talks at length about the *via negativa* and then briefly discusses the *via positiva,* which he terms "The Lesser Way." Happold is careful to emphasize that the term "lesser" does not imply inferiority, but the word "lesser" connotes and denotes meanings which undermine this assertion. The use of the term clearly reflects a theological bias that has affected the evaluation of lay sanctity in general and which is particularly evident in the scholarly treatment of Margery Kempe. As Clarissa Atkinson astutely observes, the diminuition of the cataphatic way "has led to a confusion over Kempe's mysticism, a confusion which negatively influences assessment of Margery's mysticism,"[10] and which derives in part from, and serves to compound, our misunderstanding of the very genre of her *Book.*

Margery's *Book* is not a treatise on contemplation, nor a how-to book for would-be mystics, as is *The Cloud of Unknowing,* Walter Hilton's *Scale of Perfection,* and Richard Rolle's *Form of Perfect Living;* nor is it a series of revelations from a loving God meant to be shared with all the world, as is Julian of Norwich's *Revelations.* It is autobiographical in character and obviously intended as an exemplum of the working of God's grace in the life of a sinner: "Alle þe werkys of ower Saviowr ben for ower exampyl & instruccyon, and what grace þat he werkyth in any creatur is ower profyth"

(I.Proem.7–8, p. 1).[11] In the *Book,* Margery herself is the exemplary sinner and "creatur" in question. According to Kempe, Jesus himself elected her in order to display "how benyngly, & how charytefully he meued & stered a synful caytyf vn-to hys love" (I.Proem.14–15, p. 1), addressing her with the words: "dowtyr, I haue ordeynd þe to be a merowr amongys hem . . . þat þei xulde takyn exampil by þe for to haue sum litil sorwe in her hertys for her synnys" (I.78.12–16, p. 186).[12]

Kempe can be a mirror for repentant sinners to the extent that Christ's Passion has been a mirror for her own life, which the *Book* represents as an *imitatio Christi.* In one vision, she relates Christ's promise to her that "any creatur in erthe, haf he be neuyr so horrybyl a synner, he thar neuyr fayylyn in dispeyr ȝyf he wyl takyn exampil of thy leuyng & werkyn sumwhat þeraftyr as he may do" (I.77.18–21, p. 183). The key condition for the avoidance of despair is that the sinner must *act* and *work* in accord with Kempe's example. Here Kempe makes it clear that her redemptive example is not just mystical, although it is that, but also practical. As a follower of Christ, Kempe strives daily to imitate Christ's example, and the readers of her *Book* are to take example from Kempe's life as they struggle with their own *imitatio Christi.*[13]

Following the principle set forth long ago by Evelyn Underhill,[14] we need to take Kempe's entire life into account, if we hope to assess her mysticism and her related claim to sanctity and exemplarity. As an exemplum of lay sanctity in which cataphatic mysticism plays a definitive role, Kempe provides a paradigm for the balancing of outer societal obligations with inner spiritual growth. Like most laypersons, Kempe had an active sex life. Her troubled attempts to reconcile her marital past and present with her new devotion to God create the basic tension in her book and ultimately demonstrate how sexuality—if not sex per se—can be a help, rather than a hindrance, to devotion. Unlike many mystics, Kempe was both a wife and a mother and thus necessarily concerned with ordinary household occupations, but these concerns did not impede but rather promoted her spiritual growth. Kempe's cataphatic mysticism sanctified the ordinary in her life and thus helped prepare her for an uncloistered life of service to her fellow man. Finally, as her *Book* bears witness, she did not hide her light under a bushel, no matter how much trouble she endured on that account, and the rejection she experienced as a consequence powerfully aligned not only her sufferings, but also her whole life, with Christ's.

Sexuality: Problematic and Positive

What makes Kempe unique is sex. Simply put, the likes of her had never been seen before in England. It was not unusual for a woman to marry and bear fourteen children, nor was it unusual for a woman to consecrate her life to God and take a vow of celibacy after being widowed. What was unusual was to combine these two roles while the husband was still breathing. In the current state of scholarship, as Janel M. Meuller notes, Kempe's "dual spousal—to God and to John Kempe concurrently" appears "distinctive, the more so in an Englishwoman."[15]

Both Kempe and her contemporaries, at least, found it hard to reconcile her marital status with her claim to mystical espousal. As Karma Lochrie has demonstrated, medieval women were associated with the "flesh," not the "body." The body merely housed the soul, but the flesh was associated with fallen, sinful mankind.[16] In a society which held very strict views on female spirituality and female flesh, Kempe was a public abomination whose mere physical presence drew attention to her status as a married, and hence a "defiled," woman. Unlike Julian of Norwich (1342?–1415?), who housed herself in a wall of stone as a form of *imitatio Christi* and self-abnegation, Kempe chose a secular environment and consequently became an epicenter of negative secular attention, a lightning rod for charges of sexual promiscuity, Lollardry, and sedition.

Kempe compounded matters by wearing white clothes, an apparently blasphemous action by a nonvirginal woman.[17] As a result, the mayor of Leceister accused her of sexual indiscretions and of attempting to lure the townswomen away from their husbands (I.48.11–14, p. 116). When the archbishop of York, Henry Bowet, first interviewed Kempe, he asked whether she was a virgin, and when she replied that she was not, he sent for a pair of fetters for "sche was a fals heretyke" (I.52.19, p. 124). Her white clothes were associated with a heretical sect known as the *Albi* or *Bianchi*, about which the civic authorities had been warned as early as 1399.[18] Furthermore, upon her return from Compostella in August 1417, the notorious Lollard Sir John Oldcastle (Lord Cobham) was loose and hiding somewhere in England. The combination of Oldcastle's flight from prison (1413) and treasonous plots and the heretical connotations of Kempe's white clothing led to charges that she was "Combonis dowtyr" and a seditious carrier of letters who had never actually been to Rome (I.54.12–16, p. 132). So frightened was the citizenry over the Lollard threat that Kempe was arrested three times and released three times in a macabre farce that would have been amusing were she not in very real danger of being burned to death as a Lollard.

That Kempe's sexuality was a challenge not only to others but also for herself, however, is evident even upon the most cursory examination of her book. Her postconversion agreement to an assignation and the seducer's subsequent rejection of her demonstrate that the sexual lure was strong for her (I.4, pp. 13–16). She admits and feels guilt for having taken youthful pleasure in her husband John's body (I.76.10–12, p. 181). Such struggles with a sexuality she could only see as sinful necessarily troubled her, so that she constantly battled against a negative self-image based upon her lack of virginity. Beginning in June 1413, she won her husband John's consent to live continently. When she lamented that she was not a "holy maiden," God reportedly told her, "I lofe wyfes also," and then assured her that he loved her "as wel as any mayden in þe world" (I.21.1–8, p. 49). But Kempe was not satisfied. God finally resolved her dilemma by declaring her to be "a mayden in [her] sowle" who will "dawnsyn in Hevyn wyth oþer holy maydens & virgynes" (I.22.26–30, p. 52)—an incident which prompted one scholar to note that Kempe is the "first woman on record to recover her lost maidenhead."[19] Virginal in soul but not in body, Kempe continued throughout her life to wrestle with the "sin" of her sexuality and with sexual temptations, represented in her visions of clerics and their genitalia (I.59, pp. 144–46).

Within the larger context of Kempe's whole religious experience, however, her sexuality cannot simply be considered in negative terms, however great the societal and personal problems it posed for her. Kempe incorporated her sexuality into her spirituality so that it actually helped, rather than hindered, her spiritual growth, to the extent that her experiences as a married woman shaped her perception of the *Brautmystik*. In chapter 35 of the *Book*, she describes a vision of the Trinity, in which the First Person, the Father, proposes marriage to her. She goes on to envision her union with the Godhead on November 9, 1414, in the literal terms of a medieval wedding ceremony, complete with a wedding party including Jesus, Mary, and a host of saints, holy virgins, and angels. The words God the Father uses to seal the mystical marriage come straight from the familiar matrimonial rite: "I take þe, Margery, for my weddyd wyfe, for fayrar, for fowelar, for richar, for powerar" (I.35.18–19, p. 87).

Kempe's visions further reflect her married sexual experiences. Because husbands and wives are intimate, God tells his bride, Margery, that he will lie in bed with her and that she should respond passionately: "boldly take me in þe armys of þi sowle & kyssen my mowth, myn hed, & myn fete as swetly as thow wylt" (I.36.24–26, p. 90). Such imagery is less a sign of sexual repression in Kempe than the logical outgrowth of a literal-minded woman relying upon her own life experiences to give order and meaning to her visions of the Divine.

In another vision, Christ thanks Kempe for all the times she bathed him in his manhood and harboured both Christ and Mary in her own bed (I.86.1–5, p. 214). Although her bathing Christ in his "manhood" could be read as sexual repression,[20] it is easier to assume that Kempe had a true-life correlative of this experience. When John slipped down the stairs and became disabled, incapable of controlling his bladder and colon, Kempe was forced to bathe him and change his linen. She thought it only fitting that she should be punished by the same body with which she had enjoyed inordinate sexual pleasure as a young woman; thus, she "seruyd hym & helpyd hym . . . as sche wolde a don Crist hym-self" (I.76.14–15, p. 181). Like many late-medieval women saints who (in Caroline Bynum's words) cared for the bodies of the sick "as a substitute for Jesus' own," Kempe identified John's body with Christ's.[21] The story of John's fall and Kempe's subsequent caring for him occurs only ten small chapters before the talk of washing and bathing Christ, and although much of Kempe's book is chronologically convoluted, we can nevertheless infer that, since the two incidents appear so closely together in the book, Kempe herself might have seen a relation between them. After all, Jesus himself had told Kempe "to kepyn [John] & helpyn him in hys nede" out of love for Christ (I.76.26–29, p. 180).

Sexuality helped define Kempe's spirituality further in her role as nurturing mother. In one vision, Mary showed her how to swaddle the infant Christ (I.85.19–24, p. 209), while in another vision Kempe witnessed the Virgin presenting the infant John the Baptist to St. Elizabeth for nursing (I.6.1–4, p. 19). In an earlier vision, Kempe was St. Anne's maidservant, and later, when St. Anne gave birth to Mary, Kempe became Mary's servant. She procured white cloths and kerchiefs to swaddle Christ and arranged bedding for Mary and the infant Christ (I.6, pp.18–19). Kempe physically swaddles Christ several times in her contemplations. Most assuredly such imagery springs from her duties as a mother and, in later life, as a devoted wife who had to care for her invalid husband.

Sanctification of the Ordinary

Kempe's *Book* is filled with scenes from her everyday life—partly, perhaps, because of a temperamental "pettiness" that lends habitual attention to detail.[22] Kempe's homely detail, however, arguably reflects Franciscan spirituality, which is associated with cataphatic mysticism and which had made strong inroads in England before and during Kempe's time. Franciscan piety asked one to use Christ's life as a model for one's own, and encouraged the correlation of everyday events with specific scenes from Christ's life in order to personalize his message and make him more real.[23] Even as Kempe's sexuality and marital status seem not only to have helped to shape and define her mysticism but also actually to have prepared her for the spiritual path she subsequently followed, her use of the ordinary in her book is not merely a sign of "pettiness"; rather, it suggests an active mind seeing the immanence of God in the mundane, much as the metaphysical poets of the seventeenth-century were able to infer ideal marital love from a mathematical compass. For Kempe, God's presence would have permeated every aspect of her world, transforming even the most common images into symbols of His great love.

Whereas her famous contemporary Julian of Norwich is concerned with "higher" concerns, such as reconciling the concept of an all-loving God with the concepts of hell and damnation (a slippery subject at best), Kempe seems more interested in practical matters, such as money and the accumulation of credits in heaven. As a middle-class entrepreneur, Kempe tended to perceive God in like terms, as someone keeping a ledger of debits and credits. Thus, when Kempe gave God power of attorney to disburse her good works and their credits as he saw fit, and when God promised in return to be a "trew executor . . . & fulfyllyn all [her] wylle" (I.8.4–7, p. 21), Kempe demonstrated that even the most worldly, commercial images can be sanctified and employed toward spiritual growth.

In her visionary accounts, Kempe similarly employs domestic images, drawing on items that were readily found in households in Lynn. When God warns her of the tribulations that she will have to undergo, he prophecies that she will be like a stockfish gnawed by rats: "þow xalt ben etyn & knawyn of þe pepul of þe world as any raton knawyth þe stokfysch" (I.5.16–17, p. 17). Stockfish imagery arises again when God praises Kempe for her faithful obedience to him: "þu art so buxom to my wille & cleuyst as sore on-to me as þe skyn of stokfysche cleuyth to a mannys handys whan it is sothyn" (I.37.14–16, p. 91). Other cooking imagery is employed when God commends Kempe for her willingness to be chopped up like meat for the sake of others: "þu woldist ben hakkyd as smal as flesche to þe potte for her lofe" (I.84.27–28, p. 204). In one of her more famous visionary experiences, Kempe prepares a "good cawdel" (a hot drink made of gruel and spiced wine) to comfort the Virgin after Christ's death and burial (I.81.7–8, p. 195). Just as Margery, an ordinary housewife, becomes a "new creature" through God's grace, so do the ordinary household images become "new" in her religious experience.

Perhaps a crucial image that best explains Kempe's use of the ordinary in her book occurs shortly after her restoration to sanity following the fateful vision of Christ sitting on her bed. At her request, John Kempe returns to Margery the keys to the buttery, an act symbolic of her return to sanity (I.1.25–35, p. 8). The keys are a metaphor for her position in society, the return of which reifies her societal status as a medieval housewife with definite responsibilities. Margery's job as wife was, after all, to oversee the household, prepare the meals, purchase goods at the market, secure their proper storage, and so on.

Uncloistered Service

Kempe would not have been nearly so controversial had she remained a dutiful wife at home or become an anchoress "closyd in an hows of ston" (I.13.32, p. 27). Indeed, the people of Beverley advised her to forsake her white-clad public life "and go spynne & carde as oþer women don, & suffyr not so meche schame & so meche wo" (I.53.34–37, p. 129). Convinced that she had a vocation to be a "mirror" for others, however, Kempe turned toward the world. Everything she did, everything she said, and everywhere she went was in plain sight and within hearing of a largely hostile secular and ecclesiastical world.

Kempe's three major pilgrimages to Rome and Jerusalem (1413–14), Compostella (1417), and Aachen (1433) are replete with examples of her social apostolate and service. During these pilgrimages, she publicly witnessed for God, rebuked people for swearing oaths, and spoke many tales designed to turn people to God. While in Rome, her confessor commanded her to serve a peasant woman, which she did for six weeks, sleeping on the floor with only her mantle to cover her, begging food and drink for the woman, fetching firewood, etc. (I.34, pp. 85–86). Later, when God instructed her to give away all her money, she did so, trusting that all would be well (I.37.13–27, p. 92). Similarly, Margery served lepers in Lynn, kissing them for the love of Jesus and speaking kind words to them for his sake (I.74.1–18, p. 177).

In Lynn, people who despised her well enough in life begged for her company at their deathbed. She was asked to pray for the seriously ill and, later, to determine the state of their souls if they had passed away. Margery prayed for one virgin beset by sexual temptations and claims to have facilitated relief for her (I.74.18–28, p. 177). A man approached Margery when she was under arrest in Beverley with the petition: "Damsel yf euyr þu be seynt in Heuyn, prey for me" (I.53.14–15, p. 130)—to which she replied with a word of blessing and hope for his own holiness.

Perhaps her most notable service, however, was to a young wife who, like herself many years earlier, suffered from postpartum depression. The woman roared and cried and was manacled to prevent her from harming herself or others. She was placed in a room on the farthest reaches of the town so that no one could hear her. At the request of the woman's husband, Margery met and prayed for her as often as twice a day. The young mother acted sane only with Margery, whom she saw surrounded by angels and welcomed as "a ryth good woman" (I.75.11–13, p. 178). When anyone else approached, however, the woman "cryid & gapyd . . . & seyd þat sche saw many deuelys a-bowtyn hem" (I.75.15–16, p. 178). Margery claims that she was also able to facilitate this woman's eventual return to sanity.

Kempe kept herself busy doing the Lord's work, but her white clothes, her incessant weeping, and her ten-year bout of "roarings" tended to alienate and frighten others and exposed Margery herself to danger. Perhaps the greatest fear of which Kempe speaks is rape (II.7.9–10, p. 241). Her fear of violation seems only to have intensified with age; as a woman in her sixties, she must have young maidens sleep with her at night to help protect her chastity (II.7.14–17, p. 241). Kempe recognized that rape is a crime of violence, not a crime of lust, and sensed that her white clothing made her an easily identifiable target of hatred and hostility. Kempe's fear, moreover, was evidently not self-delusionary, for those in whom she placed her trust also feared for her safety and chastity. For example, Richard, the broken-backed man, was afraid that Kempe would be taken away from him and raped (I.30.4–13, p. 77). In addition, when the steward of Leceister intimated that he would rape her, Kempe was so frightened that she related certain mystic experiences to him, bringing a halt to the whole ordeal and eliciting the steward's cryptic response, "Eyþyr þu art a ryth good woman er ellys a ryth wikked woman" (I.47.30–31, p. 113).

For safety reasons and in keeping with societal expectations, Kempe was obliged to travel with a man on her journeys at home and abroad. She was fond of making small trips in England, and if she could find no other man (usually a religious) with whom to travel, she could always get her husband John to accompany her (I.15.20–23, p. 33). Women, it would appear, were expected to travel with their husbands. After returning from Compostella, Kempe was accosted by clerics and asked for a letter from her husband giving her permission to be on pilgrimage (I.51.11–18, p. 122). When she asked to go to Aachen with a company of poor folk, they asked why she did not have a man with her (II.6.15–16, p. 237). Having the company of a single male, although preferable to a woman's traveling alone, was still questionable, however. A good wife advised her that she should not travel alone with a man (in this case, a friar), but should instead travel in a wagon with other pilgrims (II.7.24–27, p. 239). The age of a man accompanying a woman was also important, for after Margery successfully defended herself before Henry Bowet, archbishop of York, he dismissed several men who volunteered to be her escort out of his diocese, noting, "ȝe ben to ȝong; I wil not haue ȝow" (I.52.15–16, p. 128). Clearly, the woman's honor was at risk, a fact reinforced when the mayor of Leceister accused her of sexual indiscretions (I.48.24–26, p. 115).

Even in the company of others, however, Kempe remained vulnerable. In fact, she faced the most difficulty on her pilgrimages not from strangers but from her own companions and fellow countrymen. On the way to Constance, her fellow pilgrims cut her gown so short "þat it come but lytil be-nethyn hir kne & dedyn hir don on a whyte canvas in maner of a sekkyn gelle, for sche xuld ben holdyn a fool" (I.26.14–17, p. 62). These same companions, in fact, exiled her from their company, a very harsh and potentially deadly punishment in a strange and hostile land. Later, before she sailed to Compostella, her companions threatened to throw her into the sea if they experienced foul weather (I.45.15–17, p. 110).

Many obviously feared and despised Kempe. Although living a life of service to God and others, Kempe's mantle of virginal white clashed with her underlying, suspect sexuality as wife and mother, and people resented her "for sche weryd white clothyng mor þan oþer dedyn whech wer holyar and bettyr þan euyr was sche" (I.33.26–28). Although not everyone reacted unfavorably toward Kempe, many were ambivalent, and their feelings for her could swing from praise to condemnation in an instant. At such times, she found herself in hostile, even life-threatening, situations.

In spite of such trials, she persevered. Indeed, Kempe's *Book* paradoxically turns her failure to gain popular acceptance and support as a saint—despite her cataphatic religious experiences of bridal union, her characteristic consecration of ordinary things, her mortifications and charitable service—into her strongest claim of sanctity, by patterning her trials and persecutions as an *imitatio* of Christ's own trials, rejection, and condemnation. Margery's "Purgatory" is the "slawndyr & speche of þe world" that rejects her (I.22.15, p. 51).

A Share in Christ's Passion

We know that Kempe's first "roarings" coincided with her visit to Calvary in 1413. Although she had exhibited tears of compunction prior to that time, she had not previously been subject to the intense "roarings" which caused her to writhe upon the ground, moan and exclaim in agony, and turn as blue as lead. It was only when she visited the actual site of Christ's death that her compassion intensified in the form of the "roarings" that were to continue for ten years, and over which she claims to have had no control, noting that she could delay them but never prevent them: "sche myt not kepe hir-self fro krying & roryng þow sche xuld a be ded þerfor" (I.28.22–23, p. 68). They led to public mockery, rebuke, and scandal, all of which, Kempe relates, she accepted willingly as the fulfillment of God's will and a share in Christ's own suffering: "For euyr þe mor slawnder & repref þat sche sufferyd, þe mor sche incresyd in grace & in deuocyon of holy medytacyon of hy contemplacyon" (I.Proem.29–31, p. 2).

In her meditation, Kempe is preoccupied with the manhood of Christ. When in Rome after returning from the Holy Land, Kempe relates how she would "cryin, roryn, & wepyn" if she saw any male babies (I.35.25–28, p. 86). She would, moreover, avoid looking at any handsome man, lest she might "seyn hym þat was boþe God & man. & þerfor sche cryed many tymes & oftyn whan sche met a semly man & wept . . . in þe manhod of Crist" (I.35.31–35, p. 86). Her attachment to the person of Christ was such that she was at first reluctant even to enter into her mystical union with the Godhead, out of fear that oneness with the Father would somehow separate her from the Son who mediated that union: "And þan sche wold not answeryn þe Secunde Persone but wept wondir sor, desiryng to haue stille hymselfe & in no wyse to be departyd fro hym" (I.35.7–10, p. 87).

Kempe's preoccupation with Christ's physical nature is rooted in his Passion and her conscious imitation of that Passion. Simply put, Kempe focused on the historical Jesus as the uniquely valid exemplar for her own personal form of *imitatio Christi*. She wished to suffer as he had suffered; hence she wore a hair shirt, went on three grueling pilgrimages, denied her flesh by abstaining from meat and sex, kissed lepers, and suffered rebuke and scorn. Like Christ, Kempe was unjustly brought to trial and accused of treason; like Christ, she told parables, although very earthy ones; like Christ, she ever sought to be submissive to God's will.

Christ urged His followers to give up the vanity of the world, and so Kempe did. She confesses that she loved "pipings" and bright clothing during her younger years, and had even retorted to her husband that she was a mayor's daughter and would dress as such, whatever their financial situation. As she admits, her ambitions for financial success had led her to ill-fated investments in a mill and a brewery. Her conversion, however, prompted Kempe to trade in her fancy clothing for a hair shirt and white clothing, and she never dabbled in business again (I.2, pp. 9–11).

Perhaps the most striking facet of Kempe's *imitatio Christi* is her abstinence from sex. Christ was celibate, and thus she, too, became celibate—at the cost of becoming (in her husband John's words) "no good wyfe" (I.11.23–24, p. 23). After hearing a heavenly melody one night, she claims to have lost the "desyr to komown fleschly wyth hyre husbonde"; indeed, she says, from then on the "dette of matrimony was . . . abhominabyl to hir" (I.3.35–36, p. 11). She struggled to convince her husband to relinquish his conjugal rights, a feat that took several years and a few children to accomplish. Next, she had to suffer the scandalous gossip of her townsfolk who believed that she and her husband were hypocritically still having sex. As we have already noted, Kempe had to overcome her own not insignificant carnal desires. She suffered guilt because of her loss of virginity in marriage, and anxiety that that loss barred her from Christian perfection. Finally, however, she was able to enter into a marriage with God that not only mirrored her marriage with John but also served to redeem it.

As the *Book* presents them, the obvious parallels between Christ's life and Kempe's own result from both conscious decisions on Margery's part to imitate Christ and the positive and negative reaction of others to her attempts. Her *Book* insists, however, that Margery Kempe's *imitatio* led to a significant achievement: her old self having "died" in, with, and through a share in Christ's Passion, she has been "resurrected" as a new "creature"—the striking term she often uses to refer to herself.[24] Her book is a record of this long and often times painful rebirth, and is meant as an exemplum for other laypersons who, "seeing through a glass darkly" (cf. 1 Cor. 13:12), are feeling their way to God. This is both the example she leaves and the mirror she proffers. A perilous mirror, her account of herself tests the claim to and the very definition of sainthood, both hers and ours—and this is how *The Book of Margery Kempe* should be read.

The Pious Infant:
Developments in Popular Piety during the High Middle Ages
PATRICIA HEALY WASYLIW

*Let the little children come to me, and do not hinder them, for of
such is the Kingdom of God.*
Luke 18:16

*Children too should have their own apostolic activities. According
to their abilities, they also are true and living witnesses of Christ.*
Vatican II: On the Lay Apostolate

The explosion of popular piety in the high Middle Ages, which produced an increase in the diversity of social groups represented
within the cult of the saints, also significantly affected children. The
appearance of specific child saints and the attribution of pious behavior to children—members of a segment of society rarely associated with sanctity—attest to the depth of the transformation of
popular religious attitudes and expectations. Concepts of sanctity
in this period were affected by multiple factors: the development of
new religious orders, the growth of urban society, an enhanced attention to popular religious devotion, and increasing papal control
over the process of canonization, which introduced stricter criteria
for the formation of saints' cults.[1] The character of the saint as an
object of fervent popular veneration was necessarily transformed as
a result, with increased representation being given to lay saints,
women, and the poor. Children, as members of another such "marginal" group in medieval society, also found a recognized place
within the panoply of popular sanctity.[2]

Child saints have maintained a presence in both official and popular Christian devotion, which is as old as the cult of the saints itself,
yet the position they have occupied is somewhat obscure. The child,
commonly viewed as lacking in moral understanding, self-control,

and education, is not an obvious candidate for spiritual role model. Historically, children have qualified for sanctity almost accidentally, as a result of a premature and usually violent death, rather than on any spiritual qualities exhibited during life. Within these parameters, the child saint has taken on distinct characteristics at different times.

The child martyr of the early church was portrayed as a *puer senex,* remarkable for the courage to face a fate which many adults feared.[3] Many of the most well-known of the early Christian child martyrs, such as Agnes, Faith, Pancras, and Vitus, are not commonly recognized as children today, although their youth was clearly a factor in the *passiones.* Accounts of heroic behavior, however, were triggered only by the threat of imminent martyrdom; child saints acted like saints at the point of death and not before. In such circumstances, child martyrs were often portrayed as passive instruments of divine grace, rather than as active figures. St. Cyricus, a child of three, was martyred by being dashed to the floor when he repeated the words his mother spoke under torture, "Christianus sum."[4] One might argue that such behavior exhibited only the capacity of toddlers for mimicry, rather than spiritual understanding and acceptance of martyrdom.

Early medieval society adapted this image to its own peculiar understanding, and created a set of child "martyrs" who were really victims of secular violence, but were considered to have been slain unjustly and in a state of innocence. Kenelm, a young prince, was slain by a henchman of his sister, and Edward by an accomplice of his stepmother. Tremorus was killed by his stepfather, Melor by his uncle, and Gerulph by his godfather.[5] These children and others were clearly slain for political motives, and without any way to escape by renouncing either political or religious beliefs.[6]

By the eleventh century, martyrdom as a route to sanctity was practically unattainable in western Europe, and the veneration of murder victims was increasingly considered inappropriate. Thus only one avenue was left open for the creation of new child saints, the practice of pious behavior on the model of adults. Both child saints and adult saints in childhood appropriated the behavioral model of the confessor, with only the age of death to distinguish them. The hagiographical model of the *puer senex* was revived and combined with practices which were difficult for any normal individual to sustain and which were seen as particularly so for children. Yet increasingly in this period the vitae of saints report the childhood pursuit of prayer, fasting and other asceticisms, mystical experiences, and dedication to a life of chastity. The *Golden Legend,* for example, recounts the childish pieties of Elizabeth of Hungary and St. Dominic.[7]

Of the many individuals who followed this path, a very few died at a young age, often because of the fervor of their devotions, and so became venerated as the child saints of this era. They are unique in the field of medieval hagiography as the only children venerated as saints who may have actively sought such recognition. As such, their existence indicates an increase in religious interest and activity among children during this period, which may be an outgrowth of an increased societal awareness of, and interest in, the state of childhood.

Childhood and religion intersected in many ways during this period. The cult of the Holy Innocents was promoted by such figures as Peter Abelard[8] and Bernard of Clairvaux,[9] and it gained popular exposure through the *Legenda Aurea* of Jacobus de Voragine.[10] Popular devotion to the cult was expressed through celebration of the feast of Childermas. Festivities increasingly took the form of a carnival, as the custom of the boy-bishop developed in England, France, and Germany.[11] The cult of the infant Jesus was developed, primarily under Cistercian influences.[12] A rise in the worship of the Virgin Mary was accompanied by increasingly domestic depictions of her role as the mother of God, with emphasis on the physical aspects of childcare, such as nursing, cuddling, and play.[13] Such developments presented both a mutual devotion between mother and child, and an increasingly naturalistic emphasis on the raising of children.

The growth of such images may have been a reflection of the increasing popular interest in childhood seen in secular life. Authors such as Bartholomeus Anglicus, Vincent of Beauvais, and Ramon Lull, provided guidance in both the physical and moral development of children.[14] As the behavior of children was subjected to increasingly realistic scrutiny, however, the recognized behavior of saints in medieval society was subjected to increasingly superlative expectations.[15] As the gap between the two became more apparent, only a few child saints between the years 1000 and 1500 were able to develop popular followings based on pious behavior.[16] These few cases represent, however, a significant development in the spiritual activities of medieval children.

The child saints venerated in this period can be divided into two categories. The first group conformed to the ecclesiastical model for canonization; the vitae stressed piety, zeal, and asceticism, and focused on children who exhibited such characteristics and died of natural causes. Saints belonging to the second group were murder victims, representatives of the earlier model of popular veneration, upon which elements of religious significance were superimposed.[17] Only four children, three of whom were technically adolescents at the age of death, were promoted through the formal canonization process; most never achieved greater than local fame, and little information on their lives or cults survives. In the latter group, especially, ecclesiastical influences can be seen at work to produce a more doctrinally acceptable image of sanctity. The success of the cults would argue for popular acceptance of these standards.

The most successful cults of pious children were those of Nicholas the Pilgrim, Rose of Viterbo, and Peter of Luxembourg. All died in adolescence but exhibited the pious behavior for which they were known while still in childhood. In each case, the element of youth played an important role in the contemporary recognition of their sanctity and in the later promotion of their cults.

Nicholas Peregrinus, honored in both the Western and Eastern churches, was born in Greece in 1075 of a humble peasant family and was raised near the monastery of St. Luke at Stira.[18] His vita records that he was virtuous and pious from infancy. One day at the age of eight he began to cry "Kyrie eleison" while tending his mother's sheep. He repeated the cry throughout the day and night for four years until his mother threw him out of the house. He was first taken in by neighboring monks, but his sanity was questioned there, as it had been by his mother. He next embraced a hermetic existence on a mountaintop,[19] where he was visited by the angel of the Lord, who brought him across the sea to Lombardy, and told him that he would find great glory there.[20] As he traveled across Italy, crying "Kyrie Eleison," he collected a large following, principally of young boys, who also took up the cry. He worked many miraculous cures and cast out demons. Eventually he made his way to Trani, where he died at the age of nineteen, surrounded by an adoring crowd. He was considered insane by those who did not follow him, but the proliferation of miracles at his tomb led to his canonization by Pope Urban II in 1098.[21]

The canonization of Nicholas demonstrates contemporary recognition of those qualities which the papacy intended to promote in candidates for sanctity; papal intervention in such matters in the eleventh century was by no means widespread or uniform. Public acceptance of Nicholas as a saint, however, was not subject to papal decree. Throughout his career, popular opinion was divided on the question of whether he was holy or insane.[22] Certainly his appeal, based at least in part upon his youth, was genuine and sufficiently widespread to attain for him a substantial cult and an almost immediate official recognition after his death.

Rose of Viterbo, who died in 1251 at the age of seventeen, exhibited signs of miraculous devotion at a similarly young age.[23] When she ate bread as a little child, the birds flocked around her to pick up the crumbs.[24] She was also much given to piety and asceticism, and abhorred the vanities of worldly existence.[25] She was also noted for her gifts of prophecy, generally of a political nature.[26] From her earliest years she expressed a desire to align herself with the Franciscans, and she became a tertiary in the Order of St. Francis before her untimely demise.[27]

While Rose of Viterbo was portrayed in her vita as a *puella senecta,* "in eius pueritia senilem habens sapientiam,"[28] whose actions contradicted the typical activities of children, her life was also more directly related to that of other children than was the *puer senex* of an earlier era. One of her miracles involved the miraculous repair of a water jug accidentally broken by another little girl, in order to spare the child from the wrath of her parents: "The Blessed Rose hurried to the spot where the broken jug was, and brought together the bits and pieces, and through the merits of this Virgin, the omnipotent power of God was demonstrated through her, so that all the pieces which were scattered and divided were replaced in their proper place, and it was no longer broken. And she gave this jug back to the girl whole and sound."[29] Although Rose was set apart from the other children by her virtuous and unchildlike behavior, she was still a part of their world.[30]

The Blessed Peter of Luxembourg was eighteen years old when

he died in 1387, and by that time had accumulated a reputation for piety which was perhaps the greatest and the most well-documented of the saintly children of the era.[31] This "puer itaque famosus & celeber" would not join other children in games, but instead remained at his studies. He evinced an aversion to comforts of the flesh. He was the only one of the children attending church who participated in the Mass instead of running around in play. Other manifestations of holiness from his childhood are more magical, such as the transformation on one occasion of bread into roses.[32] Popular devotion to Peter was both strong and sustained, despite his failure to achieve formal canonization; he was considered both a saint and a thaumaturge, and was declared patron of Avignon in 1432.[33] Ecclesiastical investigators recorded hundreds of miraculous cures achieved through his intercession.[34]

More localized cults exhibited the same elements of fervent piety and premature death. The influence of the Dominicans combined with the power of a noble Bolognese family to promote the cause of Imelda Lambertini, who died in 1333 at the age of eleven. A child much given over to pious acts from her earliest days, at the age of nine she entered a Dominican convent in Val de Pietra. She distinguished herself not only by her delight in prayer but also by her fervent desire to experience first communion. Although the custom of the region and time was to reserve this sacrament until the age of twelve, an exception was made for Imelda. After receiving the wafer on her lips for the first time, she died at the altar.[35]

The actual cause of death as well as its precise timing may be open to question. The themes of Imelda's legend reflect the growing fervor over the sacrament of the Eucharist, as well as the vogue for childish piety and sympathy for a premature death. What is certain is that a young girl of noble birth died while in a convent, and the Dominican sisters inserted her life into the martyrology of the establishment: "Obit soror Imelda cui in vita hostia de coelo sibi demissa a sacerdote accepta communicata fuit coram multis."[36] They also began to recite an antiphon in her honor, and her cult was sustained through both popular interest and the interest of the order. The cult of the Blessed Imelda remained, however, limited in popularity for many centuries. Evidence for the process of canonization was not collected until the eighteenth century, under the pontificate of Benedict XIV (1740–58), who was born Prospero Lorenzo Lambertini "of noble but impoverished parentage."[37]

The Dominican order also promoted the cult of Saint Fina of San Gimignano, who died in 1253 at the age of fifteen. Her life, recorded in the early fourteenth century by Giovanni del Coppo,[38] is described as brief, but intensely religious. At age ten, she was struck by an illness which left her with little movement. Her mother died soon afterwards. Fina's reputation for piety developed because of her practice of increasing the suffering natural to her condition through additional asceticisms. She exhibited devotion to the cult of the Passion of Jesus, to the Virgin Mary, and to St. Gregory the Great, on whose feast day she died after announcing her imminent death.[39] The cult developed at once, because of the numerous miracles reported at her tomb. She became the patron of her native town, and was venerated as an example of patience in adversity.[40]

Imelda Lambertini and Fina of San Gimignano were children who died young and whose cults were promoted by a powerful religious organization. Both were credited with reputations for unusually intense piety, although popular knowledge of their zeal would necessarily have been limited by the cloistered existence of the former and the paralysis of the latter. Detailed contemporary inquiry into their lives, such as was conducted for Rose of Viterbo and Peter of Luxembourg, does not exist. It is therefore impossible to state with any certainty that these were anything other than "constructed" saints, whose vitae reflected contemporary ideals, but not necessarily the actual behavior of young girls. These cults may represent nothing more than the veneration of young and innocent death in a highly disguised form.

Other cults of child saints present an even more ambiguous picture. The blessed Achas of Thourout died at a young age in the year 1220, after having given signs of extraordinary piety. No vita was generated to elaborate on this theme, however, and his cult remained limited to the area surrounding Thourout in Flanders.[41] It is therefore impossible to separate actual behavior from the popular sympathy surrounding an untimely death.

The city of Venice advanced the fame of a blessed child of the noble family of Teleapetra, who died in 1308 at the age of thirteen. Known popularly by her aristocratic title as "Contessa" or "Comitissa," she lived a simple life dedicated to God, to the apparent consternation of her parents. Forbidden one day to go to Mass, she miraculously walked across water, and dying soon afterwards, she was buried with honor and venerated for her piety. Her legend was preserved by Flaminio Cornaro in the eighteenth century after the cult had been in existence for some four hundred years.[42]

The blessed Agnes of Bavaria, who died in 1352 at the age of seven, also clashed with parental authority over devotion to religious ideals. The daughter of Ludwig IV of Bavaria, Agnes was sent at the age of four to the Klarissenkloster St. Jakob in Munich for an education. She soon expressed a desire to remain within the religious life and, like Imelda Lambertini, showed a great devotion to the Host. Her father, who wanted to use her for marriage alliances, tried to remove her from the cloister at the age of seven. The child vowed that she would rather die than be taken away. Ulcerous sores appeared all over her body, and she died.[43] Again, as in the case of Imelda, all that can be ascertained with certainty is that behind the walls of a convent, a child of important parents died at a young age. Like Contessa, and like so many other saints of the twelfth, thirteenth, and fourteenth centuries, Agnes clashed with her parents over the proper manifestation of piety. Perhaps stories such as these were intended, among other edifying purposes, to caution parents against discouraging religious vocations in their children.

The move to attribute lives of unusual piety to popularly venerated children can be seen also in the cases of child saints which more clearly reflect the earlier medieval theme of secular murder and, in particular, domestic violence. The cults of Lié of Savins, Reinildis of Reisenbeck in Westphalia, and Panacea of Novara originated in the murder of children by family members, but were enlarged by the addition of hagiographical romance. The cults of Lié and Reinildis remained localized and gained relatively few hagiographical embellishments, but that of Panacea gained greater fame.

Saint Laetus, or Lié, who died in 1169, was the product of popular canonization and was that rare creature, a male martyr to chastity.[44] Laetus was a young boy of great beauty, whose attractiveness moved a member of his own family to attempt acts of unnatural lust. He died resisting these base advances, and his relics were preserved at the church of Savins near Provins.[45] The legend of Reinildis[46] records that she was killed in 1262 by her mother, at the instigation of her stepfather, who wished to take control of her father's inheritance. While both the general theme and the particular circumstances more clearly reflect patterns of popular veneration of murder victims found in the early medieval period, the cult managed to sustain itself into the modern period through the characterization of the girl as unusually pious.[47]

Panacea of Novara, who died in 1383 at the age of fifteen, was born at Quarona, in Valseria, in 1368, to Lorenzo de' Muzzi and Maria de' Gambini. Her mother died when she was three, and her father married a widow with daughters of her own. Panacea was regularly abused by the stepmother and her daughters, and was beaten so severely by them that her father once found her unconscious under the straw in the stable.

Panacea was finally killed by her stepmother in a violent rage after the girl had been gathering firewood and the sheep that she was supposed to have been tending returned alone to the sheepfold. On her return, she was beaten repeatedly by her stepmother with various objects, and then finally stabbed to death with a spindle. Panacea's excuse, as preserved in the legend, was that she had lingered on the hilltop to pray.[48] Without this detail, the legend of Panacea would be little more than a variant of the Cinderella story without the happy ending. With the growth of her cult, she acquired a reputation for unusual piety from her infancy.[49]

The cults of child saints formed in the eleventh through fourteenth centuries thus reflect two major developments stemming from the increased emphasis upon piety as a quality of sanctity. The cases presented in the first part of this essay indicate a popular acceptance of the stricter definition of piety promoted in this period, through its reflection in the precocious behavior of children.[50] The second group of examples, which suggests the cloaking of popular victim cults in vaguely religious motifs, also illustrates a shift in popular expectations of sanctity.[51] Conformity to papally promoted standards became the norm, but to what extent was this change the result of popular acceptance rather than ecclesiastical pressure?

The continued veneration of murder victims, their stories thinly disguised with a veneer of piety, indicates the difficulty of altering longstanding popular belief. Hagiographical elements may have been inserted by ecclesiastical authorities rather than desired by the faithful. Certain elements, however, indicate a true shift in popular belief. This trend can be seen even more clearly in the legends of alleged child victims of ritual murder by Jews; such children were popularly venerated throughout Europe from the mid-twelfth century into, in some cases, modern times.[52] The case of William of Norwich, who died in 1144 at the age of twelve, and who provided the first charge of ritual murder by Jews in medieval Europe, may have developed precisely because of higher standards of lay piety. The *passio* composed by Thomas of Monmouth some time after 1150 for the purpose of promoting the cult laid guilt directly upon the Jews of the town, but also told the story of a young boy found dead in the woods after certain miraculous signs, and of clerical interest in promoting the cult of the innocent youth whether or not he was slain by the Jews.

> [T]he blessed William's innocence preserved his boyhood and . . . the purity of his virginity exalted it; and by the certain marks of his wounds, whoever may have inflicted them, he is proven as it were by sure arguments to have been indeed slain; and who can believe that, young as he was and innocent, he can have deserved death, since no previous fault is known?[53]

Thomas took care to construct a pious *pueritia* for William, but this was not enough to win popular acceptance for the cult. "Not the suffering but the cause of suffering makes the martyr,"[54] said detractors; in other words, one had to do more than die an innocent death. Others cautioned that it was "presumptuous to maintain so confidently that which the Church universal does not accept and to account that holy which is not holy."[55] Ecclesiastical intervention in the determination of the validity of a popular cult was recognized and accepted. It therefore became necessary to prove a martyr's death at the hands of the only non-Christians available, and thus the notion of Jewish culpability was stressed.

The cults of child saints, therefore, although generally representative of marginal objects of popular piety, nevertheless strongly illustrate the impact of ecclesiastical reform upon lay piety in the high Middle Ages. Even in cases where formal canonization failed to occur, and veneration remained at the popular level, the effect upon the laity was such that even these saints were pushed into the mold formed by ecclesiastical standards. Although the extent to which each individual case conformed in reality to societal expectations was questionable, the need to conform is clear in all cases and marks a significant change from popular practice in earlier centuries.

Children seeking sanctity have not disappeared with the Middle Ages. Since the visions at Lourdes which appeared to the fourteen-year-old Bernadette Soubirous in 1858, many of the principal Marian apparitions in western and eastern Europe have been witnessed by children.[56] Two of the three children who witnessed the appearance of the Virgin at Fatima in 1917, Jacinta and Francisco Marto, died of influenza soon afterward; Francisco in 1919 and Jacinta in 1920. Both have been declared venerable, and the cause of Jacinta, especially, is still being promoted for beatification. During her extended illness, she prayed repeatedly, and showed her love for God by drinking milk, which she disliked, and refusing grapes, which she loved.[57]

The most famous child saint of the modern age is undoubtedly Maria Goretti, the daughter of an Italian peasant who died at the age of twelve in 1902. She was stabbed to death during an attempted rape by the son of her father's partner, and was canonized for her purity in 1950.[58] Although her death itself was, like those celebrated in early medieval popular cults, completely lacking in a specifically religious significance, numerous popular biographers have stressed her unusual piety, her obedience to her parents, and her forgiveness of the murderer on her deathbed.

Such are the ingredients of hagiography, past and present. Children of the modern age, like their medieval predecessors, become saints both through design and accident. While the behavior of modern children is more subject to societal conceptions of innocence, the extreme difficulty of sustained pious behavior still plays a part in the recognition of child saints today. While children actively seek sanctity and mimic the behavioral patterns of sanctity, the element of chance still plays a significant role. Illness, accident, and murder as forms of early death shape the child saint in the present as in the past.

Elizabeth Leseur: A Strangely Forgotten Modern Saint

JANET K. RUFFING, R.S.M.

One form of the individual apostolate . . . is the witness of an entire lay life which is rooted in faith, hope and charity.
Vatican II: On the Apostolate of the Laity

Since Vatican II began to shift the attention of all members of the church to their universal call to holiness, so eloquently and persuasively argued in *Lumen Gentium,* lay members of the church, both theologians and people in the pews, have been critiquing the process of canonization, reviewing the list of officially recognized saints, and asking "Where are we?" Most recently, the complicated issues related to canonization both as a social process and as a pedagogical tool of the papacy have been skillfully and accessibly described in Kenneth Woodward's best-seller, *Making Saints: How the Catholic Church Determines Who becomes a Saint, Who Doesn't, and Why.*

His is only the latest of a series of popular and scholarly treatments of this question since the council.[1] The teaching in *Lumen Gentium* crystallized the suspicions of the majority of the laity over the centuries. If all are called to one and the same holiness, then why the paucity of canonized lay saints? Even more, when the record is analyzed with an eye to who these "lay" saints are, they turn out to be a strange lot. Their lives seem to bear little resemblance to the normal structures and concerns of lay life. The married are scarcely represented at all, and for those who are venerated, the reasons for their canonization have nothing to do with marriage as a path of holiness.[2]

Although much could be said about the clerical church's ambivalence about sanctity and sexuality, the issues are perhaps a bit more complex. Lawrence Cunningham aptly describes the long-standing tensions in the tradition on sainthood, in which martyrdom

117

became the first category of saintliness, followed by the confessor, who as type combined the ascetic with the miraculous. Hence, the role of saint as model or exemplar, someone to be imitated or at least admired as a guide to one's own holiness of life, became obscured by the saint as intercessor, a miracle-worker, a locus of religious power.[3] Finally, when the ideal of celibacy came to dominate all models of holiness, sanctity or the life of heroic virtue came to be identified with virginity, thus successfully excluding the majority of Christians as candidates for sainthood.

Nevertheless, the process of saint-making remains rooted in two separate streams: the authenticating process of the magisterium and the recognition by the people of those they choose to imitate, as well as those to whom they pray for intercession. Despite the official process's bias for the miraculous rather than the paradigmatic, the faithful long for the example of saintly people who have confronted similar cultural or personal situations in their lives and demonstrated the action of God's grace working in and through them. Whether canonized or not, people instinctively revere those who offer concrete models of holiness of life that can in some way illumine their own callings and serve as positive encouragement toward their Christian discipleship. It is in this context that I present a noncanonical, saintly married woman whom I believe is a credible model close enough to our own times to offer such hope and encouragement to women today.

A contemporary of Thérèse of Lisieux and Charles de Foucauld, Elizabeth Leseur (1866–1914) was a married woman and mystic who offers a compelling model of saintliness, lived in the context of marriage and a thoroughly secular milieu in France. Having undergone a spiritual conversion in her early thirties, several years after her marriage to Felix, a journalist, diplomat, and unbeliever, she appeared to have taken for granted that she was to live out this deepening life of union with God precisely in her married life and the secular social milieu within which she had heard and heeded this call. Like Thérèse of Lisieux, whose sanctity was already being promoted shortly before Elizabeth's death at the age of forty-eight of generalized cancer, Elizabeth embraced a path of hidden union with God while radiating to those around her a loving presence. Elizabeth's world, unlike that of Thérèse, was not a cloistered world but one peopled primarily by those who were hostile to religion and incapable of appreciating or sharing the deep spiritual core which alone gave meaning to Elizabeth's life. Her marriage to Felix was a happy and loving one. Her sole complaints were their inability to conceive children and to share faith. Both of these were sources of considerable suffering for Elizabeth. A final source of suffering was her chronic ill-health from the early days of their marriage and the physical pain which resulted from the cancer which caused her death.

Elizabeth kept a spiritual journal from the time of her conversion through her terminal illness. She wrote a series of letters to friends which were brought together in two collections under the titles *Lettres sur la souffrance* and *Lettres aux incroyants*. Her husband, inconsolable in his grief, was converted by her writings and an occasional uncanny sense of her presence after her death. He became a Dominican priest, wrote her biography, and published her writings, which were translated into a number of languages before his death in 1950. Although these writings circulated widely through the thirties in Europe, England, and America, there has been little public mention of Elizabeth in the past thirty years.[4] Indeed, Elizabeth's biography is poorly known, although the cause for her beatification was first initiated in 1936 and, after a delay due to the war, was reopened in 1990.[5]

As a saint for the laity, she demonstrated the following characteristics: (1) an apostolic strategy in a hostile, secular milieu; (2) a redemptive and transformative use of her physical and emotional suffering; (3) a mature sense of agency and surrender; (4) an active intellectual life; (5) devotion to her husband and family; (6) a lay pattern of devotional and ascetical life; and finally, (7) a relationship of mutuality and support in her friendship with Soeur Gaby.

Apostolic Strategy

Elizabeth, well-to-do by birth and marriage, participated in a social group that was cultured, educated, and largely antireligious. So secularized was the circle around her husband that she herself was gradually led away from the active faith of her childhood, and absented herself from the sacraments and personal prayer for a period of time. After her conversion in her early thirties, which occurred in 1898, she felt a call to minister in a loving and hidden way to those who seemed incapable of faith. She wrote: "I want to love with a special love those whose birth or religion or ideas separate them from me; it is they whom I want to understand and who need that I should give them a little of what God has given me."[6] She realized from experience that argument or discussion was futile and would never be persuasive with the kinds of unbelievers she knew. Understanding that faith was a gift that only God could give, she trusted in the power of prayer and had a profound sense of the communion of saints.[7] Thus she developed an apostolic strategy of allowing the divine presence to touch others through her without direct conversation. In 1904 she resolved:

> To go more and more to souls, approaching them with respect and delicacy, touching them with love. To try always to understand everyone and everything. Not to argue, to work through contact and example; to dissipate prejudice, to show God and make Him felt without speaking of him; to strengthen one's intelligence, enlarge one's soul; to love without tiring, in spite of disappointment and indifference. . . . Deep unalterable respect for souls; never to do them violence if they are sensitive, but to open wide one's soul to show the light in it and the truth that lives there, and let that truth create and transform, without merit of ours but simply by the fact of its presence in us. (*Journal,* p. 78)

And to that end, she developed her personal asceticism. To live such a vision required an almost absolute silence about the interior life that thoroughly animated her. By 1910, she is even more convinced of the need for silence:

> To be gentle and smiling outside, keeping for God alone the inner life. In what concerns God: to suffer and offer. In what concerns others: to give myself, to pour out myself. In what concerns me to be silent and forget myself. (*Journal,* p. 33)

She actively embraced the suffering resulting from being isolated from other believers and from hearing her own beliefs ridiculed and mocked. She wrote to Soeur Gaby on December 1, 1911, when she was already quite ill:

> Try, my dear sister, to smile at all that He sends: joy or sadness, illness, consolations or heavy aridity of spirit . . . this is how it is for me—these small social duties, totally external, often weigh heavily on a soul desirous of being more with God. There is, deep

within me, an ardent desire for retreat, for a life hidden and silent that the world and even Christians don't understand. But I have made of this "superficial" life, accepted, and led with apparent good grace . . . a most intimate oblation to God. It is a constant source for me of renunciations and sacrifices; and since this takes place in secret, I hope that these poor offerings will benefit and serve souls well.[8]

Her circle of unbelievers could not guess the cause of her serenity but found themselves mysteriously attracted to her. One man reported sending his wife to Elizabeth for a "bath of serenity,"[9] so remarkable was her personal presence.

Naturally introverted by temperament, and preferring a life of solitude and seclusion for reading and prayer, Elizabeth chose instead to make herself an out-going, attractive, and joyful hostess. She considered their busy social life of parties, dinners, theater, and other events part of her duty and vocation as Felix's wife, and fulfilled this role as well as possible. So well did she conceal her intense devotional life that not even Felix ever guessed how costly it was for her to live this way. When he read her journals, he understood for the first time the divine source of her love, peace, and silent endurance of physical and emotional pain, which she offered for his conversion and the conversion of other nonbelievers.

Redemptive Use of Suffering

Elizabeth made a virtue of necessity in her preoccupation with the theme of redemptive suffering. Elizabeth herself claimed her two favorite spiritual writers were Catherine of Siena and Teresa of Avila, both of whom emphasized the role of suffering in the spiritual life. Elizabeth seemed to have profoundly appropriated Catherine's sense of the redemptive value of suffering on behalf of others.[10] Elizabeth became extremely ill shortly after her marriage and suffered from ill-health the rest of her life. She experienced periodic flare-ups of hepatitis and went through a series of physical crises, including surgery, radiation, and the progression of cancer from 1911 until her death in 1914. Amazingly, few realized how ill she was much of the time, since she received visitors, sometimes traveled with her husband, and maintained an active social life until her final illness. Her letters and journals also reveal that she considered physical suffering to be the least of her suffering. From her conversion experience until her death, she constantly described as her most severe suffering either the pain of living in a spiritually hostile environment or her efforts to overcome her emotional re-actions to this constant "given" of her life.

Several streams of spirituality converged in her to support an ab-solute conviction that, although she could not personally experience the beneficial effects of her suffering for other people, nonetheless, she could offer her suffering for the conversion and sanctification of herself and others. She had appropriated Catherine of Siena's mys-ticism of suffering, the theme of reparation carried in the Sacred Heart devotion popular in her times, and the themes from the Gospels which emphasize the life-giving nature of the cross of Jesus transformed by the resurrection. She frequently connected these themes to the communion of saints.

Supported by these convictions about the meaningfulness of suf-fering, accepted and offered but not necessarily deliberately sought, Elizabeth prayed incessantly for the conversion of her husband, for her mother to experience a spiritual reality beyond her conven-tional Christianity, and for all unbelievers known and unknown to her. During her final illness, she reported making a pact with God, offering her sufferings for the conversion of her husband, which she expected to effect after her death and to which end she wrote him a "last testament." This conviction about the efficacy of suffer-ing in the communion of saints and the correlative hope in a re-union with the living and the dead in the next life was supported by the spirituality of her times. However, as anyone knows, when one is actually suffering acutely without any signs of fruitfulness apparent in oneself or others, one walks by a blind and often purifying faith in order to maintain hope in the midst of the darkness and the spiri-tual aridity which often accompany severe illness.

A Mature Sense of Agency and Surrender

Correlative with this active surrender to God's will and oblation of her suffering, Elizabeth Leseur also clearly demonstrated a mature sense of personal agency. She expressed a well-delineated sense of self in her activities and in her relationship to God. This sense of herself as a woman in France in the late nineteenth century was largely shaped by a sense of duty, yet this implied the full develop-ment of herself as a person. She wrote in July of 1900 of her vision for French women, a vision which she knew was not yet widely shared:

> Woman, whose immense power of influence is not yet understood by the French, and who does not understand it herself always, should from now on realize her task and consecrate her life to it. To recoil from duty and sacrifice is a dishonor. Now, to bear children is a duty and often a sacrifice; it is a duty to develop unceasingly one's intelligence, to strengthen one's character, to become a creature of thought and will; it is a duty to view life with joy and to face it with energy. Finally it is a duty to be able to understand one's time and not despair of the future. All this a woman can do. As much as man she is a thinking being, acting and loving; she can proudly reclaim her right to duties. (*Journal,* p. 51)

She connected this sense of a realized person to her Christian vocation. Such duties as she outlined in the quotation above must be affected by union with God. She clearly sensed that in order to surrender herself entirely to God and God's will for her, she had a responsibility to cultivate and develop her fullest potential. The following year she reflected on how she had realized these ideals in her own situation:

> I have seen clearly what I can do in my own corner of life. Above all, to try and develop in myself the instincts God has given me; to strengthen my will by regular work; to lift up my heart in the acceptance of my perpetual sufferings, and in unfailing tenderness and sympathy for all who come near me. To do the humblest things and thus possess the truth and beauty for which I long. To love and seek duty, however obscure or painful, whether intellectual or material; to miss no opportunity for an act of devotion, especially if it will not be remarked. Never willingly to give up any sacrifice unless it brings me praise or flatters that subtle pride which so quickly prevails. To go always to the little ones, the suffering, those for whom life is hard; but to have no scorn for the gay who live for themselves. (*Journal,* p. 59)

Elizabeth clearly distinguished between the healthy self-development needed by the mystic and the inflation or self-preoccupation that she named a "subtle pride." It was Elizabeth's strength of will that enabled her to fulfill her vocation of prayer and suffering, to be so lovable and attractive to those who knew her, despite her almost constant physical pain from her various illnesses. Contemporary developmental psychologists would agree that hers was the sense of self that is required for the kind of surrender to God that she demonstrated so clearly in her letters to Soeur Gaby during the last four years of her life.[11]

She wrote constantly of her abandonment to God's will. As her health became more fragile, she accepted with equanimity her inability to be active. She wrote in 1911: "I desire to live only for God, to generously do all I can in his service, and above all to abandon myself entirely to his will" (*Lettres,* p. 115). Yet she recognized that "what is possible and seems to be the divine will for me is action by means of suffering and prayer" (*Lettres,* p. 116). She developed this theme in an extended metaphor of herself as a boat floating on the waves, guided by God, confident she would reach the safe harbor of union with God and reunion with the beloved dead in the communion of saints.

Her letters are so consistent in her description of the alternation of consolation and desolation, of deep spiritual joy in one part of the self while experiencing pain and distaste in other parts of herself, that one is utterly convinced that this surrender is real and not merely a pious convention. In January 1912 she wrote:

> Let us follow Him where His gentle hand leads us: in darkness or light, illumined on Tabor or at the foot of the Cross. . . . There is great sweetness in this total abandonment and detachment which God works in us little by little through every consolation, every personal striving. I am far from having arrived, but if God brings this work to completion in his poor servant, . . . I will be totally abandoned to him. (*Lettres,* pp. 172–73)

Intellectual Life

Although not university educated, Elizabeth exhibited a certain intellectualism which was closely related to her developed sense of self. Prior to her conversion, she disciplined herself to spend time each day in intellectual pursuits. She mastered several languages including Russian, traveled extensively, and prepared for those trips by reading art and history. Not surprisingly, her conversion process included a strong intellectual component.

At the time when she was immersing herself in languages and had lapsed in church attendance, she ran out of reading material and asked her husband for something to read. He gave her Renan's *Life of Christ,* a diatribe hostile to belief, in order to stabilize Elizabeth in her growing agnosticism. Elizabeth, much to Felix's dismay, rejected Renan's faulty argumentation and began studying the Gospels to support her intellectual assessment of Renan. For the rest of her life, Elizabeth read and meditated on the New Testament; this shaped her spirituality as much as the standard devotional piety of the times. After the Gospels, she undertook a reading program which included a number of serious writers such as Thomas Aquinas and Jerome, as well as the classical mystical literature. Like so many women before her, who found themselves in an atmosphere of religious bigotry, she reinforced herself by solid study so that she could adequately defend her position as well as nurture her faith and spiritual development.

After her conversion, she did not limit herself solely to theological material. Feeling that philosophical study was appropriate for women and deploring its neglect, she began to study philosophy, which she valued for the way it helped to order and focus her mind:

> I set myself to study philosophy, and it interests me greatly. It throws light on many things and puts the mind in order. I cannot understand why it is not made the crown of feminine education. What a woman so often lacks is true judgment, the habit of reasoning, the steady, individual working of the mind. Philosophy could give her all that, and strip from her so many prejudices and narrow ideas which she transmits religiously to her sons, to the great detriment of our country. (*Journal,* p. 44)

Clear thinking remained an important aspect of Elizabeth's approach to life.

Marriage and Family

One of the most appealing characteristics of Elizabeth as a saint for the laity is how well she integrated her family life and spirituality. Tutored in the Salesian spiritual tradition, she fully accepted Francis De Sales' teaching that a life of devotion was fully compatible with marriage.[12] Since her conversion occurred several years after her marriage, she assumed that this call to a deeper, more intimate relationship with God was to be lived as Felix's wife. Despite the pain she increasingly suffered from Felix's inability to share faith with her as they shared everything else, every reference to her husband suggests a loving and mutually respectful relationship. She felt herself to be deeply loved by Felix, supported by his presence, companionship, and expressions of affection. For instance, she wrote: "Some joyful days, because of a present from Felix, and more because of the words that accompanied it—words so full of love . . . I do not deserve this, but I rejoice in it" (*Journal,* p. 55). She felt comforted in her grief at her sister's death from tuberculosis by Felix's love, and they enjoyed one another's company when they traveled together, visited friends, and summered in the countryside with Elizabeth's family. Despite their childlessness, Elizabeth consistently described a healthy and mutually loving marital relationship. In her letters, she remarked frequently on how busy her husband was, with no trace of resentment on her part. From his side, Felix was devoted to her and remained constant in his love and affection for her throughout her multiple illnesses. The devastation he experienced at her death evidenced the depth of his love and his emotional reliance on her.

She accepted the gender expectations of her role, managing the large household and supervising the servants, planning the necessary round of dinner parties, and responding to the charitable needs of the poor. She involved herself with her extended family, her mother, her sisters and their children. The children were welcome for long periods of time at her mother's country home in Switzerland, where they enjoyed being together. Elizabeth took an active role in encouraging the faith life of her niece and nephew by preparing them for first communion and writing spiritual treatises for both of them on this occasion.[13]

Pattern of Devotional Life and Ascetical Practices

Elizabeth developed a flexible rule of life that organized her devotional life and ascetical practices, which she outlined in the part of her journal titled "Book of Resolutions," which spanned the years 1906–12. Although she gave her life a specific structure, she adopted the two principles of flexibility and charity as determinative of her practice. Her devotional life was never to interfere with either the comfort or needs of those she loved. She rigorously adhered to her program when she was alone and did not need to consider the rest of the household, and she was entirely flexible where others were concerned.[14] There was a daily pattern of morning and evening prayer, including meditation. She went to confession and communion every two weeks. She desired to communicate more often, if she could do so "without troubling or displeasing anyone" (*Journal*, p. 112). Monthly, she gave one day to a spiritual retreat. For her this meant as much solitude as possible, more time in meditation, an examination of conscience, reflection on her life, and preparation for death. Annually, she tried to make a few days of retreat. Her letters indicate that by 1911, she felt herself fortunate to communicate three times a week.

She also developed a clear approach to her outer life. She considered family and social responsibilities first. She lovingly placed Felix at the head of the list. She carefully monitored what she said to him about matters of faith, and by 1906 she resolved to say as little as possible. Since she was relatively healthy at this time, she adopted work she felt she could do, was actively involved with the poor, and sought to treat her servants as warmly as possible without crossing the boundary of familiarity. Finally, she developed an asceticism based on silence, self-giving, and austerity, which she defined for herself.

Silence meant not troubling others with her illness, pain, or even graces. She thus actively sought to conceal her suffering and to refrain from self-absorption in her suffering. She spoke about her interior experience only if she judged it to be beneficial for someone seeking spiritual guidance from her. By self-giving she meant a radiant and active charity—real love expressed in every relationship and activity in her life. And for personal austerity, she avoided anything harmful to herself physically.

> I must . . . watch and improve my health since it may be an instrument in the service of God and of souls. But in this illness . . . the precautions I am obliged to take, the discomforts it brings and the privations it imposes, there is plentiful source of mortification. (*Journal*, p. 116)

Anything else she chose for the sake of personal austerity would generally have been of actual benefit for someone else. As mentioned earlier, she continually tried to be gracious, lively, and good company in social situations and chose to conceal and embrace the pain caused by religious hostility on many of these occasions. There was in her ascetical choices a careful ordering of all of them to charity. If they did not serve love or increase her intimacy with God, she did not embrace them.

Spiritual Friendship with Soeur Gaby

Finally, Elizabeth revealed her side of a profound spiritual friendship with Soeur Gaby, a nun at l'Hotel-Dieu in Beaune, in the correspondence later titled *Lettres sur la souffrance*. This friendship was primarily epistolary, in letters written from 1911 until shortly before Elizabeth's death in 1914. The two friends managed to visit in person once or twice a year, but the letters indicate a profound spiritual communion. For Elizabeth, this was her first and only soul-friend. She poured out her heart to Soeur Gaby, who did the same. When Elizabeth lifted her veil of silence, she offered a more intimate chronicle of her interior life, her spiritual theology, and her consummate tact.

Elizabeth wrote as often as every ten days or as infrequently as once a month. It is clear that within these letters, Elizabeth felt understood. Felix had met this sister and liked her. He appeared to have approved of this friendship, helped them visit one another, and acquired Elizabeth's letters after her death.

The letters suggest a deep spiritual and affective bond and an extraordinary respect for their different vocations. Elizabeth frequently wished she could have been more active, as her friend was, in caring for the poor, yet she always affirmed her own vocation to "pray and to suffer," recognizing this as God's will for her. Elizabeth also described her increasing abandonment to God, a growing union, yet without glossing over the periods of aridity, darkness, and suffering one would expect from someone as ill as she was. When Soeur Gaby was unable to write because of a problem with her eyes, Elizabeth felt the lack of the emotional support she had experienced from her friend's letters. Occasionally, there was a letter of spiritual direction when Soeur Gaby asked Elizabeth's advice on a particular issue. To such invitations, Elizabeth was discerning and clear in her assessment of the issues, yet she couched such advice as if she were taking it herself. There was such mutual understanding and respect that neither thought it unusual that a nun should have sought such advice from a married woman. And indeed, Elizabeth helped her friend resolve her conflicts.

This friendship with Soeur Gaby, enjoyed only during the last three years of Elizabeth's life, finally overcame the spiritual isolation she experienced from her conversion. It was in this relationship that Elizabeth experienced the communion of saints on earth. She was completely convinced that Soeur Gaby, Felix, and herself would all be reunited someday in the heart of their Divine Master. The two women prayed for one another, prayed for one another's intentions, affectively participated in one another's lives, and supported one another on their distinct yet common journeys. Long before other laywomen and nuns began to overcome the barriers to friendship and mutuality, Elizabeth and Soeur Gaby had enjoyed such freedom and support.

Elizabeth's life and teachings offer considerable guidance as a saint for the laity. When Elizabeth's journal, "lost to the world for decades," was reissued in 1996 under the title *My Spirit Rejoices: The Diary of a Christian Soul in an Age of Unbelief,* its publisher called attention to Elizabeth's virtues, her apostolate of good example, her holy simplicity, her gracious silence, and her "incredible power of prayer." The catalogue went on to describe "the pages of her diary" as charting "a path to holiness for all who find themselves among persons indifferent or hostile to the faith."[15] Surely, that applies in particular to the laity, whose vocation entails living "in the world" and working "for the sanctification of the world from within, in the manner of leaven."[16]

The reopening of Elizabeth's cause for beatification in 1990 offers hope that she will be recognized officially by the church.[17] Whether or not she is canonized as a saint, however, we can learn a great deal from a remarkable and holy woman like Elizabeth who offers a credible model of married sanctity and of spiritual transformation through the suffering occasioned by serious illness and an uncongenial social milieu.

Lay Apostolate and the *Beruf* of Gertraud von Bullion

ANN W. ASTELL

> *The ideal model of this apostolic spirituality is the Blessed Virgin Mary, Queen of the Apostles.*
> Vatican II: On the Apostolate of the Laity

The life of Gertraud von Bullion (1891–1930) suggests a saintly genealogy. Her membership in the nascent Schoenstatt movement as well as her ancestry confirm the observation of John Stratton Hawley that "saints typically come in flocks" and bear witness to "a nuturant family of faith spanning the seen and unseen realms."[1] Hailed as a "heroine" at her funeral and remembered by her local community at Augsburg as a "new saint living in our midst,"[2] Gertraud was, in the words of Joseph Stimpfle, bishop of Augsburg, "one of the most radiant persons of the Catholic and Schoenstatt apostolate in the first years of this century."[3] In 1991 the process of her beatification began. Gertraud herself, however, had wished for something quite different. In a prayer that sounds a postmodern note, she requested for herself a noncanonical, selfless anonymity: "Mother, if I am to become a saint, see to it that no one notices, and I the least of all."[4]

Much of Gertraud's short life was spent in a search for her *Beruf*—a multivalent German word, the semantic range of which includes "profession," "vocation," and "calling." Her professional frustrations led her not only to discover for herself and to co-create with others a new communal vocation for the laity, but also ultimately to hear and fulfill the intimate demands of her own personal calling. As we shall see, the gradual clarification of the *Beruf* of Gertraud von Bullion not only anticipates the teaching of Vatican Council II on the vocation of the laity in general, but also suggests avenues of approach to the open questions surrounding the problem of individual vocations to the lay apostolate.

The documents of Vatican II echo the theological reflections of Yves Congar, Karl Rahner, and others to define the vocation proper to the laity. According to *Lumen Gentium,* "The laity, *by their very vocation,* seek the Kingdom of God by engaging in temporal affairs and ordering them according to the plan of God." They live "in the world," and they "are *called there by God* so that by exercising their proper function and being led by the spirit of the gospel, they can work for the sanctification of the world from within, in the manner of leaven."[5] Similarly, according to the "Decree on the Apostolate of the Laity," "Since it is proper to the layman's state in life for him to spend his days in the midst of the world and of secular transactions, *he is called by God* to burn with the spirit of Christ and to exercise his apostolate in the world as a kind of leaven." Therefore, "the laity *must* take on the renewal of the temporal order as their own special *obligation.* . . . Everywhere and in all things they *must* seek the justice characteristic of God's Kingdom."[6]

As Jesuit theologian John Gerken points out, however, this description of the vocation and obligations of the laity in general inevitably raises the problem of the individual's vocation *to* the laity: "If there are tasks in the world, and the world is to come to perfection in Christ, then there must be some people whom God wants to be laymen, and there must be some people God wants in one apostolate . . . rather than another. How does one discover what one must do?"[7] If, in answer to the call of God, "some people are obliged to become laymen," that being lay by vocation is clearly not the same as being lay "at birth"; nor does it result simply from not having received (or from having refused) a call to the priesthood or religious life.[8]

The idea of an actual, positive, obliging vocation to the lay state and apostolate is, however, relatively new. As C. A. Schleck observes, "For legal and historical considerations, vocations are normally divided into religious and clerical."[9] The reasons for this traditional binary (rather than tertiary) division of vocations are many and complex. In the context of the present discussion, Karl Rahner's imagistic language is helpful.

Rahner distinguishes between the clerical and religious "apostolate constituted by a sending-out" and the lay "apostolate of man *in* his original place-in-the-world."[10] The two vocations that require persons to "leave the world," "follow," and "go forth" are visible to the church and world in a way that the lay vocation to "stay" and "remain" is not. Unlike priests and religious, laypersons do "not go out (in a spatial or spiritual sense), but work 'on the spot'" in order to Christianize the original pre-Christian situation of their existence.[11] The "radiating power" of the lay apostolate thus remains "rooted in its 'domicile'; it is not sent-forth," and precisely that "limitation" is its "strength."[12] Working "in the manner of leaven," the lay apostolate is and remains relatively invisible, and the vocation to it is correspondingly difficult for the individual to discern.

Rahner's categories evoke two different biblical models for Christian vocation. The first, which corresponds to the religious and clerical calling to "leave," "follow," and "go forth," appears in the Gospels in the various scenes where Jesus calls the individual apostles and disciples (e.g., Matt. 4:18–22; 8:19–22; 9:9; 10:1–42; Mark 1:16–20; 2:13–14; 3:13–19; Luke 5:4–11, 27–28; 9:1–6). The second, which corresponds to the vocation of the laity, appears in the scene of the Annunciation (Luke 1:26–38). Mary, in her home at Nazareth, receives the angel's message, and her "on-the-spot" acceptance of God's will for her actually draws God down "into the world" and makes Him "present" there in a new way.[13]

As I hope to show, the *Beruf* of Gertraud von Bullion is assimilated to this second, Marian model both outwardly in her commitment to Schoenstatt as a lay movement of renewal and inwardly in the realization of her personal ideal. In the early stages of Gertraud's search for her *Beruf,* the "home"—as a symbol for her father's authority, her social obligations, and her increasing confinement due to illness—stands in opposition to her hopes and dreams of discipleship as a "sending-forth." Later, her spiritual "home," the Schoenstatt shrine, becomes analogous in Gertraud's experience to Mary's home in Nazareth, the place of Mary's "local attachment" and activity, and an outward sign of the domiciled apostolate of the laity to which she freely commits herself.[14] This "home" becomes the intimate realm of her unique calling-by-name, her personal ideal, as she hears and answers it in an ongoing dialogue between herself and God.

The "Home" against *Beruf*: Obstacles in Augsburg

The fourth of six children, Gertraud was deeply attached to her aristocratic family, and her upbringing fostered her general vocation (in the familiar words of the catechism) "to know, love and serve God" (p. 191).[15] As she herself wrote, "It was already my ideal as a little girl to become someday good 'through and through,' from the very bottom of my heart" (p. 421). She received her earliest formal education in Augsburg at the school run by laywomen belonging to the Institute of Mary Ward.[16] At age twelve, on March 22, 1903, she received her first Holy Communion and gave an initial indication of her own wish for her future and the opposition she anticipated. Worried about her beloved father, Arthur, a lapsed Catholic, she offered up her reception of the Eucharist "for the conversion of [her] father and eldest brother," and she prayed, "Dear God, let me never commit a mortal sin. Let me become a missionary sister."[17]

Expressed in the form of a wish on her part, rather than a "yes" to a definite call of God, the idea of becoming a missionary stayed with Gertraud throughout her adolescence, when she studied abroad at the Sacred Heart Institutes in Riedenburg bei Bregenz, Austria (1906–7), Fontaine l'Évêque, Belgium (1907–8), and Leamington, England (1908–9). In Leamington she gave another expression to her sense of vocation. Received into the Marian Sodality there, she had the word "Serviam" ("I shall serve") engraved on her medal.

Upon her return in 1909 to her parents' home in Augsburg, she joined the Marian Sodality for working-class women at St. Sebastian's, the nearby Capuchin church, where she attended daily Holy Mass at 5:00 A.M., even after having danced the whole night through at Fasching. Six years passed, during which Gertraud participated with family and friends in the charmed social life of a young countess without, however, losing sight of her high religious ideals. Gertraud's father wanted to see his pretty, well-educated daughter suitably married. When to his amazement she flatly refused and reaffirmed her wish, "Let me become a missionary sister," the two reached an impasse—he refusing permission, she unwilling to go without it, each troubled about the other's resistance and hoping for an eventual change of heart.

The outbreak of World War I gave Gertraud an opportunity to realize her ideal of service in a secular sphere acceptable to her parents. Her father and her brothers, Gottfried and Konrad, were army officers, and already in 1914 Gertraud enlisted as a Red Cross nurse. In July and August 1915, she attended the sick on crowded military hospital trains. On September 13, 1915, she was called to the western front to serve at Fénelon Hospital in Cambrai, France. There, for more than two years, she witnessed the horrors of war and worked to alleviate them with so much courage and resourcefulness that she was awarded the Red Cross Medal on January 19, 1917. In February of that same year the hospital was moved to Mons, Belgium, where Gertraud served for eight months as a laundry nurse in an infectious cellar. In Mons she had her first introduction to Schoenstatt through some young soldiers, among them, Franz Salzhuber, Alois Zeppenfeld, and Nikolaus Lauer.[18] The contact, as we shall see, directed her toward the discovery of her true vocation.

Frustrated in the fulfillment of her *Beruf* and deeply troubled in conscience about her opposition to her father's wishes, Gertraud obtained from Salzhuber the address of Father Joseph Kentenich (1885–1968), the young founder of Schoenstatt, and wrote him a long letter, explaining the situation and requesting spiritual direction from him. In a reply dated September 13, 1918, Father Kentenich assured her that in his opinion her conduct toward her father was "not self-willed stubbornness, but obedience to an inspiration of grace that required a great personal sacrifice from [her]."[19] Reluctant, however, to declare the matter of her vocation *(Berufsangelegenheit)* settled, he encouraged her to endure the struggles surrounding her life-decision and put her in contact with Father Michael Kolb, the current provincial superior of the Pallottine Fathers, who agreed to serve as her spiritual director.

Father Kentenich helped her to see her "strong-willed stubbornness" in a positive light, as a protection against temptations and faults and as a source of moral courage in an oppositional environment, and he assured her that, under more supportive circumstances, her will would "more easily be purified from selfish motives and rendered capable of a complete surrender to the will of God, as well as great sacrifice in his service" (p. 10). He concluded the letter with the advice to fulfill faithfully her duties as a nurse and remain conscientious in her prayer life and personal asceticism "so that the dear God can help you find the right vocation *[den rechten Beruf]*."

At the end of 1918, after a brief term at the hospital at Hasselt, Belgium, Gertraud returned home to Augsburg. The situation of the family had changed considerably, however. On March 8, 1916, Gertraud's mother had died. Shortly thereafter, her father's health

began its steady decline. Her brother Gottfried had contracted a
lung disease on the battlefield, and he, too, needed her care. The
rampant inflation and civil unrest after the war necessitated careful
management of the family's estate. Although she did not realize it
until January 1921, Gertraud herself was already ill with the tuberculosis that would eventually take her life. Her ailing father continued to oppose her wish to join a missionary order.

Gertraud's writings during this period (1918–26) reflect her
gradual, painful detachment from the dreams of her youth concerning her *Beruf* and, on the other hand, her ever deeper acceptance of a new vocation to the lay apostolate in and through
Schoenstatt. In a letter of March 30, 1919, Gertraud could still speak
optimistically of her desire for a career in music. As a wartime nurse
she had bolstered the morale of patients and nurses alike by form-
ing choirs and rehearsing hymns and carols for the various feast-
days, and she thought of exercising this vocal talent professionally:

> My heart's wish to continue in music, especially in singing, has
> failed me up to now whenever I stood before its fulfillment, and I
> definitely hope to be able to begin studies soon. Perhaps this is
> also a proud ambition out of natural urges, but nothing hinders
> us from "converting" them [into God's service]. (p. 72)

This dream too, however, like her wishes to become a missionary
and/or a registered nurse, remained unfulfilled. In a letter to
Nikolaus Lauer, dated April 20, 1920, she speaks about her tor-
menting inner restlessness:

> Is this heavenly fire not at once our greatest happiness and our
> greatest suffering? How long will I have to wait for my direct vo-
> cation? If only I won't be fruitless in between! Yes—"As God wills
> it, so you bow"—often we sang it out there [during the war]; now
> we don't sing it, but live it. (p. 93)

Repeated hospitalizations for treatment for tuberculosis punctu-
ated the intervening years. Finally, in a letter to a friend dated
March 18, 1926, Gertraud connects the death of her father with the
final surrender of her earlier ideas about her *Beruf*:

> On Jan. 7 God called our good father forth from us and left me
> behind, alone and homeless. To be sure, I still inhabit the old

rooms and Miss Betz, who has been in the family already 21 years now, looks after me; but the emptiness makes itself daily more palpable. . . . And the future? What I had earlier dreamed for my-self at this point of life is no longer possible, due to my bad health, and that means the plans must be set aside. (p. 285)

In that same letter, however, she also claims for herself a new free-dom to respond to God's call and a new understanding of it:

Dear J., if you want to do a favor, something loving, for me, then pray an Ave now and then so that I might know what God now ex-pects from me. Actually I am now free, so that he should take the undisputed first place in my future life. Only he must take care of the many concerns that stand, hindering, in the way! My purpose inclines toward full-time lay apostolate. . . . Help me pray for light and strength to follow through.

The "Home" As *Beruf*: Gertraud's Vocation to Schoenstatt

Gertraud's strong inclination in 1926 toward the lay apostolate and away from religious life had been fostered negatively by her father's long-term opposition to her becoming a missionary and positively by her close association with the Schoenstatt movement, beginning in 1917. Indeed, in her writings as a member of Schoenstatt, she al-ways uses the word *Beruf* as "vocation" with a happy confidence that contrasts sharply with her frustrated sense of *Beruf* as "profession."

As we have seen, she addressed her initial letters to Father Kentenich from Mons in 1917–18, a correspondence that he later called "the first milestone in the history of the women's movement in Schoenstatt" (p. 11). In June 1920, Gertraud was the first woman to join the Apostolic League of Schoenstatt. Later that same year, on December 8, she and her cousin, Marie Christman, made a conse-cration to our Lady of Schoenstatt that marks the foundation of the Apostolic Federation for Women. As a result of Gertraud's leader-ship, already in 1921 (August 13–17), the first Women's Convention of the Apostolic Federation took place in Schoenstatt. On April 16, 1925, five years after the foundation of the Women's Federation, twenty women consecrated their lives to our Lady of Schoenstatt in the service of her work, using the words of a prayer written by Gertraud von Bullion. As a result of that consecration, a second women's community, the Secular Institute of the Schoenstatt Sisters of Mary, was founded in October 1926. Gertraud remained active as a group leader in the federation until her untimely death in 1930.

Reflecting in 1940 on the rapid growth and international development of the large women's movement within Schoenstatt, Father Kentenich stressed the singular contribution of Gertraud von Bullion, the first woman in Schoenstatt: "I stand reverently before her greatness. Despite many shadows, she stands before us as a truly great woman. . . . She also had a mission *[Aufgabe]* in life, as we all have a mission, and this mission is not lost. Gertraud von Bullion has not lost her mission [which she continues among us]" (p. 12).

How did Gertraud herself see her mission in life, her *Beruf* to Schoenstatt? A vocation implies that God has called, that the individual has heard and accepted that call, and that others have confirmed it. As Gertraud understood it, she was called by Jesus through Mary into a timely participation in Mary's own unending apostolic vocation as the Christ-bearer. Gertraud was called to be an *altera Maria* for God and others. She received this vocation in a concrete manner in the shrine of our Lady of Schoenstatt, a holy pilgrimage place to which Mary had "attached" herself in order to make Christ "present" in the contemporary world and bear him into the world through Marian apostles. This calling was, moreover, confirmed within the Schoenstatt movement indirectly by the manifest fruitfulness of Gertraud's consecration, both during her lifetime and afterwards, and directly by Father Kentenich, the founder of Schoenstatt. From him, Gertraud received the vocational blessing which her own father had withheld. On April 16, 1925, Gertraud invited Father Kentenich to bless her and her companions before they made their life-consecration. He did so, she writes, and "it was like when parents bless their children before they take the most important step in life" (p. 268).

Gertraud made the consecration in 1925 in a spirit of intimate surrender to God and total dedication to the Schoenstatt apostolate. In 1924, when the women of the federation gathered in Schoenstatt to begin preparations for their consecration, Gertraud was already "at home" in her vocation, as her diary entries indicate. The chapel of the Mother Thrice Admirable had become her spiritual home and the means and expression of her calling:

> The first moment in the shrine was so beautiful! I knelt down and only said: "Here I am, Mother, and I have also brought along

something for you—my heart. But also something that pleases
you even more—my will, my world, my "I." Give it to the Savior!
How happy this makes me! (pp. 247–48)

She goes on to marvel: "How grace works in me!" The Savior, she
writes, has implanted in her soul such a "hunger for cross and suffering, and thereby filled [her] soul with such an elation of freedom
and joy that [she] cannot put the feeling into words" (p. 248). She
feels moved to "spread out [her] arms and sing" a song like Mary's
own Magnificat (Luke 1:46–55). Her trust in God and her "hunger
for cross and suffering" have cast out any remaining fear about accepting her vocation and given her strength to encourage others:

> Some of the sisters of the Federation came crying to me, shaken
> by what they had heard and without courage and afraid on ac-
> count of the high demands; but I had to hide my joy forcibly and
> could only comfort them with a word that makes me so happy:
> "Through my impotence *[Ohnmacht]* shall God's omnipotence
> *[Allmacht]* be glorified!" Therein lies my complete happiness.
> (p. 248)

In a letter dating from that same period, Gertraud reenacts this
memorable scene in the form of an imaginary dialogue in which
she uses very specifically the language of "call" and "vocation." First
she poses the problem and makes it her own:

> My dear sisters, it is true: concerning the renewal of the world, we
> must want to strive for the greatest possible perfection. But who
> would not be overcome by anxiety and dread, if he stands before
> this steep, sky-high cliff? Look, I feel the same if I consider the
> coming consecration and take a look at myself. Like poisonous
> snakes the doubts coil close: "Have you too then really a vocation
> to the Federation? Your action and still more your suffering stand
> so far from the goal!" (p. 264)

Then she rejects this train of thought, recalling the "hour of grace"
when she first received her calling. The "basic question," she says, is
this: "Why has the Blessed Mother, by order of the Savior, led *me* into
the Federation? *Me,* who am nothing . . . and unlikely to accomplish
anything for the moral and religious renewal [of the world]?" The
answer Gertraud hears from Mary's lips affirms the paradox of powerful weakness: "Then the Mother says, 'My child, just because you

are nothing and can do nothing . . . therefore God chooses you for his work. Not because you should accomplish something, but because *God* wants to work and create! . . . Your impotence *[Ohnmacht]* shall indeed glorify the omnipotence *[Allmacht]* of God!'"

Gertraud's genius consists in keeping the loving and powerful Caller, rather than the call per se, in the foreground of her spiritual vision. In times of discouragement, she asks herself, "Should I throw everything away because I never bring anything to perfection? The choleric in me would like to do so" (p. 466). She rejects this option, based on her response to the call alone, turning her attention instead to the Caller: "But is it not better that I retain my poverty, my incapacity for good, for anything more than mediocrity, and say, full of humility, to my Mother: 'See, I am not capable of serving and following your Son as I should. You, however, have called me. Here I am.'" In that same prayer, Gertraud goes on to place the main responsibility for the fulfillment of her mission in life on the Mother who has called her:

> Take the striving and stumbling of your child. Mother, help me that I at least attain to mediocrity, since I manage to do nothing better. And, Mother, if you and my Savior expect more from me, give me the glowing flames of Love that overcome the obstacles of my pride and lead me to the cross. Give me each day anew the will to strive. (p. 466)

In an attitude of radical, childlike dependence, Gertraud looks away from herself, even in a certain sense away from her calling, to focus instead on the personal source of her vocation, Jesus and Mary, whom she begs to live and act within her. The prayer concludes with the extraordinary petition: "Mother, if I should ever become a saint, grant that nobody notices it, and I the least of all!"

Precisely because of this existential detachment from self and attachment to her Caller, however, Gertraud experienced an enormous freedom to do and dare much in the fulfillment of her call. As her own physical health rapidly declined, the growing Schoenstatt work became her extended self. She found her own strong "urge to be apostolically active" (p. 420) alive in Schoenstatt—so much so that she identified herself completely with the young community she had co-created: "The awareness 'I am the Federation; the Federation is I,' often awakens serious thoughts in me, [and I ask myself]: Am I cooperating faithfully with the grace of God?" (p. 249). She offered her life and death for its vitality and fruitfulness: "We must let ourselves be crucified for the Federation" (p. 426). In this way Gertraud fulfilled her "vocation to be a mother of souls" (p. 213), a maternal vocation that "a woman bears . . . in her very nature" and lives out in "self-giving to the point of self-forgetfulness" (p. 197).

Her journal entries and her many letters to federation members give a detailed account of the spiritual formation she and her co-sisters were receiving in Schoenstatt during the conventions, days of recollection, and retreat courses they attended. After the initial women's convention of August 1921, she wrote in summary: "The spirit of the Apostolic Federation expresses itself outwardly in the apostolate, in devotion to Mary, and in the striving for self-sanctification" (p. 119). Her notes on the lay apostolate anticipate the formulations of Vatican Council II:

> The Apostolic Federation is a community of education aimed at the formation of lay persons who constantly concern themselves with the salvation of immortal souls. It can accomplish this through the indirect apostolate in which we through prayer, example, word or deed contribute to the free development and expansion of the Church (whose mission is the care for souls) or through the direct apostolate. (p. 117)

In her elaboration on the indirect apostolate, Gertraud emphasizes the importance of good example: "People want to see men and women who prelive Christianity for them; therefore the absolute necessity of self-sanctification." This striving for personal holiness has a communal, rather than an individualistic, character. As Gertraud recognized, one of the distinctive features of Schoenstatt's spirituality and lay apostolate is the guiding idea: "I sanctify myself *for others*" (emphasis mine), the "communal coloring" that "unites the care for the individual soul with the care for the souls" of others (p. 117).

As a member of the apostolic federation, Gertraud attached great importance to this communal dimension: "We are and remain an educational community; we are all striving people and none of us are finished" (p. 427). Repeatedly, she reminded her fellow sisters of the federation: "The vocation to the Federation is not only a calling to serious striving for holiness and apostolic work, but also to communal work in the groups. . . . It should also be said about the sisters of the Federation: 'See how they love one another, understand one another, help one another'" (p. 429). And she exhorted them, "Do not forget that you must believe wholeheartedly in your vocation, despite all inabilities, poverty and weakness" (p. 426).

Gertraud's notebooks show her, as one of Schoenstatt's cofounders, to have reflected deeply on the idea of lay sanctity. Under the guidance of Father Kentenich, she and her federation sisters devoted their energies to developing a personal and communal style of life, tested by experience, that realized the evangelical counsels of poverty, chastity, and obedience in a novel way in a secular setting. This practical asceticism was inspired by Marian ideals, animated by prayer, and informed by repeated pilgrimage to the shrine at Schoenstatt. The pilgrimage graces Gertraud and others received there—the graces of being "at home" with the Divine, of personal transformation, and of apostolic fruitfulness—later gained expression in Schoenstatt's threefold spirituality, which includes covenant spirituality, everyday sanctity *(Werktagsheiligkeit)*, and instrument piety.

Gertraud knew herself to be Mary's instrument. As her repeated hospitalizations—in Bad Lippspringe (1921), Schömberg (1922 and 1927), Geislingen (1929), and finally, Isny (1929–30)—increasingly limited her ability to travel, she devoted herself all the more to correspondence with fellow federation members. In an undated diary entry she admits, "Sometimes it seems to me as if my apostolate consists only in letter-writing" (p. 436). She suffers under her inability to do more than "patchwork" (p. 465) and wishes "never to grow tired in writing and saying how blessed it is to be an instrument of the Blessed Mother for the salvation of souls" (p. 425).

In two long letters to the sisters of the federation, dated May 5 and September 8, 1927, she offers an extended meditation on the position of Mary as the most fitting leader of the young women's community and the best possible model for their apostolic work and striving for personal holiness. Again and again, she identifies the Caller with the call by indicating that their vocation is a participation in Mary's own continuing vocation as the God-bearer, and results from and expresses outwardly their intimate oneness with her, their mother, exemplar, and intercessor. In Gertraud's view, Mary's own love for Christ necessarily supports and animates all those who follow him. Mary, moreover, models for them the threefold apostolate of word, example, and deed. As Gertraud puts it, "In every situation we can, I think, find an example, a model, if we correctly picture to ourselves Mary's life" (p. 334).

Gertraud accordingly weaves into her portrait of Mary a series of contemporary applications. She speaks, for instance, of the Marian "apostolate of silence": "How much less anger, lovelessness, bitterness, hate and envy would be in the world (and often particularly among so-called devout souls), if we in silence observed an apostolate of kindness and love!" (p. 335). The hiddenness of Mary's life in Nazareth inspires Gertraud's call for a heroic mastery of the "little things of everyday life" as a faith-filled contribution to the work of salvation:

> What contemporary humanity needs are heroic souls who conquer the everyday, whose lack of personal needs answers the need of our present time for a source of supernatural strength; heroic souls, who, good and faithful, fulfill their duty exactly, whether they earn for it honor and promotion or demotion and ridicule; heroic souls, who can renounce pleasurable eating and drinking, the theatre, conveniences and amusements, because they scoop their happiness out of deeper wellsprings. (p. 335)

Similarly, Mary's stance beneath the cross of Jesus models for Gertraud the indispensable "apostolate of suffering" (p. 336).

More than anything else, however, Gertraud sees Mary as apostolic through the radiant beauty of her very being. Hers is an "attractive holiness," a "natural" holiness that Gertraud wishes to emulate. Unlike a merely ethical striving and straining for virtue that too often affects people "in a repulsive way," the Marian apostolate works through the transforming power of love. The natural and supernatural "gracefulness" of Mary "draws people closer, so that they, attracted by such sweet virtue, are enthused to become just as gentle, humble, kind and mild, just as pure and ethical, just as selfless and ready to serve" (p. 335).

In Mary, the great exemplar of the federation, Gertraud found an image of her personal ideal, an embodiment of her own unique calling. She was fascinated by the theory of the personal ideal, as Father Kentenich explained it to the members of the federation, and her quest to recognize and realize "the creative idea of God concerning [her] person" (p. 427) essentially redefined for her the problem of her *Beruf*.[20] She concerned herself less with the question "What am I to *do*?" and more with "What does God wish me to *be*?"[21] The attempt to put her ideal into words led Gertraud into an ever deeper self-knowledge as she considered her temperament; her strong natural inclinations and characteristic behaviors; her favorite stories, symbols, and prayers. Her personal ideal, in turn, then became the basis for her decision-making and the standard according to which she reviewed her past actions. "Our goal," she told her co-sisters, "is the realization of our personal ideal" (p. 309).

In a diary entry, probably dating from November 1922, Gertraud copied a poem about an autumnal leaf falling to the ground. Interpreting the richly hued leaf as a symbol of herself, Gertraud prays: "Grant such a fulfillment also to me, Eternal Father, when you call me to yourself" (p. 189). She explicitly associates this final calling ("Du *rufst* mich"), this last vocation, with the realization of her personal ideal: "Everything depends on faithful work with the P. I."

What, then, was the personal ideal of Gertraud von Bullion? By her own admission, she had two passions: "the first is to help all people, each one where he or she has need; the other: to see God honored and loved everywhere by everyone" (p. 420). She expressed these two passions in a short, oft-repeated prayer of self-offering that summed up the fundamental orientation of her soul and thus gave expression to her other-centered personal ideal: "Lady, Mother, as your instrument, my whole love to your Jesus! My whole strength for souls!" (p. 422). On April 14, 1930, two short months before her death, Gertraud wrote to her spiritual director, Father Kolb, in order to renew her federation consecration and with it, her P. I.: "How seriously the Mother has taken our surrender! For a year now I have been sick and I see no end to it. But I do not take back a single word of the consecration. Tell that to the Mother in the shrine!" (p. 414).

Thus Gertraud von Bullion answered her calling in the end, and the beloved Mother who had called her, in fulfillment of her own prophecy: "My love shall ripen to its full maturity—yes, to its completion in my death-offering!" (p. 466). The obstacles to the fulfillment of her *Beruf* had led her to the discovery and generous fulfillment of a new vocation, both communal and personal, for which Gertraud herself has now become an exemplar. Having answered her own call, she calls to others. The jubilation of the thousands of women who gathered to celebrate the opening of her beatification process in September 1991, confirms the word Father Kentenich spoke in 1945 concerning her and the other Schoenstatt "saints" of the founding generations: "The dead are not dead. They live among us. . . . They live for us" (p. 13).

Contemplation along the Roads of the World
The Reflections of Raissa and Jacques Maritain
ASTRID O'BRIEN

> *The spiritual life of lay people . . . ought to take its distinctive quali-*
> *ties from their marriage and family life, their single or widowed*
> *state, their conditions of health, and from their involvement in their*
> *own professional and social lives.*
> Vatican II: On the Apostolate of the Laity

When Raissa and Jacques Maritain were baptized in June 1906, two years after their marriage, they were determined to be genuine followers of Jesus rather than mediocre Catholics of the type their godfather, Léon Bloy, denounced in his books. For them there was no middle ground; it was either mediocrity or the total self-surrender characteristic of the saints and mystics they had come to love.[1] Even before their conversion, they had read in Surin's *Spiritual Catechism* the requirements and stages of the development of the life of the spirit, for which they had hungered since finding hints in Plotinus and Pascal. Raissa writes that it seemed to them there was no way for them to "be alive and human in [their] spirit as well as in all [their] acts" (*Memoirs,* pp. 122–23). In comparison with that of the saints, their own interior lives seemed powerless, uncertain, and aimless.

They learned from Surin that the truth they sought so earnestly—indeed, three years earlier they had decided they would have to commit suicide if it proved unattainable—was, in fact, personal: to seek truth is to seek the God Who is Truth (pp. 64–68; 96), and the way to attain him is by a total, loving surrender leading, through his grace, to union with him.[2] Surin also taught them that, though they could not reach God merely by their own efforts, neither could they come to him *without* any effort: what was necessary was to root out of one's heart all attachment to any lesser goals (p. 123).[3]

What does this mean in the concrete? The history of spirituality

has been a chronicle of differing interpretations of this require-
ment: it has meant lifestyles as varied as that of the hermit and that
of the Little Sisters of the Poor. Almost always it had been understood to mean embracing the religious state in one form or another: the overwhelming majority of canonized saints who were not
martyrs were either religious or clerics. Even further, all the treatises
on the spiritual life had been written by such persons for—with only
a few exceptions—other such persons. But the Maritains felt no call
to the religious state; they were, on the contrary, convinced that
marriage was their vocation. Thus their immediate challenge was to
fashion for themselves a way of living which would be faithful both
to the gospel and to their duties as married laypersons in the world
(*Notebooks,* p. 34).

The general direction, "to love God and serve Him with all your
heart" (*Journal,* p. 105; *Memoirs,* p. 138; *Notebooks,* p. 20) was clear
enough. But how to adapt the "tried and true" practices of the religious orders to the lay state could only be discovered by experience—even, to some extent, by trial and error. Initially their "rule of
life" resembled that of the monastery (*Notebooks,* pp. 43, 73), even
though they were aware of the danger of becoming "secularized
monks rather than . . . laymen given to God" (p. 56). They were anxious to find a spiritual director,[4] believing—erroneously, as they
soon came to realize—that perfection would be easy to attain once
they had someone to show them the way (*Memoirs,* pp. 173–74).
They fully expected to be given explicit instructions which they
need only follow obediently to be assured of living *in* the world without conforming *to* the world (p. 176).

Only gradually did they come to see that such docility was im-
prudent—it presupposes a director capable of "the purest discrimination between those things which are God's and those which are
Caesar's" (p. 313). Raissa adds that such perfect discrimination is
impossible to find. Even more important, it is an abdication of the
directee's own responsibility; after receiving wise counsel, the latter
must bring his own good sense, life experience, and prudence to
bear on the issue in question (*Notebooks,* p. 183). "Spiritual direction
has for its object to teach us to form wisely, and not to elude, the
judgment of our conscience" (*Memoirs,* p. 314), writes Raissa.

Jacques gives a vivid description of their experience of "coming
of age" spiritually:

We have the impression that here we are, the two of us, in spite of ourselves, in high seas and forced to judge for ourselves, as autonomous beings. . . . It is necessary to be ready to receive advice, but not to *count* on it . . . to have one's own point of view, the only one from which can be judged certain values referring to the place which in His providence God has assigned us. (So it is, for us, a question of what is suitable for lay life with respect to intellectuality and faith and the spiritual life.) . . . Our lot henceforth is a greater trembling and at the same time a greater liberty and self-sufficiency. (*Notebooks*, pp. 146–47)

Reaching this point took them sixteen years—a not abnormal period in comparison with that of reaching social independence. They might have come to it even earlier were it not the case that the priest on whom they became dependent was in so many other ways a considerable help (*Memoirs*, p. 134). A learned and holy Dominican, he was convinced that "Christian life is based on intelligence" (p. 177). It was he who introduced them to the writings of St. Thomas Aquinas (p. 180). Jacques states that he was given to them by God to give them "very perfect intellectual guidance" (*Notebooks*, p. 58) and calls him "that great master in the illuminative life" (p. 68). It was also he who, during the first year they knew him, confirmed their vocation, telling them that they must not hesitate to follow the way of contemplation in the world (p. 57).

The term "contemplation" is problematic: within the spiritual tradition it has come to mean either meditation on spiritual things—often called active, acquired, or ordinary contemplation—or an experiential perception of God, a state of awareness of God's being or presence, often called passive, infused, or extraordinary contemplation.[5] The first names an attentiveness to God and his activity in history arising from one's own efforts; the second, a state of absorption produced in the soul by God. The boundary, however, is not hard and fast: what begins as primarily an intellectual activity leading to a prayerful response and a practical resolution becomes increasingly less active, with more prolonged periods of quiet and loving attentiveness to God.

In her letter to Charles Henrion (*Journal*, pp. 355–61), Raissa wrote that, ontologically, infused contemplation is a passive state, that is, "one produced in virtue of union . . . by a special will of God which leads him to give us, in some manner, knowledge of his love for us"

(p. 357). Psychologically, it is experimental knowledge: one *experiences* God's infinite love and responds with love, a love which longs to be ever more total, to keep nothing for oneself. Writing later, after Raissa's death, Jacques speaks of it as coming from love, tending to love, and a work of love, a "mysterious knowledge given by love."[6]

Whether all Christians are called to this latter type of contemplative prayer has been much debated, and the debate has been complicated by the fact that various extraordinary graces—visions, foreknowledge, etc.—sometimes accompany infused contemplation.[7] Ordinarily such graces are not given to all. Yet all are called to union with God—this no one denies—and it is difficult to believe that one who earnestly desires this above all else will be refused all experience of it while on earth. So reasoned Jacques and Raissa, though they recognized that some ways of life seem more congenial to contemplative prayer than others.

Raissa, who had given up her own university studies when she married and was, moreover, plagued by poor health, had neither the responsibility nor, indeed, the possibility of professional activity outside her home (*Memoirs,* p. 180). Yet this very restriction gave her greater opportunity for reflection and prayer (p. 142) than Jacques, called to serve God and the common good in lecturing and writing, could enjoy (*Notebooks,* p. 79). Her inner life developed rapidly. Therefore, when it became important for Raissa and Jacques to share with those who through their influence came to Catholicism and to Thomism the principles upon which a solid lay spirituality depended, they had very few authors but considerable personal experience upon which to draw (*Journal,* p. 235, #33).

Together they wrote a little "spiritual directory" (*Notebooks,* p. 145)—its English title is *Prayer and Intelligence*—which they describe as "an attempt to disentangle and state as clearly as possible, in the spirit of Christian tradition and of St. Thomas, the main directions which seem suitable to the spiritual life of persons living in the world and occupied in intellectual pursuits" (*Prayer,* p. v). It was completed in July 1922 (*Notebooks,* p. 147), but this was by no means their last word on contemplation in the world; they returned to it again and again in *The Situation of Poetry* (1938) and *Liturgy and Contemplation,* published in 1957.[8] *Raissa's Journal,* edited by Jacques after his wife's death in 1960, shows her constant effort to be more and more docile to the action of God in her life and prayer. *Notes on the Lord's Prayer,* also published posthumously, was meant to be the first part of a book on prayer which she thought of as "Contemplation along the Roads of the World."[9] Jacques deals with the topic in an article entitled "Love and Friendship (A Marginal Note to 'Raissa's Journal')" included in his *Notebooks* (pp. 219–57), published in 1965, and one final time in *The Peasant of the Garonne,* published in 1966.

The doctrine which emerges from these writings is decidedly different from that found in the overwhelming majority of treatises on the spiritual life. The latter promote a "double standard" very reminiscent of the Manichean distinction between the elect and the hearers, according to which holiness is only for clerics and religious.[10] The most laypersons can hope for is a lengthy purification in purgatory to render them fit to enter heaven (*Notebooks,* pp. 177, 275). Jacques explicitly rejects this view, insisting that "what is *normal* for the Christian—is to go straight to Paradise, to rejoin the Lord. Not only rejection into Hell, but even also passage through Purgatory . . . represents *abnormal* cases" (p. 273). Even if, because of our sinful condition, the abnormal be more common, it nevertheless remains abnormal. Jacques does not hesitate to take St. Thomas to task for following the pessimistic view of St. Augustine regarding the small number of the chosen, finding the argumentation "extraordinarily unconvincing" (p. 270).

He was no less emphatic in his rejection of the view that the function of the laity in the Mystical Body is merely to sin and go to confession (p. 175). On the contrary, they are called "to participate in the sanctity of Jesus and in His redemptive work" (p. 177), and it is the duty of the clergy to aid the faithful to become conscious of this vocation. Jacques states:

> What matters in a very special way, and perhaps more than anything else for our age, is the life of prayer and of union with God lived *in the world* . . . by those who are called to this life in the common condition of lay people with all its turmoil, its risks, and its temporal burdens. (*Peasant,* pp. 196–97)

He adds that such people are not as rare as one might think, and the reason why they are not even more numerous is that they either lack wise spiritual guidance or have guides who actually dissuade them.

Yet further, he disagrees strongly with another version of the "double standard"—the claim that *only* those in the religious state are consecrated to God—arguing, on the contrary, that a "Christian family is in itself a community consecrated to God in the lay order, just as an abbey or a Carmelite convent is in the religious order. . . . it belongs to the spouses themselves, in a long and patient novitiate, to discover . . . the path which must be theirs in order to progress towards God" (*Notebooks*, pp. 180–81). Absolutely nothing can replace this discovery, though they may be helped by the counsel of a wise and holy spiritual director, as well as by the companionship of similarly motivated friends. According to Raissa, the director's function is to aid the couple to sift out the illusions of self-love (*Memoirs*, p. 312). Jacques sees like-minded friends as so important that he is convinced it is Divine Providence that is active in what appear to be "chance meetings that [crop] up all along the roads of the world" (*Notebooks*, p. 182).

Not only is it the case that marriage is not a lesser vocation: "There are," he writes, "even probably particular cases in which the state of marriage . . . offers to certain married persons more propitious moral conditions than the state of religion offers to certain religious" for growth in holiness, because of "the perpetual mutual attentions and the daily sacrifices which marriage requires and . . . the innumerable occasions for compassion and . . . fraternal help which life in the midst of men entails" (p. 247). The evangelical counsels are but a means; they are not ends in themselves. Consequently, the vows of religion cannot be required for the perfection of charity (*Prayer*, p. 16). Raissa asserts that the grace of infused contemplative prayer is given not only to cloistered religious, but also "it is frequently the treasure of persons hidden in the world" (*Liturgy*, p. 74).[11]

Having thoroughly demolished the "double standard," they begin to develop their own position, reasoning that if contemplation—"A silent prayer which takes place in recollection in the secret of the heart" (*Liturgy*, p. 36; *Notebooks*, pp. 233–34)—is directly ordered to union with God then, since all are called to this union, this type of prayer cannot be as extraordinary or abnormal as most think, even if, whether for lack of wise guides or our sinful nature, it is not common (*Prayer*, p. 3; *Liturgy*, p. 31; *Journal*, p. 323). Neither can it be the case that involvement in the day-to-day affairs of the world renders it impossible, even for those who are deeply committed. It is the inner disposition, not the outer situation, which is essential. In fact, writes Raissa, God wills that this spiritual union be realized in quite diverse forms of life—of immense activity and minimal solitude as well as minimal activity and great solitude (*Journal,* p. 324). Indeed, it is those in the former state who have the greater need for it, so that in their activity they may be guided by it. Those whose access to the highest forms of contemplation is made more difficult because of their many responsibilities will not be denied it in substance (*Prayer,* p. 54).

Very few dedicated Christians seem to experience God's loving presence in the vivid, immediate forms traditionally associated with mystics and visionaries; instead they live by faith, not seeing but believing. Their prayer is clearly not that type of infused contemplation described by St. John of the Cross and St. Teresa of Avila (*Liturgy,* pp. 35–39). Yet there are many among them who live in the simplicity of the "little way" taught by St. Thérèse of Lisieux "without visions, without miracles, but with such a flame of love for God and neighbor that good happens all around them without noise and without agitation" (p. 74). Can it be that the type of prayer that nourishes such a life is other than contemplative? Jacques and Raissa are convinced that it cannot. They solve the dilemma by distinguishing two forms of infused contemplation: one conscious, the other unconscious.

The conscious form is that found in the great medieval mystics; this they speak of as "open." Initially they term the unconscious form "masked" and include under this heading both those who are not conscious that their prayer is contemplative and those other devout persons who recite prayers learned by heart.[12] Jacques later states that this was "a serious error" (*Peasant,* p. 228, n. 103). The type of prayer which Father Osende in *Contemplata* speaks of as so silent and so rooted in the depths of the spirit that it may be described as unconscious is truly "open," but not like the type described by the medieval mystics.[13] That is why it is not recognized as contemplative. Nevertheless, Jacques asserts that it is a typical form of contemplation and, indeed, one of the most precious.

He describes it as "an unformulated act of love that can be constantly present, like that of a mother who, while she sleeps, still watches over the infant in the cradle" (*Peasant,* p. 228). We see how, even in the natural order, one whose heart is dominated by a great love is focused on what he loves, even when his whole attention is on the work he is engaged in. How much more, then, is it possible in the order of grace? Made without the attention actually being fixed on it, this prayer is not in the order of knowing but in that of love. No matter how many things occupy the conscious attention, the heart is fixed on God (*Liturgy*, pp. 33–37).

In support of this conclusion, Jacques and Raissa cite both in *Liturgy* (p. 37) and *Prayer* (p. 27) Cassian, who quotes Abba Anthony the Hermit's comment that "there is no perfect prayer if the religious perceives that he is praying."[14] Later, in *Peasant*, Jacques speaks of it as "uninterrupted prayer, which is carried on even in sleep by a mental activity inaccessible to consciousness" (p. 228, n. 104), and concludes that this is how we can best fulfill the precept to pray constantly. Here he names this type of contemplation "arid," distinguishing it both from the classical form, which he calls "consoling," and from that atypical form which is not silent or wordless but vocal, for which he retains the term "masked." Both the arid and the consoling types are open or typical (p. 231).[15]

"Masked" contemplation, on the other hand, is atypical. Having established that all are called to contemplation, he needs to find a way to distinguish deeply committed Christians enmeshed in, and perhaps burdened by, temporal responsibilities from nominal Christians who do no more than the bare minimum. Surely "a businessman or a factory worker, or a doctor overwhelmed by his practice, or a family father bent under his burden" (*Peasant*, p. 229) is not barred from advancing toward God. But for them to aspire, in this life, to transforming union and spiritual marriage seems quite impractical, and in St. Thomas and St. Bonaventure, Jacques finds a distinction which helps to justify his position.

They recognize both a "distant" and an "immediate" call to contemplation. *All* are called in a distant way, for contemplation is "the normal flowering of the grace of the virtues and the gifts of the Holy Spirit" (p. 230, n. 107). What is required of all, then, is to set out on this journey; it is not necessary that the choice be conscious and explicit. "Whoever has within him, even in the feeblest degree, the will to pray to God, whether by mumbling paternosters or crying out to God, is without knowing it on the way to contemplation" (p. 230, n. 108).

The call becomes immediate only when the three signs mentioned by Tauler and St. John of the Cross are present.[16] To respond to that call is to enter into the contemplative life. Maritain asserts that it is simultaneously entering into the life of the spirit. It is the culmination of a transitional phase during which, in a manner inaccessible to consciousness,[17] the person has been gradually introduced to a new way of living. Whereas before, the gifts of the spirit were given only occasionally, "in order," writes Maritain, "[for the soul] to extricate itself from some exceptional difficulty" (pp. 230–31), the soul now begins to be *habitually* aided by these gifts.

Equating infused contemplation with being habitually aided by the gifts of the spirit allows Maritain to explain the difference between open and masked contemplation on the basis of which of these gifts predominate. Since these gifts have different objects, there are different ways in which those who have set out on the path of the spirit can advance: "In some, it is . . . Wisdom, Understanding, and Knowledge which are at work in an eminent way. These souls represent the mysterious life of the spirit in its normal plenitude, and they will have the grace of contemplation in its typical forms, whether arid or consoling" (p. 231).

In others, the gifts at work will be Counsel, Fortitude, Fear of the Lord, or Piety—gifts, says Maritain, which are principally related to action. Such persons "will live the life of the spirit . . . with respect to their activities and their works, and they will not have the typical and normal forms of contemplation." However, since, as St. Thomas teaches,[18] all the gifts are linked to one another, the gifts related to action cannot exist in the soul without the gift of Wisdom "which is at . . . work, though in a less apparent way. These [persons] will have the grace of contemplation, but [in] a masked, not apparent [way]. . . . Mysterious contemplation will not be in their conscious prayer, but perhaps in the glance with which they will look at a poor man or . . . at suffering" (p. 231).

Maritain concludes his analysis with the comment that we will fail to understand contemplation if we do not take into account these atypical or disguised forms, as well as the hope that his explanations will help his reader, "even one trained by the clergy of today" (p. 232), to be less uncomfortable with the idea that contemplation, whether open or masked, lies in the normal path of Christian perfection.[19] In any case, what is important is not the type of prayer but the degree of love. This is the only true measure of perfection. Whoever attains the perfection of love must have entered into infused contemplation "in one way or another" (*Liturgy*, p. 46).

What, then, is perfect love? This is most clearly explained in Raissa's *Journal* and Jacques' *Notebooks*. Raissa distinguishes between love and friendship: "The essence of love is in the communication of oneself, with fullness of joy and delight in the possession of the beloved. The essence of friendship is in the desire for the good of one's friend, strong enough to sacrifice oneself for him" (*Journal*, p. 163). Jacques, in his explanatory note, speaks of this friendship as "the love of mutual goodwill," and this love as "mad, boundless love, the love of total self-giving" (p. 162, n. 2).[20] Raissa continues, "The friend of God keeps his commandments but the lover of God goes further, giving himself from the bottom of his heart in such a way that no other love ever dwells in it" (p. 163).

Mad, boundless love is, by its very nature, exclusive: "It is the very person of the lover which is the gift, simple and unique and without any possible reserve, made to the beloved" (*Notebooks*, p. 122). It is spousal love; it does not exclude loving others in addition, but it does exclude loving them *in this way:* "The total gift that the lover makes of himself entails and requires an absolute exclusiveness" (p. 250). A married person who comes to love God in this way will have to renounce mad, boundless love for the human beloved. Jacques writes, "If a man loves a woman with mad, boundless love, he will not consent to give her so far as immolation, even to God. (He will struggle against God . . .)" (p. 251).[21] If the surrender to God is mutual (as in the case of Raissa and Jacques, it clearly was), the couple will, instead, be bound together by "a unique and perfect friendship rooted in charity and the grace of the sacraments" (p. 251). Thus, the fact of being married does not constitute an obstacle to the mystical state into which one enters when one begins to love God with mad, boundless love.[22] Neither is it the case that carnal intercourse between spouses constitutes an obstacle to even very high contemplation. Among both the canonized saints and those never officially canonized, one may find mystics who were both married and parents (pp. 248–49). Hence it does not follow that the reception of this grace requires them to renounce sexual intercourse and the begetting of children (pp. 249, 251, n. 3).[23]

However, those who devote themselves to the active life, while no less called to contemplation than those in the contemplative orders, will be more likely to experience it in the "masked" form (pp. 233–34). For them, no less than those who experience the "open" form, contemplation will have an habitual directing role, although they will be nourished by it unconsciously, spreading its fragrance about them without being themselves aware of doing so (p. 243; *Liturgy*, p. 45). Whereas those who lead a contemplative life in the classical sense bear witness to "the mad, boundless love of God for men and His desire that the soul become a single spirit with Him," those whose contemplation is masked bear witness "to the service of one's neighbor, which is a consequence of this love, and to which this love wishes that some will devote themselves" (*Notebooks*, p. 235).

Both love God with a love that is totally self-forgetful, seeking only him. It is the absence of any return on oneself which is the essential condition of contemplation (*Liturgy*, p. 67; *Prayer*, p. 28). All that matters is "To love, to abandon oneself" (*Journal*, p. 125). *Nothing* else is necessary, not even silence with God if real obstacles, whether interior or exterior, make that impossible. In the words of Raissa, "The soul can be sanctified without . . . realizing it, and find itself at last united to God without having had the leisure to practice what it would have thought most necessary for this" (pp. 125–26). Even mad, boundless love is not necessarily conscious; a person may believe that he has not reached this kind of love for God when he actually did so a long time ago. "In such a case," writes Jacques, "what appears to consciousness . . . is very secondary" (*Notebooks*, p. 236). In fact, such persons are not much given to self-scrutiny. Preoccupation with their own interior state no longer attracts the attention of conscious thought; it "is another that they are interested in" (*Notes*, p. 72). Thus it is by virtue of contemplation that the supreme degree of self-forgetfulness is attained. Such souls are preoccupied instead with extending the kingdom of God on earth, so that all may come to love and serve him (n. 1; *Liturgy*, p. 68). To those "ordinary Christians" living the life of a committed layperson whose hearts are burning to go further while being ignorant of how to do so, or afraid to aspire to do so, Jacques offers some practical advice.[24] In *Liturgy* (p. 76), Raissa had written, "in this contemplation on the roads . . . it seems that [first] constant attention to the

presence of Jesus and [second] fraternal charity are called to play a
major role, as regards even the way of infused contemplative
prayer."

Concerning the first, Raissa observes that the conviction of some
spiritual writers is that the highest contemplation is one which does
without images of any kind, even that of the man Jesus. However,
this is a profound error, betraying a serious misunderstanding of
the Incarnation. When the Word assumed human nature, everything which belongs to this nature—suffering, pity, compassion,
hope—became attributes of God. Thus, in contemplating these
things in Jesus, we are contemplating the attributes of God.

> And the soul must not be afraid of passing through the human
> states and the human pity of Jesus, and of making requests of
> Him and of praying for the cure of a sick person, for example—
> all these things being participations in the desires and the com-
> passion of Christ, which belonged to the divine Person itself
> (*Journal*, p. 362).

In confirmation, Jacques quotes Père Nicolas: "The humanity assumed by the Word has no separate existence which would make of
it a creature between the world and God. *To love the man Jesus, to
unite oneself to the man Jesus, is to love God.*"[25]

Regarding the second characteristic, Jacques observed that it is
possible only to the extent that "love-prayer can and must be pur-
sued in those very relations with men in which those who live in the
world are constantly involved" (*Peasant*, p. 236). This means that, in
listening to another attentively, with compassion, we will not only
strive to love them as Jesus loves them, but also we will be opening
ourselves to being drawn into a more intimate union with him. "If
we give them all the attention we can from our hearts, that is not
much, to tell the truth. But what counts much more, for us and for
our brothers, is the fact that at the same time Jesus' love for them,
which gives them His very heart, is drawing to Him the gaze of our
soul and the depths of our heart" (*Peasant*, pp. 236–37). In looking
at our brothers and sisters, loving them to the point of wearing ourselves out for them, we come to penetrate a little of the very mystery
of Jesus himself and his love for each of us. It "is the fulfillment in
act of the love of God and union with Jesus, and it is love that makes
contemplation grow, deepen itself, exult" (p. 237).

Jacques admits that putting this advice into practice is not easy for one engaged in the labors of the world, whether man or woman;[26] one is constantly exposed to difficulties created by lack of time. However, in every person's life there are periods of "dead" time—in the train, on the subway, in the dentist's waiting room— and even in the busiest schedule there are pauses long enough for the short prayers called ejaculations. In fact, the desert fathers made use of this kind of prayer constantly (p. 238, and n. 115). The material obstacles encountered at each moment by one who lives the life of prayer in the world are an integral part of this life; they make up its sorrowful side. He concludes, "I do not think that it is impossible, since one still finds quite a bit of time for chit-chat or television, to give every day a little time, *however little it might be,* to praying in private, door closed" (p. 239). That is the only more or less fixed rule; some days, even this will be impossible. However, there always remains the desire of the heart. One will, then, find a way to spend some time in prayer on most days.

But it is not all sorrow and struggle; we come, as well, to know the beauty of the world. We see not only the foolish ways of our nature but also its grandeur and dignity—not only natural love run amok but also its sweetness and nobility. Even though, in the world, one may be less well-armed against temptation than one would be in the desert or cloister, one is in a better position to recognize the beauty of nature, created by God, especially on those occasions when, in order to be faithful to our calling, we must set aside something good and perhaps even noble in itself. This involves, it is true, dying to ourselves. But by accepting such a death, we make room not only for the love of God, but also for the love of creatures according to divine charity (*Journal,* p. 61; *Peasant,* p. 242). Our task is to transform all love into Love. The one who prays in the world is in a better position to understand what that means than one who prays cut off from the world (*Peasant,* pp. 242–43).

And it is especially such persons who, by their selfless service, bear witness to God's love. Their vocation, like that of Jacques himself, is to "take part in the life of the city [and try to] establish all things in Christ." After all, the world order Christianity seeks to introduce "is not for the good of the few; it is for . . . the common good" (*Journal,* pp. 92–93; *Notebooks,* p. 79). Largely because of what Jacques terms "a progressive collapse of the practical exercise of the virtue of hope" (*Notebooks*, p. 275), laypersons have been persuaded by the "double standard" that they are not the stuff of which saints are made and have not aspired to put their faith into practice in secular affairs. This the Maritains emphatically reject, asserting that "The great need of our time . . . is to put contemplation on the roads of the world" (*Liturgy*, pp. 74–75).

The Political Holiness of Dorothy Day
Eschatology, Social Reform, and the Works of Mercy
PATRICIA M. VINJE

> *Lay people . . . must greatly respect the works of charity and devote their energies to them.*
>   Vatican II: On the Apostolate of the Laity

A Platonizing mystical theology has long associated the contemplative life of prayer, on the one hand, with religious, clerics, and the eschatological dimension of the church; the active life of the corporal and spiritual works of mercy, on the other hand, with the laity and the cosmological dimension of the church.[1] Matthew 25:31–46, however, calls this simple binary into question by enumerating the works of mercy in a specifically eschatological context: the Last Judgment when the Son of Man comes as king and reveals to the just and unjust alike that he has visited them in the poor, the naked, the hungry, the thirsty, the sick, the strangers, and the imprisoned.

Inspired by this passage from Matthew's Gospel, the life and writings of Dorothy Day (1897–1980)—social activist, journalist, and cofounder of the Catholic Worker movement—trace a timely, biblically inspired path of lay sanctity that is simultaneously cosmological and eschatological, active and contemplative, cataphatic and apophatic, in its discovery of Christ in the urban poor and its explicit, revolutionary challenge to existing social structures. The "time" of Day's reformist work is, as Edith Wyschogrod puts it, "the time-before-it-is-too-late."[2] Beholding Christ incarnate in the needy and living in his/their constant presence, Day practiced a self-emptying, cataphatic contemplation that rivaled the so-called "higher" forms of prayer in its fervor and depth.[3] That vision of Christ invested her political activism with prophetic force.[4] Indeed, her "excessive" desire to alleviate the boundless suffering of others through selfless service may be said to constitute, in Wyschogrod's terms, a peculiarly postmodern kind of ecstasy, which extended, expressed, and realized her lifelong quest for God.[5] The tendency of Day's religious experience to cross normative boundaries—cosmological/eschatological, active/contemplative, cataphatic/apophatic—is all the more striking because, as we shall see, she originally found religion and social action, prayer and politics, incompatible.

The Long, Lonely Journey toward God (1897–1927)

As Jesuit John A. Coleman has rightly observed, the story of Dorothy Day, as we know it, exhibits a new "style of hagiography" in its public intimacy and autobiographical thrust—a hagiography formally akin to the autobiographical novel (such as Day herself wrote); it nevertheless configures itself to certain classical patterns in the lives of saints.[6] As Wyschogrod indicates, "For hagiography, childhood is an impressionable age in which there is often a premonitory vision of a later mission articulated in terms of an earlier, more pristine tradition."[7] In Day's case, there were numinous childhood experiences of books and almsgiving that foreshadowed her future path.

Dorothy Day was born in Brooklyn Heights, New York, on November 8, 1897.[8] Her father and mother had been raised as a Congregationalist and an Episcopalian, respectively, but the Day children had no formal religious affiliation, because the parents felt that selecting church membership was a very private matter. Thus the direct impact of the divine on her life first occurred independent of an institutionalized setting.

In 1904 the family moved to California, where they lived temporarily in a furnished home in Berkeley. One Sunday afternoon Dorothy and her sister Della were playing school in the attic. Able to read since the age of four, Dorothy began to read from a Bible that they had found, and she suddenly experienced the presence of God. Afterwards, remembering "that Sunday afternoon up in the dim attic, and the rich, deep feeling of having a book, which would be with [her] through life," Day remarked:

> I knew that I had just really discovered [God], because it excited me tremendously. . . . Here was someone that I had never really known about before and yet felt to be One whom I would never forget, that I would never get away from. The game might grow

stale; it might assume new meanings, new aspects, but life would never again be the same.[9]

Having discovered at once both God and the "book, which would be with [her] through life," Day was oriented toward a vitally biblical spirituality through a childhood experience that foreshadowed her own vocation as an author, prophet, and teacher. Henceforth her course was set in a direction from which she could never retreat.

The family soon relocated in Oakland, and Day took it upon herself to attend Sunday services at a neighboring Methodist church. In 1906 tremors from the San Francisco earthquake cracked the Day home down the middle. Separated from the rest of her family, Dorothy had to make her own way to safety. Her father's newspaper office was destroyed. Immediately, within hours of losing their home and business, the Days began to feed and clothe homeless refugees worse off than themselves—an event that left a lasting impression on the future founder of houses of hospitality and farm communes for the homeless and unemployed.[10]

Poverty-stricken by the quake, the Day family moved to Chicago. Here Dorothy encountered the homeless, who walked the streets of the neighborhood. The family relocated four times in Chicago. Continually uprooted from friends, she had "much time alone" and found inner strength in reading Dostoevski, Augustine, and the Bible. She remembers her childhood as "a happy time . . . in spite of moods of uncertainty and even of hopelessness and sadness": "Our parents did nothing to offer us distraction or entertainment. We were forced to meet our moods and overcome them. . . . The Psalms became part of my childhood" (*LL*, pp. 27–28).

Thus the precocious child quietly taught herself the *lectio divina* of the monasteries, practiced prayer, and began her meditations on (if not contemplations of) Christ in the homeless and displaced. Gradually she affiliated herself with an Episcopal church and received the sacraments of baptism and confirmation there at the age of twelve.

Her college days, however, brought a slackening of liturgical participation and the reading of books other than the Bible. As she recalls, "I had read Wesley's sermons and had been inspired by them. I had sung hymns from the Episcopalian hymnal. . . . I had read the New Testament with fervor. But that time was past" (*LL*, p. 41). Instead, Day absorbed the depiction of poverty and endorsed the radical social criticism of novelists like Jack London and Upton Sinclair and found their dark political realism "in conflict with religion, which preached peace and meekness and joy" (*LL,* p. 41). As a child, the "happy peace" of her Methodist neighbors had "appealed to [her] deeply"; but "now the same happiness seemed [to her] to be a disregard of the misery of the world." Feeling that her "faith had nothing in common with that of the Christians around [her]," she decided that "religion was something [she] must ruthlessly cut out of [her] life":

> I felt at the time that religion would only impede my work. I wanted to have nothing to do with the religion of those whom I saw all about me . . . I felt it indeed to be an opiate of the people and not a very attractive one, so I hardened my heart. It was a conscious and deliberate choice. (*LL,* pp. 42–43)

Day perceived the incongruity between the Gospel message preached on behalf of the poor and the lack of social concern that was tolerated by church members in their own ranks. Choosing to separate herself from a complacent religiosity, she devoted herself all the more to political activism and direct service to the poor.

Deciding to pursue a career in journalism, Day left college and moved to New York. She frequented coffee shops, where she rubbed elbows with playwrights, artists, union strikers, pacifists, and suffragettes. She observed the activities of the draft boards and government officials, the confrontations of labor and management. She tripped over the bodies of the unemployed homeless on her comings and goings, and the stench and ooze of New York's slum neighborhoods horrified her. Nothing could have prepared her for the disease-infested cardboard-box homes of the city's destitute. She herself lived in various rented rooms without heat and on a meagre diet, supported at intervals by small paychecks. When World War I broke out, Day's pacifist principles led her not only to protest publicly the involvement of the United States in World War I, but also to study nursing at King's County Hospital in Brooklyn in 1918, in order to prepare herself to care for the wounded (*LL,* pp. 88–93).

From this point on, Day's personal life became more complicated. Shortly after the November 11, 1918, armistice, she moved in with newspaperman Lionel Moise, by whom she became pregnant. In a vain attempt to retain a hold on his wavering affections, she

agreed to abort the child. When the relationship with Moise failed
nonetheless, she entered into a short-lived marriage with Tobey
Berkeley, only to divorce him in 1921, at which time she returned to
Chicago. There she involved herself with communists and communist sympathizers—an association that resulted in her spending a
brief time in jail (*LL,* pp. 105–08).[11]

During the years 1923–25, Day began little by little to move back
into the arena of religious piety. She spent the winter of 1923–24 in
New Orleans with her sister Della and communist friend, Mary
Gordon. There she supported herself by writing a series of articles
for the *New Orleans Item.* In between stints, she found herself stop-
ping regularly at the Catholic cathedral for quiet prayer. When her
novel, *The Eleventh Virgin* (1924), was awarded movie rights, she had
a nest egg with which to purchase a beach cottage on Staten Island.
Very soon thereafter she entered into a common-law marriage with
Forster Batterham, a marine biologist, who revealed to her the won-
ders of nature. She began again to read the Bible and other religious literature and found herself praying spontaneously: "I am
surprised that I am beginning to pray. I began because I had to. I
just found myself praying."[12] She could not "get down on [her]
knees," however, without facing a host of doubts and recalling her
earlier rejection of religion:

> I think, "Do I really believe? Whom am I praying to?" And a terri-
> ble doubt comes over me, and a sense of shame, and I wonder if
> I am praying because I am lonely, because I am unhappy. . . . And
> over and over in my mind that phrase is repeated jeeringly,
> "Religion is the opiate of the people." "But," I reason with myself,
> "I am praying because I am happy, not because I am unhappy. I
> did not turn to God in unhappiness . . . to get something from
> Him." And encouraged that I am praying because I want to thank
> Him, I go on praying.[13]

During this period of gradual religious reawakening, when Day
"went on praying," she not only reexamined her previous ideological positions but also began to sift through the painful memories
connected with her abortion. Her happy relationship with Batterham
had turned her heart back to the Lord, and she began to hope that
it might also heal her of the guilt and the sense of loss and violation
that continued to haunt her. Feeling "unfruitful, barren," Day had

"for a long time . . . thought that [she] could not bear a child, and the longing in [her] heart for a baby had been growing." A "blissful joy," therefore, filled her when in June 1925 she learned that she was indeed pregnant with a second child: "I could not see that love between man and woman was incompatible with love of God, and the very fact that we were begetting a child made me have a sense that we were made in the image and likeness of God, co-creators with Him" (*LL,* pp. 135–36). Free of the sadness and despair that had colored all her past life, Day's new-found happiness led her to conclude in retrospect that she "had not known real freedom nor even had a knowledge of what freedom meant" before (*LL,* p. 135).

For his part, however, Batterham remained ambivalent about bringing a child into a too-troubled world and, disapproving of any formal religious affiliation, he directly opposed Day's wish to have the baby baptized as a Catholic. In the face of his obstinance, Day felt that she would have to disassociate herself from Batterham if he could not support her decisions for the child's birth, baptism, and religious upbringing:

> I knew I was going to have my child baptized, cost what it may. I knew that I was not going to have her floundering through many years as I had done, doubting and hesitating, undisciplined and amoral. I felt it was the greatest thing I could do for my child. For myself, I prayed for the gift of faith. I was sure, yet not sure. I postponed the day of decision. (*LL,* p. 136)

The birth of a daughter, Tamar Teresa, on March 3, 1926, led not only to the child's baptism, but also Day's: "When I was unhappy and repentant in the past, I turned to God, but it was my joy at having given birth to a child that made me do something definite" (*LL,* p. 144). Baptized as a child in the Episcopal Church, Day now took instructions in preparation for her baptism as a Roman Catholic—a decisive action that had important consequences for her personally.[14] She knew that it meant the termination of her common-law marriage with Batterham, since he would avoid the sacraments at all cost, and without the sacrament of matrimony she could not in good conscience cohabitate with him, once she joined the church.

Day turned to the church, moreover, with open eyes, knowing its human imperfection and still critical of its lack of practical commitment to the work of social justice: "I loved the Church for Christ made visible. Not for itself, because it was so often a scandal to me. Romano Guardini said that Church is the Cross on which Christ was crucified; one could not separate Christ from His Cross, and one must live in a state of permanent dissatisfaction with the Church" (*LL,* p. 149). She remained scandalized by "businesslike priests, . . . collective wealth, the lack of responsibility for the poor, the worker . . . even the oppression of these" (*LL,* p. 150). Nonetheless, she believed that the church possessed a vision that the world needed, and a divine power that could not be tapped in any other way except through its sacramental means:

> "Am I my brother's keeper?" [the priests] seemed to say in respect to the social order. There was plenty of charity, but too little justice. And yet the priests were the dispensers of the sacraments, bringing Christ to all men, and enabling us all to put on Christ and to achieve more nearly in the world a sense of peace and unity. (*LL,* p. 150)

In December 1927 Day joined the church, in and through which she found Christ made sacramentally present and active in the world. In the real presence of Christ in the Eucharist, she discovered a Lord who was in our midst as a vital, divine, and human force with the power to work revolutionary political and social change. In so doing she joined together in her own vision of things the transcendental, liturgical religiosity and the acute, this-worldly social awareness that she had earlier considered irreconcilable.

The Communal Journey to God-in-Others (1927–80)

Not long after her conversion, Day was able to translate her prophetic vision into concrete action through her collaboration with Peter Maurin in the founding of the Catholic Worker movement. In 1933 the first edition of *The Catholic Worker* appeared. The regular publication and growing circulation of this newspaper served to promote the establishment of houses of hospitality, which provided food and shelter to the homeless, and farming communes, which allowed the unemployed to share in the dignity of labor. These establishments were designed, moreover, to help their guests to reenter and eventually transform the mainstream of the labor force through ongoing education: roundtable discussions, classes, and the use of in-house libraries.

In addition to influencing the economic and cultural arenas, Day hoped to have an impact in ecclesiastical circles:

> Many times we have been asked why we spoke of *Catholic* workers and so named the paper. Of course, it was not only because we who were in charge of the work and edited the paper were all Catholics; we also wanted to influence Catholics. They were our own, and we reacted sharply to the accusation that when it came to private morality the Catholics shone, but when it came to social and political morality, they were often conscienceless. (*LL,* p. 210)

Consciousness-raising was indeed a major part of the movement's task. Day wanted to influence the church from the grassroots up through all the levels of the hierarchy. She hoped to renew interest in the medieval practice of all bishops overseeing hospices for the poor.[15] Inspired by a suggestion from St. Jerome, the movement also encouraged each Christian home to have a Christ-room reserved for the poor and urged each parish to have facilities for the homeless.[16]

Day's philosophy of Christian personalism permeated her endeavors. Each guest in the houses of hospitality was to be treated as someone possessing the dignity of Jesus, and each Catholic Worker, in turn, was to represent Christ to every guest and coworker, especially through the practice of generous hospitality.[17] The works of mercy enjoined in Matthew 25:31–46 gave a concrete cast to the mission of the Workers, even as the communal life of the early church provided a model for their social interaction. All members were called to voluntary poverty, so that more people could receive the support of the community, in accord with the radical patristic dictum: "The bread you retain belongs to the hungry, the dress you lock up is the property of the naked. . . . What is superfluous for one's need is to be regarded as plunder, if one retains it for one's self."[18]

This radical witness of generosity bestowed credibility on the Catholic Worker movement in the eyes of the world and church alike. Day won the respect and trust of the poor, because she and the other Workers treated them with dignity. She elicited the approval of the Catholic hierarchy, in spite of their uneasiness about her leftist political leanings, because her staunch identification with the church served to purify and renew the church from within, even as it enabled the church to fulfill its evangelical mission in the world.

Within the ranks of the Catholic Workers themselves, there emerged an ever clearer sense of their personal and communal calling as lay members of the church: "We are developing the idea we long had of the lay apostolate, and there are now enough fellow workers to send out into the fields and factories to work and attract new followers."[19] Filled with a sense of *missio,* of being "sent forth," Day interpreted the vocation of the Workers as an apostolic calling: "Just as the Church has gone out through its missionaries into the most obscure towns and villages, we have gone too. . . . We have lived with the unemployed, the sick, the unemployables . . . [who have been] stripped . . . not only of all earthly goods, but of spiritual goods, their sense of human dignity" (*LL,* p. 215).

Evangelizing the poor necessitates a literal sharing in their physical and spiritual poverty. Indeed, true poverty of spirit presupposes literal, material dispossession. Only voluntary poverty changes social structures and enables one actually to identify with the poor; to share their needs, their living conditions, their lives, afflictions, and aspirations:

> Going around and seeing such sights [of poverty] is not enough. To help the organizers, to give what you have for relief, to pledge yourself to voluntary poverty for life so that you can share with your brothers is not enough. One must live with them, share with them their sufferings too. Give up one's privacy and mental comforts, as well as physical [ones]. (*LL,* p. 214)

In Day's understanding, only this kind of radical self-emptying allows one, on the one hand, to make God present to the poor and, on the other, to encounter Christ in the poor, in whom he lives out his passion. The poor, who are always with us (John 12:8), are the surest guarantee for the abiding presence of God in the midst of the world, both in his crucified abandonment and in the kenotic exchange of love between persons, each of whom gives to and is enriched by the other.

This loving exchange of material and spiritual goods with Christ-in-the-poor is a form of contemplative prayer that is confined neither to the cloisters and monasteries nor to moments of silence; that is entered into, not just with mind and spirit, but with the whole of one's fleshly body.[20] As Day insists, "Christ is always with us, asking for room in our hearts. But now it is with the voice of our contemporaries that

He speaks."[21] The Christocentric mysticism such a statement implies is cataphatic because our senses—sight, hearing, touch, smell, and taste—necessarily mediate our experience of God's presence in the poor. On the other hand, it is "dark" with a darkness that rivals the apophatic mysticism of the hermits and ascetics because the poor in whom Christ comes to us are often unwashed, unkempt, and disagreeable. In Day's words, "[Christ] is disguised under every type of humanity that treads the earth."[22]

The theme of the "disguised" Christ is readily evident in Day's eucharistic writings and helps to explain the central importance of the Eucharist in the spirituality of the Catholic Workers. As they see it, the work of praising God in liturgy inspires other works in the service of God and neighbor. Seeing Christ disguised in the symbols of bread and wine prepares one to see his veiled presence in the human faces one encounters throughout the day. Responsibility for others, in turn, always moved one back to the liturgy for support and strength. From Mass to Mass, the eucharistic Christ thus lives and acts in the Workers, in keeping with the unforgettable words Jesus in the Eucharist once spoke to Dorothy Day: "This is my Body broken for you; will you give your body to Me in return to serve the needs of My people? This is my Blood shed for you; now will you shed your blood for Me?"[23]

This same Christ came to Day "disguised" in the brokenness of her own life and work. Sometimes the houses of hospitality ran short of rations. Squabbles occasionally broke out in the homes and communes. Yet even these weaknesses, Day recognized, were crucial to her success and ensured a divine sanction, for they kept her and the Workers reliant on God. As Day prayed, "I do know how small I am and how little I can do, and I beg you, Lord, to help me, for I cannot help myself."[24]

Even more difficult, perhaps, were the personal challenges that came to Day as a moral and spiritual leader because of the radical fervor that set her so much apart from ordinary laypeople and because of her difficult social status as a single mother with a checkered past. At age thirty-eight, for instance, Day was experiencing difficulties in the movement and wishing she "were married and living the ordinary, naturally happy life." About that same time a priest from the Midwest criticized her, saying that the things she "wrote in *The Catholic Worker* about community and personalism would have

more validity" if she were "a woman of family." Day at first enter-
tained the validity of his criticism, but then became indignant,
telling herself, "But I *am* a woman of family. I have had a husband
and home life. I have a daughter, and she presents problems to me
right now. . . . I am a mother, and the mother of a very large family
at that" (*LL,* pp. 235–36).

Day fulfilled her mission heroically, not perfectly. Indeed, as
Wyschogrod reminds us, the very "infrastructure of saintly experience" includes the painful recognition that "the suffering of the
Other . . . is always greater than the intention that strives to relieve
it."[25] The ecstatic quality of Day's life derives precisely from the
sheer impossibility of supplying the infinite needs of the poor to
whom she devoted herself in an attempt to offer them not only
food, shelter, and education, but also the experience of God's loving presence. No human being can represent God to others just as
he is, because human beings are flawed and limited and because
the divine nature is, as Wyschogrod puts it, "inherently refractory to
representation."[26] And yet, precisely because "saints" like Dorothy
Day have emptied themselves in an excess of giving, God has been
made tangibly present in our midst.

As we have seen, her life crosses boundaries, and challenges the
normative assumptions that the cosmological ("in the world") dimension of the church necessarily excludes the eschatological
("end of the world") dimension; that the active life precludes the
contemplative; that the cataphatic way is "light," and the apophatic,
"dark"; and that emphasizing God's immanence rules out the experience of his transcendence.

Day's spirituality is eschatological in both theory and praxis, and
one might say that she called the church back to its own eschatological, world-ending and world-re-creating vocation. When she
linked the works of mercy and the practical service of Christ in the
poor to the promised Second Coming of Matthew 25:31–46, she espoused what Jesuit Jon Sobrino has called "political holiness," a
term he uses to describe the reflexive dynamic of belief shaping culture and society, providing a contemporary arena in which to practice holiness.[27] Like Day, Sobrino upholds the necessity of joining
faith and politics, which is tantamount to joining the realms of es-
chatology and cosmology, realms heretofore considered mutually
exclusive. Through the outstanding heroic practice of virtue—in

particular, the infused virtue of charity—the unjust world as we have known it passes away, to be replaced by a more just social order that anticipates the "new heaven and new earth" (Rev. 21:1) of the eschaton.[28]

Day's life among the poor is both cosmological and eschatological because it points to God's abiding presence in the world and reveals it precisely in those human beings who empty themselves in kenotic service and in those who are destitute, at the margins of society, and "at the end" of their own existence. Day's future-time is always "the-time-that-is-left in which to alleviate suffering before it is too late."[29] A political "saint," Day acts and speaks in a way that tells the poor and oppressed that Christ is coming again in order to save them, both now and forever.

Through a saint like Day, Christ comes to the needy, precisely because, in the eyes of the saint, Christ is already there. The saint identifies with the poor to the extent that their hunger is palpably hers, their nakedness is hers, their debasement and humiliation are hers—and Christ's. Entering into the life of the poor, the saint participates in the *kenosis* of Christ, who "emptied himself, taking the nature of a slave" (Phil. 2:7). If contemplation is union with God, then this entering into the vulnerability of the poor through *caritas* is also entering into the God who has loved us to the point of complete self-abandonment on the cross (Mark 15:34; Matt. 27:46). Such a dying to self for the sake of others, such a self-denial—as the extraordinary life of Dorothy Day shows—is divinely effective, life-giving, and does in fact renew the face of the earth.

A Life between Two Fires
Chiara Lubich and Lay Sanctity
DONALD W. MITCHELL

Among the phenomena of our times worthy of special mention is the growing and inevitable sense of solidarity of all peoples. Lay people in their apostolate should earnestly promote this sense of solidarity and transform it into a sincere and genuine fraternal love.
Vatican II: On the Apostolate of the Laity

"Unity," the watchword of the Focolare movement, sounds a new note within the Christian mystical tradition. In a recent interview, Chiara Lubich, the foundress of the Focolare, first defines Christian perfection in classic terms as "the mystical union of the soul with the Trinity within itself," a "transforming union" in which "the person, while remaining a separate individual, becomes 'one' with God."[1] She goes on, however, to describe a "new way" to achieve this union.

Referring to Thomas à Kempis, whose *Imitation of Christ* advises solitude and the avoidance of other people, Lubich remarks, "Times have changed . . . and it is possible to reach union with God in other ways."[2] In support of her claim, she interprets the documents of Vatican II as indicating to "the faithful" that our neighbor should not be seen as a distraction to the spiritual life, or as an impediment to union with God; rather, he or she must be understood as a way to go to God. Indeed, she insists, the graced unity among persons that results from loving one's neighbor is not only a sign of, but also a sure means for, personal and interpersonal union with the Triune God. The "great attraction of today," she says, is "to reach the highest contemplation while sharing in the life of every person, being one among many."[3]

Both theoretically and in practical application to her own foundation, Lubich recognizes the great importance of this development for the history of Christian spirituality. On March 9, 1995, in a public address on the topic of the significance of the Focolare movement,[4] she pointed to an essay by Karl Rahner, in which he contrasts the church of the past, where persons "have been spiritually formed in an individualistic way," with the church of the future, in which "the element of fraternal spiritual communion, of a spirituality lived together, can play a more decisive role." Pentecost, Rahner observes, certainly "did not consist . . . in the casual meeting of a collection of mystics who lived individually, but rather in the experience of the Spirit made by the community." As I hope to show, and as Lubich herself asserts, the new "collective way" to union with God which characterizes the special charism of the Focolare and informs its notion of lay sanctity answers directly to Rahner's vision of the spirituality of the church of the future, even as the life and striving of the Focolare's worldwide membership realize his dictum that "slowly but surely, we must proceed along this way."[5]

The flames of Pentecost, as a symbol of a transforming, collective experience of God, have their counterpart and continuation in the hearth fire of the Focolare. In Italian, the very word "focolare" denotes a family fireside. The interplay between this communal fire and the inner fire of the Spirit has formed the spiritual life of Chiara Lubich and that of the whole Focolare movement. Since Christian spiritualities and the concepts of sanctity that they imply are best understood through looking at the lives of their founders, I will begin with an account of Lubich's own quest and then turn to a three-part examination of the notion of lay sanctity in the Focolare spirituality which has resulted from this quest.

Chiara Lubich was born in 1920 in Trent, Italy. When she was nineteen years old, she attended a student convention of Catholic Action in Loreto. At that time she was searching for her vocation. Little is known about her religious experiences before this visit to Loreto, but the particular experience she had at that conference has been described in some detail because of its importance to Lubich's discovery of her lay vocation.[6] Briefly, when she went to visit the little house at Loreto, said to be the house in Nazareth where Jesus lived with Mary and Joseph, she contemplated for some days the great mystery of the life of the Holy Family. At the end of the conference, she understood that she had found her vocation, and it was not one of the three "ways" open to women at that time, namely, the religious life, marriage, or a personal dedicated life as a layperson. Rather, Lubich said that what she discovered in Loreto seemed to be a new "fourth way" which contained some elements of the other three. It was based on the model of the *family* of Nazareth, of Mary and Joseph living *consecrated* lives as *laypersons* with Jesus in their midst. However, what this meant concretely would not be clear for some years.

Soon World War II reached Italy, and Lubich found herself in Trent with a small group of young women friends whose ages ranged from fifteen to twenty-five. In 1943, Lubich made a "choice" of God as the ideal of her life. When she shared this decision with her companions, they all made a similar choice of God in solidarity with her. In return they received a communal "charism" from God. This spiritual "gift" entailed a special awareness of God's love, a realization of God as Love for each of them in a very personal and intimate sense. In December of that year, Lubich was running an errand for her parents and passed a shrine dedicated to the White Madonna. In that moment, she experienced God calling her to take the further step to consecrate her life to him. On December 7, 1943, she did so, and this date came to be considered the "birth" of the spiritual movement she was to establish, namely, the Focolare. A few days later, her young women companions joined her in consecrating their own lives to God. When they did so, they began to be "inflamed" by the charism of their new ideal of God-Love from the spiritual "fire" that burned in Lubich's heart. In both their choice of God and their consecration to God, the group of young women found themselves drawn together in unity in a new spiritual reality that God was sharing with them through Lubich.

Meanwhile Trent came under heavy bombing. In May of 1944, Lubich's house was destroyed and her family decided to leave the city. Lubich made the very difficult decision to remain in Trent to be with her young companions. She understood that through her and with her companions God was bringing about the new lay vocation that he had shown her at Loreto. All of her companions were still alive, and they continued to meet in the bomb shelters, sometimes as often as eleven times each day. Together they read the Gospels with the "light" of their ideal of God-Love to illumine the meaning of the scriptures for their lives. Then they would put into practice what they had understood. They would not only *read* and *reflect* on scripture; they would *live* the scripture in daily life.

With their hearts inflamed by the "fire" of God's love for them, and with their minds illumined by the light of this charism, they began, as Lubich says, "to recognize and love Christ in each person."[7] They understood that God as Love is not just to be contemplated in prayer but to be lived; they could "be love," be a presence of this love in caring for those in need in the war situation. This active charity, lived in each moment as if it would be their last (something that during the war was very possible), became one of the cornerstones of their lay spiritual life. As Lubich and her companions cared for the needy in Trent, they soon discovered the asceticism needed for this kind of charity that finds and loves Christ in one's neighbor. They learned the ascetic discipline of making themselves empty in a loving *kenosis* in order to be one with those in need. They also found that when they loved in this way, they passed through their neighbors into a deeper union with God in the center of their hearts: "The more we loved Christ in everyone, empty of ourselves, the more our hearts were filled with God."[8] In this way, their neighbors were not impediments to their union with God, but rather their way to a deeper union with God.

Lubich notes that when they prayed at the end of the days that they lived with this charity, they found that their union with God in prayer had increased. By living charity, their lay activities increased rather than decreased their union with God. As laypersons, they could contribute to society and further their own sanctity at the same time. How did Lubich understand this growth in sanctity? She explains it as being the result of a growth of Christ, the Saint, within them and exhorts her companions to yield to this transforming process:

> Oh! then how great will be the flame of divine charity in us. How much Jesus will grow in you and will devour you all. Let him grow, and let yourselves die. Allow the charity that he has poured into your hearts to become aflame and spread, that it might spark from your eyes, your words, and your actions.[9]

In living this life of charity together, they also made another discovery, one that would give their lay spirituality its new and distinctive characteristic. When their charity became mutual, they not only found a deeper personal union with God, but also God became the uniting center of their community. As Lubich bears witness, "Our mutual love was the powerful means of rendering him [Christ] present."[10] She and her companions found themselves living between two fires of spiritual transformation: the fire of Christ within them and the fire of Christ among them. By charity, an inner fire was fueled so that "He could destroy our egos and transform us into himself."[11] By mutual charity, a collective fire was fueled so that all were transformed into unity in God. When this unity happened, Lubich says, "we felt as if we were in heaven, as if paradise were in our midst. Christ, in whom we were sisters and brothers, now came among us spiritually. . . . he enkindled in our hearts a flame that the world did not know."[12] The presence of "Jesus in their midst"—as they, echoing Matthew 18:20, referred to this collective presence of Christ— was not only among them uniting them in him, but also penetrated each of them and contributed to their growth in personal sanctity.

In this way, personal sanctity gained a communal meaning, understood in trinitarian terms as a mutual interpenetration of persons in God and of God in those persons. Lubich says that when Christ is "among them," he is also profoundly "in them. In maintaining this unity, they can sincerely say: 'It is no longer I who live but Christ who lives in me.' "[13] Elsewhere she explains, "The words 'in our midst' intend to say that he is in us. . . . We all together share of him, as does each one of us; we partake of his presence."[14] Through this mutual interpenetration of persons in charity and in unity with God, the community is made one in a kind of communal holiness in which each member finds his or her sanctity. The flame of God among them burned in their hearts with the effect of a deeper personal sanctity in union with God; at the same time it burned away divisions, enabling them to participate in a deeper collective sanctity, in the holiness of the reign of God. As Lubich describes it, "We had the impression that the Lord was opening our eyes and hearts to the kingdom of God in our midst, to the Trinity dwelling in this small cell of the mystical body."[15]

Others, too, were warmed by this fire. Within just a few months, Lubich had over five hundred followers, who said that being with Lubich and her young companions was like being near a "focolare," or "family fireside." Thus Lubich's spirituality took the name "Focolare." In this "fireplace," people from all divisions of Italian society, from the poor to the aristocrats, became united for the first time. Transformed by this fire within and among them, they lived the communion of material and spiritual goods, so that everyone was cared for. Lubich and her companions read, illuminated by their ideal, the priestly prayer of Jesus: "May they all be one" (John 17:21). They realized that their communal lay spirituality could contribute to the realization of this prayer of Jesus, that all humankind be united, and to this end they began to devote their energies.

This life of unity was not easy, but they soon discovered that the only real way to unity is through the way of the cross. Abandoned on the cross, Jesus had identified with all who would suffer, and so they found in their sufferings and the sufferings of others a special presence of Christ that they named "Jesus forsaken." By uniting themselves with him, they found themselves passing with Christ through their crosses into a fuller participation in his resurrection—indeed, into the trinitarian life of love and unity. God revealed himself in Jesus forsaken as the "key" to unity.[16] They recognized in Jesus forsaken the apex of the love of God in and for humanity, a love that realizes through the cross the unity of God and humankind, even as it unites humankind in God.

Lubich and her companions found a relationship with Jesus forsaken in their own crosses and the crosses they encountered in the lives of others. "Embracing" him as the height of God's love for humanity and as the basis of their continued love for others, they progressed through the grace of the cross into a deeper life of union with God and unity with each other. As Lubich said, "We too . . . have experienced that in embracing the cross one does not find only suffering. On the contrary, one finds love, the Love that is the life of God himself within us."[17] Therefore, Lubich could write to her followers:

> God will live among you; you will sense his presence; you will enjoy his presence; he will give you his light; he will inflame you with his love! To come to this point however, you must devote yourselves to *him crucified.*[18]

After the war, Lubich and her companions continued to live and develop this spiritual life they had discovered as laywomen. In 1948, a men's Focolare opened in Trent. As the years passed, Focolare centers opened around the world, and in 1962 Pope John XXIII approved the Focolare spirituality in the Catholic Church. In the 1960s and 1970s, the spirituality of Chiara Lubich began to be practiced by persons of other Christian denominations, as well as by persons of other religions. Today the movement is a vital force for both ecumenism and interfaith dialogue.

As this brief history has already suggested, Lubich's notion of holiness resonates within the tradition of the Christian pursuit of sanctity, even as it renews and recasts that tradition for the laity.[19] The sanctity to which Lubich and the Focolare aspire, though indivisible, has three distinguishable dimensions: (1) personal sanctity as union with God and unity with others through Christ, (2) communal sanctity as a collective sharing in the spiritual life of the Trinity, and (3) participatory sanctity as a partaking in the creative work of God and redemptive work of Christ.

Personal Sanctity

According to Lubich, "the will of God is that each Christian becomes a saint, another Christ, the Saint."[20] Personal sanctity is here understood as a holy life animated by the sanctity of Christ; indeed, the divinization of the person by the indwelling of Christ. Lubich accepts the traditional theology of sanctity that posits the sanctity of the saint to be a "reembodiment" by "participation" in the sanctity of Christ. But given her perspective of unity, she also sees this sanctity as entailing unity with others. Since Christ is always united with God *and* with all humankind, a growth of this life of Christ advances personal sanctity as union with God *as well as* unity with others.

Lubich found this growth in personal sanctity through a corresponding growth in the inner presence of Christ to be especially nourished by two points, striving to live the "Word of Life" and to become the will of God. As Lubich and her companions lived the scriptures in the daily activities of lay life, they found that in each instance they were placing themselves in contact with the living Word of God: "To place ourselves in contact with the word of God is, then, to come into vital contact with Christ, to absorb his life. . . . He who is the Word *communicates himself* to our souls. And we are one with him! Christ is born in us."[21] To substantiate her point, Lubich quotes Clement of Alexandria: "he who obeys the Lord and follows the Scripture . . . is fully transformed into the image of the Master: he comes to life like God in flesh."[22] Lubich concludes that this sanctity of the enfleshment of God, this becoming an *alter Christus* by the grace of the Word through living the scriptures in daily life, should be a goal of the laity: "Let us live the word in the present moment, each time more and more intensely, so that for the world and for the glory of Christ, we too may be 'God in flesh.'"[23]

Living God's word moment by moment allows a person to fulfill the will of God—indeed, to become God's will—and thus become holy. As a young person, Lubich was troubled because in the church one state in life was considered more perfect than another; namely, for a woman, religious life was seen to be more perfect than lay life. But she came to understand that what was important was the will of God for each person. She was impressed with the words of St. Francis de Sales: "One who loves God is so completely transformed into the will of God that he can be called by that name: 'Will of God.'"[24] Here she found what she came to call the "way to holiness that is open to all persons," which is not just to *do* God's will but to *become* God's will: "Our primary goal now was to become *God's will for us,* and thus make our choice of God a concrete reality."[25]

This "becoming God's will" means two things for Lubich. First, it means an asceticism of moving beyond one's own limited will to embrace the infinite will of God. But since God's will is an expression of his infinite love for us, this movement is not a negative loss but a positive gain, "a divine adventure." In terms of personal sanctity, this gain also implies a movement into a deeper union with God because, as Lubich says, "God and his will are one and the same. So to live in God's will is to live in God."[26] Doing God's will concretely in each moment allows God to "'build up' himself in us."[27] And since God is love, to live in the will of God is to be inhabited by God's love, because God who is love inhabits the person who loves.

The second thing entailed by "becoming God's will" is the realization of the divine "design of love" in the life of the individual. As Lubich understands it, to find sanctity in the will of God is to enter God's design of love for each person. And since this design is one of love, to live that design is to live love and to restore thereby the image of love, the "image of God," in which we were created from the loving hand of God. As Lubich emphasizes, the sanctity to which all persons—lay and religious—are called can only be achieved by living the will of God, who has designed a plan for our lives. In this design of love, this life of holiness open to all persons, all the virtues of personal sanctity blossom: poverty, meekness, purity, humility, etc.[28]

Lubich's understanding of personal sanctity, then, includes basic characteristics of Christian sanctity: a purifying asceticism that leads to a deeper union with God, an attentiveness to the Word of God as the source of sanctity, and the practice of the "perfection of charity" in a life of kenotic love for God and others—especially the poor and needy. Lubich's genius, however, gives a fresh expression to these traditional features and blends them together, organically joining scriptural meditation with action and ascetical self-denial with charitable practice, within the context of an appealing spirituality that can be lived by laypersons in secular circumstances today.

Unlike older spiritual masters who urged the negation of the human faculties in order to find God within the self, Lubich counsels an active use of the faculties in being the will of God, that is, in being love for others. The mortifications for which she calls are other-centered, not self-centered. In being love for others, one silences or empties oneself before the other in order to receive their joys and sorrows. One sets aside his or her resistance to loving in order to care for others. As that happens, one not only finds a deeper union with God but also a fuller life of charity and unity with others.

Communal Sanctity

Using a trinitarian logic, Lubich explains how the pursuit of personal sanctity can be done in the context of a collective life. Her metaphor in this regard is that of a sun with many rays. If a ray is the particular will of God for a person, as that person follows the ray into the sun, he or she moves ever closer to others who also follow their rays.[29] Here the notion of the personal will of God for each individual takes into consideration the notion of the collective will of God for all humankind, which is that humanity live united in love as a communal image of God as Trinity. Lubich points out that God creates all humankind in the image of God. Humanity was created as one collective reality to image the trinitarian life of love and unity, and as each person follows the will of God, he or she participates more and more fully in that trinitarian life with the people of God. Speaking on this same theme, the late Klaus Hemmerle, a German bishop and theologian who was active in the Focolare, quotes St. Cyprian to affirm that the will of God for the "people of God" is to be one in the life of God-as-Trinity, in which we realize the "holiness of the people of God."[30]

This "holiness of the people of God," or the communal sanctity of love and unity as a collective human reflection of the trinitarian life, is furthered in Lubich's spirituality through the life of mutual love. This collective development of charity generates the communal presence of God among people that, in turn, transforms the community into what Lubich calls "spiritual oases" where Christ refreshes, strengthens, enlightens, guides, and penetrates each member to deepen both their personal and communal sanctity. Jesus-in-the-midst brings to them a participation in the trinitarian life of love and unity that makes them one with God and in God with each other. It is Jesus, the Saint among them, who sanctifies them, effects the holiness of the people of God, and brings about the communal imaging of God in his Mystical Body.

In this trinitarian form of sanctity, as Lubich defines it, we see a notion of sanctity that is a corrective to the individualism of modernity and the trend that individualistic thinking can produce in spirituality, namely, the tendency to see sanctity as only a personal matter that is compromised by relations with others, rather than furthered by them. With this trinitarian notion of collective sanctity, holiness can be understood more clearly in relational terms. In the inner trinitarian life, the divine principle of self-transcendence manifests itself in the immanence of mutual indwelling, and vice versa. The gap between modern self-consciousness and the other, so problematic for modern philosophy since Immanuel Kant, is thus filled by this relational dimension of God that penetrates the self, even as it relates self to others in an interpenetrating unity of love. According to Lubich, now is the time to emphasize the mutual indwelling of God in the midst of humankind as the means to overcome the field of secular individualism and recover the sense of the sacred as a source of personal as well as social transformation:

> Mutual love, lived in a radical way, generates . . . the presence of Jesus in the midst of the members of the [Focolare] Movement . . . thus helping in the sanctification of each individual. The "interior castle," as Saint Teresa called the soul inhabited by "His Majesty," . . . is the apex of sanctity sought on an individual level. Perhaps the moment has come to discover, illuminate and edify for God what we could call God's "exterior castle," with him spiritually present in the midst of humanity.[31]

Lubich's vision of "God's exterior castle" reveals a new conception of communal life and sanctity and shows the profound uniqueness of her spirituality. For Lubich, community not only has its traditional spiritual function as a place of formation, but, being an actual place of trinitarian life, it becomes a special means of communal sanctity. According to Jesus Cervera, this life of unity in the Focolare has "the savor of innovation, the wonder of newness" and "raises communitarian and ecclesial spirituality to the level of Trinitarian spirituality": "There is no doubt that a spiritual wisdom, a charism of the Holy Spirit lay at the basis of such a new and lofty discovery . . . practically unknown, unheard of up to that moment in the Church, even though it had been sensed and preached in Christian spirituality."[32]

As Cervera observes, while Lubich preaches the traditional obligation to "be Jesus . . . to die so that Jesus may live," she always presents this obligation in the "new and lofty" context of a "deeply moving communitarian experience" of a new relationship with Jesus in others. In this communal relationship of "Jesus with Jesus," there is not just an individual spiritual death enabling Jesus to live within one's soul, generating personal sanctity; rather, we also "die together so that 'Jesus in our midst' may be the life of all," generating communal sanctity—the holiness of the people of God.[33] Thus, in Lubich's words, becoming "another Christ means not only tending toward a personal perfection, but also participating in his redemptive mission for the salvation of humankind."[34]

Participatory Sanctity

In what I call "participatory sanctity," we come to the third dimension of the Focolare spirituality, which urges its members to act in such a way that the Divine can, in the powerful words of Chiara Lubich, "penetrate [humanity] as wine penetrates a piece of bread."[35] This "participatory" dimension of sanctity involves a sharing in the creative and redemptive work of God—a freely chosen, instrumental sharing which gives God a "place" in the world, consecrates the world, and thus (to echo the Japanese philosopher Keiji Nishitani) "overturns" the one-dimensionality of our "despiritualized" field of modern life and experience.[36] Indeed, the role of the modern saint is precisely to facilitate the "respiritualization" of the world by challenging a one-dimensional secularity through a life and experience grounded in a deeper (and higher) transcendent source.

As Lubich explains, the Gospel indicates the way to sanctity, and throughout history the Gospel has inspired many different leaders—among them, St. Francis of Assisi, St. Catherine of Siena, St. Teresa of Avila—to prescribe appropriate spiritual remedies for what humankind suffers in particular eras and societies. In all times, Lubich continues, there has been a need for lay spirituality and lay sanctity, but today we have a very special need for holy laypersons. Faced with the decadence of modern society and equipped with education, the laity feel the desire, and have the moral obligation, to take responsibility for the building of a more peaceful and united world. In order to support laypersons in this endeavor, Lubich insists, we need lay spiritualities that keep in mind our particular historical situation and give to humanity new ways to sanctity in answer to the personal and the social needs of today.[37]

In her 1987 address to the Synod of Bishops on the Vocation and Mission of the Laity, Lubich characterized our time as "an era of materialism and secularism" in which "Christians need a new injection of the life of the spirit in order to be faithful to Christ."[38] The ideal of the modern Western world "is the total independence of one's individual personality . . . but this search [for independence] in practice is focused more on having than on being."[39] As Lubich observes, "The plan of many people today consists in being financially well-off and having a good social position. Work is viewed as a means for acquiring more instruments of well-being."[40] As a result, free time is used to further personal well-being through tourism, amusements, shows, etc. This kind of modern lifestyle is clearly one "which is exclusively earthly, which totally lacks any Christian dimension, which gives little happiness here on earth and does not prepare us for eternal life."[41]

In order to respond creatively and courageously to the multiple challenges represented by the individualism, materialism, consumerism, and secularism of our modern society, the laity need spiritual formation. In contrast to the dominant modern Western mode of living, Christian spirituality is called to witness to another kind of life—to see life (in Lubich's terms) as a "divine adventure" by which one can participate in the creative and redemptive work of God in a manner that leads to personal sanctity and social transformation. In opposition to the individualistic life-style of modernity, Christ brings with him, because he is God, "the lifestyle of the Trinity which is love, mutual love."[42] To live this counter-cultural lifestyle and to bear it to the world is to participate in Christ's redemptive action. Expressed differently, it is to be another Mary, so to speak, who brings and bears God to the world. For Lubich, this Marian bearing of God-Love to the world has a special "preference for those most in need: those with alcohol and drug dependencies, the lonely, the handicapped, the elderly, the unemployed, the alienated, as well as those who are far from God and from the Church."[43]

Here, obviously, we are no longer talking about a lifestyle of "having" but of "being"—of being transformed by Christ in order to bear his presence to the world, and of living a trinitarian communal life of love and unity in order to "give birth" to this Christ-life in society. As Lubich says, "the lay person's vocation is to bring [the fire of Gospel love] into the world. Naturally, in order to do this, [the laity] must possess this love, they must live it."[44] Only by "being" this spirit of love in the world can laypeople grow in union with Christ, while at the same time transforming the world with the spirit of Christ. As Lubich says, "The Christian's way to holiness . . . is to get involved in one's job in a perfect spirit of service . . . to love Jesus in the collectivity, in a school, in an office, in the public service sector . . . and by so doing, renew the world and society."[45] Indeed, she tells her followers, "it is precisely by getting involved in the things of the world that you will become saints."[46]

Lubich has described this spiritual path as "the journey of monasticism towards the world," and she frequently uses monastic images in comparison and contrast to define for others the newness of the Focolare approach to sanctity:

> To become saints, you don't obey the bell of the superior that calls you to prayer. You obey the siren of a factory. That is your bell! . . . It is with your working tools that you empty yourselves so that Christ may emerge. You don't, I repeat, use cords to beat yourselves, keep strict fasting or stay up all night praying. No. You use the tools of your trade. It is with these that you become saints. . . . the pen for a professor, the chisel for a sculptor—that is your crucifix, with which you go to sanctity.[47]

Lubich affirms the universal need for asceticism, but she finds the exterior source and means of mortification for a layperson in a different place than the monastic discovers it. The penance involved in the "emerging" of Christ in the layperson's life happens in the context of the world: "Perhaps the relationships [at work] are difficult and the work demanding—but there lies our penance and purification. There lies our sanctification."[48]

> In reality, to reach perfection, they do not have to walk primarily along the path of prolonged prayers, of austere penances, or along the path of fleeing from the world. They are called to fulfill God's will perfectly wherever they may be: at home with the family, in offices, schools, parliaments, on the street, when at rest and when at work.[49]

The prayer into which a layperson enters in the world is necessarily different than the prayer to which a monastic devotes himself or herself. Lubich sees St. Francis de Sales's "vital prayer"—that is, a continuous praying in life, where one offers all one's actions and sufferings to God—as having special importance in our modern times. In the past, Lubich says, people thought of the universe as a "still" place that reflected the eternal nature of God, and they sought God's presence, therefore, principally in nature, moments of deep recollection, and before the Blessed Sacrament. Today, however, influenced by science and technological development, we see the world as being in constant evolution, and we seek contact with God in the midst of change and movement. God continues to create and calls laypersons to cooperate with him in that creative activity of building the world. In this cooperation, one does not work primarily for his or her well-being or social status, but rather with the intention of participating in the creation of God: "In this perspective, our work is sacred. We cooperate with God the Creator in . . . building the world."[50] And this, according to Lubich, is what makes daily work a continual prayer.

But even more important, Lubich emphasizes, our spiritual cooperation with God enables Christ to emerge in us and allows us to bear him to others in our work. We enable him to penetrate the world through our work; therefore, we not only cooperate with God the Father in creation, we also participate with the Son in its redemption. Thus creative work is raised to an even higher, redemptive level through which a layperson attains to what Lubich calls a "Pauline sanctity" in daily life:[51] "Through our work we cooperate with God the Father in continuing the work of creation. And through our spiritual life we cooperate with Christ in the redemption of the world, because we work at spreading the kingdom of God."[52]

When this spirituality of work has matured in a layperson, Lubich says that the spiritual life and work are brought "onto the same level."[53] The practices and activities of the spiritual life, on the one hand, and work and family life, on the other, are lived on the same level—namely, in the will of God. The will of God brings these two aspects, symbolized by Martha and Mary, into harmony:

> by underlining the need to carry out the will of God to perfection as a loving response to the love of God, the [Focolare] Movement opens to all the laity the possibility of harmonizing two aspects of their life which are often considered to be incompatible: living their Christian way of life, which is often in antithesis to the world, and remaining in the world. They know that if the will of God calls them to remain in the midst of the world, then fulfilling their family, professional, civil and social obligations according to the Gospel will lead them to sanctity.[54]

Various aspects of Lubich's spirituality thus blend together in her notion of the sanctity of work. It is a participation in God's creative work, in Christ's redemptive work, in the will of God in all situations, in a deeper life of charity, and in living the Gospel in daily life—all in a loving response to the love of God as a way of building a more united humanity and a more peaceful and just society. This participatory dimension of sanctity complements the first two discussed above, the personal and communal dimensions. As Lubich says, the spiritual aspect of Focolare life is lived so that "Christ might grow in us [personal sanctity] and among us [communal sanctity] and therefore build the Church; and then . . . we work toward permeating the various sectors of society with the spirit of Christ [participatory sanctity]."[55]

I would like to conclude this essay with some final observations on the "key" to the threefold sanctification process described above, what Lubich calls "Jesus forsaken." The process of sanctification is one of "death" and "resurrection," of dying to a limited life and rising into a new life of the spirit in union with God and unity with others. Here is the mystery of the cross, which, as Lubich points out, is little understood and practically denied in our contemporary society: "[D]ifferent forms of entertainment, television, and advertising tend to present images of well-being and security. Above all, people would like to exorcise death as if it did not exist, carefully turning attention to all they can have in this life."[56]

Lubich, in contrast, emphasizes that there is a hidden significance to the cross that we, like the saints of the past, can discover in suffering. The trials and sufferings of life allow people to "give a contribution to their own salvation and sanctification."[57] This contribution is possible because of the cross of Jesus. Lubich explains that Jesus crucified and forsaken experienced the separation from God brought about by the weight of our sins and identified in that experience with each one of us in our sufferings. He is truly present in our own crosses, and since his cross is what restores the unity between God and humankind as well as the unity within humankind, embracing Jesus forsaken in one's own suffering, or embracing him with empathy in the sufferings of others, leads to a deeper life of union with God and unity with others.[58]

Through this "divine alchemy," as Lubich calls it, suffering can actually be transformed by the way of the cross into a love that can in turn establish union with God and unity with neighbor. In Lubich's own religious experience within the fledgling Focolare community, the encounter with and surrender to Jesus forsaken proved to be life-transforming:

> Darkness, the burden of our sins, spiritual aridity, anguish, fear. . . . Everything reminded us of [Jesus forsaken]; above all, the sufferings caused by disunity in our relationship with God or in our relationship with our brothers and sisters. Each time that these sufferings came to us, we looked deep into our heart and accepted them; they were aspects of the suffering of Jesus forsaken. Then we tried to forget about ourselves in order to live the will of God in the following moment. In this way, we could re-establish our union with him, which we had broken, or we could recompose unity with others and establish peace. Joy returned to our hearts as in a continual resurrection.[59]

Thus the love of Jesus forsaken became for Lubich and her followers the "key" to a spiritual passage into the resurrection life of

God. In the Focolare, this process of sanctification results not only in personal sanctity but also in the communal sanctity of those "people of God" who are united in the trinitarian life to which Jesus forsaken gives access. Living in a deeper union with God and in a deeper unity with the people of God, a layperson has the creative opportunity to participate through his or her work in the world in the respiritualization of society, so that "the divine [can] penetrate it, as wine penetrates a piece of bread."[60]

Abbreviations

AASS	*Acta Sanctorum,* ed. J. Bollandus. 62 vols. Antwerp, 1643–; repr. Brussels, 1965–
AB	*Analecta Bollandiana*
AESC	*Annales: économies, sociétés, civilisations*
AN	*Annales de Normandie*
ANF	*Ante-Nicene Fathers.* Buffalo: Christian Literature Co., 1887–
BN ms latin	Latin manuscript, Bibliothèque nationale
CCM	*Cahiers de civilisation médiévale*
CR	*Cartulaire de l'abbaye de Ronceray,* ed. Paul Marchegay, *Archives d'Anjou* 3. Angers, 1854.
CSCO	*Corpus Scriptorum Christianorum Orientalium*
CSG	*Cartulaire de l'abbaye de Saint-Georges de Rennes,* ed. Paul de la Bigne Villeneuve, *Bulletin et mémoires de archéologique l'Ille-et-Vilaine,* 9, 1875
GC	*Gallia christiana.* Paris, 1715–
HR/RH	*Historical Reflections/Réflexions historique*
JMH	*Journal of Medieval History*
Mabillon *AB*	Jean Mabillon, ed., *Annales ordinis Sanctis Benedicti.* Lucca, 1739–1745
Mabillon *VA*	Jean Mabillon, ed., *Vetera Analecta.* Paris, 1723
MGH SS	*Monumenta Germaniae Historica: Scriptores*
MGH SRG	*Monumenta Germaniae Historica: Scriptores rerum germanicarum in usum scholarum*
MSAT	*Mémoires de la société archéologique de Touraine*

PG	J. P. Migne, ed., *Patrologiae cursus completus*, series graeca. 162 vols., with Latin translation. Paris, 1857–1866.
PL	J. P. Migne, ed., *Patrologiae cursus completus*, series latina. 221 vols. Paris, 1844–64.
RB	*Revue Bénédictine*
RHDFE	*Revue historique de droit français et étranger*
RHEF	*Revue historique d'église de France*
RHGF	Recueil des historiens de Gaul et de France
RM	*Revue Mabillon*
SC	*Sources Chrétiennes*
SPCK	Society for the Propagation of Christian Knowledge
SETTIMANE	Settimane de Studio de Centro Italiano de Studi sull'alto medioevo
Thesaurus	Edmond Martène, ed., *Thesaurus novus anecdotorum*. Paris, 1717.

Notes

Introduction

1. For a useful bibliographic note on an enormous body of scholarship, see Thomas Head, *Hagiography and the Cult of the Saints: The Diocese of Orléans, 800–1200* (Cambridge: Cambridge University Press, 1990), n33, p. 14.

2. In an apologetic commentary for the Feast of All Saints, the editors and revisers of Alban Butler's *Lives of the Saints* (1756–59) observe, "If it be a question of *canonized* and *beatified* saints, then it is true that there are far more religious than lay people, and also far more bishops than priests, and men than women" because of "some purely natural factors [that] necessarily come into play" in the selection process. The enumeration of those factors, however, shows them to be more institutional than natural. See *Butler's Lives of the Saints*, 4 vols., ed. and rev. Herbert J. Thurston, S.J., and Donald Attwater (Westminster, Md.: Christian Classics, 1981), vol. 4, p. 233. Attempts to quantify exactly the number of lay saints are practically impossible because of the imprecise boundaries demarcating the laity, the complications involved in "negotiating sainthood," and the gradual and late definition of the canonization process. See Aviad M. Kleinberg, *Prophets in Their Own Country: Living Saints and the Making of Sainthood in the Later Middle Ages* (Chicago: University of Chicago Press, 1992), pp. 13–15, for a critique of the statistical methodology employed by Donald Weinstein and Rudolph H. Bell, *Saints and Society: The Two Worlds of Western Christendom, 1000–1700* (Chicago: University of Chicago Press, 1982). I generally use the titles "St." and "Bd." as they appear in *Butler's Lives*.

3. Kenneth L. Woodward, *Making Saints: How the Catholic Church Determines Who Becomes a Saint, Who Doesn't, and Why* (New York: Simon and Schuster, 1990), p. 336.

4. There are historical and legal reasons for this. The investiture controversy of the eleventh century, which pitted Pope Gregory VII against the Emperor Henry IV, led canon lawyers to refer to civil marriage law. Arguing that if the church is Christ's bride (as the authority of Ephesians 5:21–33 affirms), then the church is also husbanded by Christ's special representatives — the pope ("vir ecclesiae"), the bishops, and priests. The analogy advanced by the jurists dictated procedural guidelines for the election of bishops, protected the inalienability of church property (as a bridal dowry), and eventually led to an obligatory celibacy for priests, who were understood to be married to the church. See my *Song of Songs in the Middle Ages* (Ithaca: Cornell University Press, 1990), pp. 42–43, 50–51.

5. For a superb study of their relationship, see Mary M. McLaughlin,

"Abelard as Autobiographer: The Motives and Meaning of his *Story of Calamities,*" *Speculum* 42 (1967): 463–88. For a review of the controversy surrounding the authenticity of their letters, see Jacques Monfrin, "Le Problème de l'authenticité de la correspondance d'Abélard and Héloïse," in *Pierre Abélard, Pierre le vénérable* (Paris: Éditions du Centre National de la Recherche Scientifique, 1975), pp. 409–24.

6. Heloise, Letter 5, in *The Letters of Abelard and Heloise,* trans. Betty Radice (New York: Penguin, 1974, repr. 1976), p. 159. Subsequent citations are parenthetical by page. For the Latin text, see Epistola VI, *PL* 178, c211–26.

7. For a discussion of the key terms "laos" and "laikos," see Jean-Guy Vaillancourt, *Papal Power: A Study of Vatican Control over Lay Catholic Elites* (Berkeley: University of California Press, 1980), pp. 19–21.

8. André Vauchez, "The Saint," in *Medieval Callings,* ed. Jacques Le Goff, trans. Lydia G. Cochrane (Chicago: University of Chicago Press, 1990), p. 324.

9. Heloise quotes 2 Cor. 12:9, "virtus in infirmitate perficitur."

10. St. Bernard, "Sermo IX," in *De diversis, PL* 183, c566.

11. See John R. Sommerfeldt, "The Social Theory of Bernard of Clairvaux," in *Studies in Medieval Cistercian History,* Cistercian Studies, no. 13 (Spenser, Mass.: Cistercian Publications, 1971), pp. 35–48.

12. St. Bernard, *De diversis, PL* 183, c634–35. See also "In nativitate Domini, Sermo I," *PL* 183, c118–19.

13. See Jacques Le Goff, introduction to *Medieval Callings,* pp. 11–12; Georges Dumézil, *The Three Orders: Feudal Society Imagined,* trans. Arthur Goldhammer (Chicago: University of Chicago Press, 1980).

14. The adjectives "lay" and "illiterate" were virtually synonymous in the Middle Ages. See Reudi Imbach, *Laien in der Philosophie des Mittelalters* (Amsterdam: B. R. Grüner, 1989), pp. 21–26.

15. Gratian crystallized the ideals of the Gregorian reform, which mandated celibacy for all priests and thus aligned them more closely with the religious, in the influential text, "Duo sunt genera Christianorum" (CorpIurCan C.12 q.1 c7). In 1888 Pope Leo XIII echoed this canonical distinction in *Est sane molestum:* "It is indeed clear and certain that in the Church there are two orders very different from one another, the shepherds and the flock." See *Clergy and Laity: Official Catholic Teachings,* ed. Odile M. Liebard (Wilmington, N.C.: McGrath, 1978), p. 1.

16. Jean Leclercq, "St. Bernard's Attitude toward War," *Studies in Medieval Social History* 2, ed. John R. Sommerfeldt, Cistercian Studies Series, no. 24 (Kalamazoo: Cistercian Publications, 1976), pp. 31–32. See also my discussion of "Ghostly Chivalry," in *Job, Boethius, and Epic Truth* (Ithaca: Cornell University Press, 1994), pp. 165–70.

17. See Richard Kieckhefer, "Imitators of Christ: Sainthood in the Christian Tradition," in *Sainthood: Its Manifestations in World Religions,* ed. Richard Kieckhefer and George D. Bond (Berkeley: University of California Press, 1988), pp. 1–42, esp. pp. 12–16.

18. Vauchez, "The Saint," in *Medieval Callings,* p. 331.

19. For a good introduction to the Beguines, see *Beguine Spirituality,* ed. Fiona Bowie, trans. Oliver Davies (New York: Crossroad, 1990), esp. pp. 3–45.

20. André Vauchez, *The Laity in the Middle Ages: Religious Belief and Devotional Practices,* ed. Daniel Bornstein, trans. Margery J. Schneider (Notre Dame: University of Notre Dame Press, 1993), p. 72. Following the example of St. Catherine of Siena, later tertiaries were especially prone to unusual ascetical (and ecstatic) excesses. Among these women are Bd. Columba of Rieti (†1501), Bd. Magdalen Panattieri (†1503), Bd. Catherine of Racconigi (†1547), and St. Rose of Lima (†1617).

21. As Vauchez has shown, the practice of marital continence was considered a proof of heroic virtue, figured strongly in late Franciscan asceticism, and contributed to the canonizations of St. Hedwig of Silesia (†1243) and St. Elzéar. See *The Laity in the Middle Ages,* pp. 185–215.

22. Their bliss was cut short, however, by Ludwig's early death while on crusade and, as Vauchez observes, their conjugal relationship played no appreciable part in the recognition of Elizabeth's sanctity, which rested instead on her almsgiving, Franciscan love of poverty, and endurance of humiliations in her widowhood. See *The Laity in the Middle Ages,* p. 185. A higher evaluation of marital affection seems attached to the recognition of later matrons, such as Bd. Louisa of Savoy (†1503), Bd. Louisa Albertoni (†1533), Bd. Victoria Fornari-Strata (†1617), and Bd. Anne Mary Taigi (†1837).

23. Vauchez, "The Saint," in *Medieval Callings,* p. 325.

24. Ibid., p. 324.

25. According to Vauchez, the phenomenon of the recognition of lay commoners as saints depended on special developments in Italy and the Mediterranean. He discusses Homobonus in particular. See "A Twelfth-Century Novelty: The Lay Saints of Urban Italy," in *The Laity in the Middle Ages,* pp. 51–72.

26. The saintly category of the "passion-bearers" *(strastoterptsy)* was highly esteemed by the Russian church, which distinguished them from the ascetics, bishops or teachers, and martyrs for the faith. The first to be so recognized were Sts. Boris and Gleb (†1015), the younger sons of St. Vladimir of Kiev, who were murdered by the adherents of their ambitious brother Svyatopolk.

27. Clarissa Atkinson has emphasized the rising cult of mother saints, such as St. Anne and St. Bridget of Sweden, in the late Middle Ages. See her *The Oldest Vocation: Christian Motherhood in the Middle Ages* (Ithaca: Cornell University Press, 1991), pp. 240–41. See also *Sanctity and Motherhood: Essays on Holy Mothers in the Middle Ages,* ed. Anneke B. Mulder-Bakker (New York and London: Garland, 1995).

28. In Daniel Bornstein's introduction to *The Laity in the Middle Ages,* he calls the fourteenth and fifteenth centuries "the golden age of the laity," pointing especially to the "new prominence of women" in the ranks of the saints (p. xix).

29. Dietrich Bonhoeffer, *The Cost of Discipleship,* 2d ed., trans. R. H. Fuller, rev. Irmgard Booth (New York: Macmillan, 1959), pp. 51–52.

30. Woodward, *Making Saints,* p. 76.

31. Ibid., p. 75.

32. Ibid., p. 76.

33. Dom Charles Poulet, *A History of the Catholic Church,* trans. Sidney Raemers (St. Louis: B. Herder, 1935), vol. 2, p. 98.

34. Robert E. McNally, S.J., *The Council of Trent, the "Spiritual Exercises," and the Catholic Reform,* Historical Series no. 15 (Philadelphia: Fortress Press, 1970), p. 11.

35. Ibid., p. 15.

36. Ibid., p. 18. Among the early modern saints who were schooled in the *Exercises* we find Sts. Charles Borromeo (†1594), Philip Neri (†1595), Peter Canisius (†1597), and Francis de Sales (†1622).

37. Ibid., p. 19.

38. Heiko A. Oberman, *The Reformation: Roots and Ramifications,* trans. Andrew C. Gow (Grand Rapids: William B. Eerdmans, 1994), p. 80.

39. Kees Waaijman, "Toward a Phenomenological Definition of Spirituality," trans. John Vriend, *Studies in Spirituality* 3 (1993): 5–57, p. 33.

40. Ibid., p. 34.

41. Peter Burke, *Popular Culture in Early Modern Europe* (New York: New York University Press, 1978), pp. 207, 212, 211. In the following paragraph I draw upon his discussion on pp. 223–234.

42. Although Protestants tended to repudiate the cult of the saints, John Foxe's *Book of Martyrs,* first published in 1563, gained wide currency.

43. For a study of St. Angela Merici and her Company of St. Ursula (founded 1535), see Dorothy Latz, "Saint Angela Merici and the Spiritual Currents of the Italian Renaissance" (Ph.D. dissertation, Strasbourg, 1986); *The Writings of St. Angela Merici,* trans. Mary Teresa Neylan, O.S.U. (Rome: Ursulines of the Roman Union, 1969).

44. St. Francis de Sales, *Introduction to the Devout Life,* trans. John K. Ryan (1950; New York: Doubleday, 1972), pp. 44, 34.

45. Pope Pius XII, "Address to the World Congress of the Lay Apostolate on Its Need Today, October 14, 1951," in *Clergy and Laity,* p. 90. In that same address, the pope refutes the charge that the church's "clerical" reaction to Protestantism inhibited the development of the Catholic laity (p. 89).

46. For a brilliant reflection on the latter, see Wolfhart Pannenberg, *Christianity in a Secularized World* (New York: Crossroad, 1989).

47. I echo Dietrich Bonhoeffer, *Letters and Papers from Prison,* ed. Eberhard Bethge (New York: Macmillan, 1953, repr. 1971), p. 362.

48. Anonymous, foreword to *The Lay Apostolate: Papal Teachings* (Boston: Daughters of St. Paul, 1961), p. 9.

49. See, for instance, Jean-Guy Vaillancourt, *Papal Power;* Ana Maria Bidegain, "From Catholic Action to Liberation Theology: The Historical Progress of the Laity in Latin America in the Twentieth Century," Working Paper 48 (Notre Dame: The Helen Kellogg Institute for International Studies, 1985).

50. Pope Paul VI reviews the history and meaning of the expression in his

April 23, 1969, General Address, "On the Layman's Task," in *Clergy and Laity*, pp. 296–99.

51. Pope Pius XII, "The Lay Apostolate Today," in *Clergy and Laity*, p. 92.

52. This phrase, from the document supporting the cause of his beatification, is quoted in the biographical entry in the *New Catholic Encyclopedia* (Washington, D.C.: Catholic University of America, 1967).

53. Pope Pius XII, "The Lay Apostolate Today," in *Clergy and Laity*, p. 92.

54. See Yves Congar, *Lay People in the Church: A Study for a Theology of the Laity*, trans. Donald Attwater (Westminster, Md.: Newman, 1957); Karl Rahner, S.J., "Notes on the Lay Apostolate," in *Theological Investigations*, trans. Karl H. and Boniface Kruger (Baltimore: Helicon, 1967), vol. 2, pp. 319–52.

55. See "The Dogmatic Constitution on the Church *(Lumen Gentium)*," in *The Documents of Vatican II*, ed. Walter M. Abbott, S.J. and Rev. Msgr. Joseph Gallagher, chapters 4 and 5, esp. 5:40, 4:31–33.

56. Rahner, "Notes on the Lay Apostolate," p. 352.

57. Pope Paul VI, "On the Layman's Sphere of Activity," in *Clergy and Laity*, p. 294.

58. See Urban T. Holmes, III, *A History of Christian Spirituality: An Analytical Introduction* (New York: Seabury, 1981), p. 150.

59. Cardinal Joseph Suenens of Belgium suggested this reform at the Second Vatican Council. See Woodward, *Making Saints*, p. 90.

60. One miracle is required for the beatification of a nonmartyr, and an additional miracle is required for his or her canonization. See Woodward, *Making Saints*, p. 95.

61. Ibid., p. 106.

62. See the listing of newly recognized saints and *beati* in the *1994 Catholic Almanac* (Huntington: Our Sunday Visitor, 1993), pp. 140–42, 544.

63. "The Patience of a Saint," a Catholic News Service report in *The Catholic Moment*, vol. 54, no. 32 (September 20, 1998), p. 11.

64. Quoted in Brendan I. Koerner, "The Making of a Saint," *U.S. News and World Report* (January 11, 1999), p. 54.

65. Bonhoeffer warns that, with the loss of the monastic ideal, "the antithesis between the Christian life and the life of bourgeois respectability is at an end. The Christian life has come to mean nothing more than living in the world and as the world" (*Cost of Discipleship*, p. 54).

66. Coleman, "After Sainthood?" in *Saints and Virtues*, esp. pp. 224, 220. See also Kieckhefer, "Imitators of Christ," in *Sainthood*, pp. 38–39; John M. Mecklin, *The Passing of the Saint: A Study of a Cultural Type* (Chicago: University of Chicago Press, 1941). St. Thérèse of Lisieux was declared a Doctor of the Church by John Paul II on World Mission Sunday, October 19, 1997.

67. Coleman, "After Sainthood," pp. 206–7, 211, 213, 222, 205. Coleman's observations about changing styles of hagiography find confirmation in Edith Wyschogrod, *Saints and Postmodernism: Revisioning Moral Philosophy* (Chicago: University of Chicago Press, 1990).

68. See John Paul II, *Crossing the Threshold of Hope*, ed. Vittorio Messori

(New York: Alfred A. Knopf, 1994), p. 177; Wyschogrod, *Saints and Postmodernism*, p. xiv.

69. On this theme, see my introduction to *Divine Representations: Postmodernism and Spirituality*, ed. Ann W. Astell (New York and Mahwah: Paulist Press, 1994), pp. 1–18; "Simone Weil's 'Affliction': Two Contemporary Spiritualities," *Studies in Spirituality* 5 (1995): 208–19; "Postmodern Christian Spirituality—A *Coincidentia Oppositorum?*" *Christian Spirituality Bulletin*, 4.1 (1996): 1–5.

70. See Barbara Newman, "The Mozartian Moment: Reflections on Medieval Mysticism," *Christian Spirituality Bulletin: The Journal for the Society for the Study of Christian Spirituality*, 3.1 (1995): 3–4.

71. Leisner was beatified by Pope John Paul II in Berlin in 1996. See Joseph Maria Klein, *Karl Leisner: For Christ and For Youth*, ed. and trans. Jonathan Niehaus (privately published by the Schoenstatt Fathers, Waukesha, Wis., in 1995).

72. Peter Brown, "The Saint as Exemplar in Late Antiquity," in *Saints and Virtues*, pp. 3–14.

73. Coleman, "After Sainthood?" p. 224.

I. Lay Sanctity and Church Reform in Early Medieval France

1. "The Martyrdom of Perpetua and Felicitas," in *The Acts of the Christian Martyrs*, ed. H. R. Musurillo (Oxford: Clarendon Press, 1972); Elisabeth Schüssler Fiorenza, *In Memory of Her: A Feminist Theological Reconstruction of Christian Origins* (New York: Crossroad, 1985), pp. 160–204.

2. Steven L. Davies, *The Revolt of the Widows: The Social World of the Apocryphal Acts* (Carbondale: Southern Illinois University Press, 1980), esp. pp. 12–13.

3. See George Williams, "The Ancient Church, AD 30–313," in *The Layman in Christian History*, ed. Stephen Neil and Hans Ruidi-Weber (Philadelphia: Westminster Press, 1963), pp. 28–56; Alexandre Faivre, *The Emergence of the Laity in the Early Church*, trans. David Smith (New York: Paulist Press, 1990), pp. 15–24; Schüssler Fiorenza, *In Memory of Her*, pp. 294–309; John Gager, *Kingdom and Community: The Social World of Early Christianity* (Englewood Cliffs, N.J.: Prentice-Hall, 1975), pp. 43, 72–73; Hans Van Campenhausen, *Ecclesiastical Authority and Spiritual Power in the Church of the First Three Centuries* (Stanford: Stanford University Press, 1969), pp. 121–23. Key primary sources include Clement of Rome, "Letter to the Church at Corinth," in *The Library of Christian Classics*, vol. 1, *Early Christian Fathers*, ed. C. C. Richardson (Philadelphia: Westminster Press, 1953), p. 62; *The Didache*, in *Early Christian Fathers*, p. 178.

4. Jacques Fontaine, "The Practice of the Christian Life: The Birth of the Laity," in *Christian Spirituality: Origins to the Twelfth Century*, ed. Bernard McGinn and John Meyendorff (New York: Crossroad, 1986), pp. 454–60.

5. Elizabeth Schüssler Fiorenza, *In Memory of Her*, pp. 246–344; Fontaine, *Christian Spirituality*, pp. 453–91.

6. Fontaine, *Christian Spirituality*, pp. 454, 464.

7. Peter Brown, *The World of Late Antiquity* (New York: Harcourt, Brace, Jovanovich, 1975), pp. 22–69; Philip Rousseau, *Ascetics, Authority and the Church in the Age of Jerome and Cassian* (Oxford: Oxford University Press, 1978).

8. Fontaine, *Christian Spirituality,* p. 468. See also Peter Brown, *The Cult of the Saints: Its Rise and Function in Latin Christianity* (Chicago: University of Chicago Press, 1981; *Egeria's Travels,* ed. John Wilkinson (London: S.P.C.K., 1971).

9. St. Gregory of Nyssa, "The Life of St. Macrina," in *Ascetical Works,* trans. V. W. Callahan, Fathers of the Church Series, no. 58 (Washington, D.C.: The Catholic University Press, 1967).

10. Peter Brown, *The Body and Society: Men, Women, and Sexual Renunciation in Early Christianity* (New York: Columbia University Press, 1988), pp. 86–102.

11. See my book, *Millennial Women: Lay Leaders of the Latin Church for the First Thousand Years* (forthcoming).

12. *Egeria's Travels,* ed. Wilkinson; Tertullian, *Apologeticum* 39, ANF III, p. 46.

13. Arthur Voöbus, *History of Asceticism in the Syrian Orient* I, *CSCO* 184.14 (Louvain, 1958); Jean Gribomont, "La monachisme au sein de l'église en Syrie et in Cappadoce," *Studia monastica* 7.1 (1965): 7–24; Robert Murray, *Symbols of Church and Kingdom: A Study in Early Syriac Tradition* (London: Cambridge University Press, 1975), pp. 4–24; Murray, "Exhortation to Candidates for Ascetical Vows at Baptism in the Ancient Syriac Church," *New Testament Studies* 21 (1974): 59–80; Elaine Pagels, *The Gnostic Gospels* (New York: Vintage Books, 1981), pp. 170–81; *Ascetic Women in Greco-Roman Antiquity: A Sourcebook,* ed. Vincent L. Wimbush (Minneapolis: Fortress Press, 1990).

14. John Cassian, *Conferences,* trans. Colm Luibheid (New York: Paulist Press, 1985), p. 186.

15. Rousseau, *Ascetics, Authority and the Church;* Brown, *Cult of the Saints,* pp. 32–49.

16. *The Life of Melania the Younger,* trans. Elizabeth Clark, Studies in Women and Religion, no. 14 (New York: Edward Mellen Press, 1984), pp. 39–45.

17. W. H. C. Frend, "The Church of the Roman Empire, 313–600," in *The Layman in the Christian Church,* p. 82; see also pp. 57–82.

18. Emile Amann and Auguste Dumas, *L'Église au pouvoir des laïques (888–1057)* (Histoire de l'église depuis les origines jusqu'a nos jours), ed. A. Fliche and V. Martin (Paris: Bloud and Gay, 1948), pp. 198–210, 231–49, 303–16.

19. Frend, *The Layman,* p. 82. See also Fontaine, *Christian Spirituality,* pp. 453–91; Faivre, *The Emergence of the Laity;* Rosamond McKitterick, *The Frankish Church and the Carolingian Reforms, 789–895* (London: Royal Historical Society: 1977), pp. 1–44, 98–114, 206–9; McKitterick, *The Carolingians and the Written Word* (Cambridge: Cambridge University Press, 1989), pp. 211–73; McKitterick, *The Frankish Kingdoms Under the Carolingians* (London: Longman, 1983), pp. 106–26; Georges Duby, *The Three Orders: Feudal Society Imagined,* trans. Arthur Goldhammer (Chicago: University of Chicago Press, 1980), pp. 76–80; Pierre Riché, *Daily Life in the World of Charlemagne,* trans. Jo Ann McNamara

(Philadelphia: University of Pennsylvania Press, 1978), pp. 81–84, 203–29, 259–68; Thomas Noble, "The Monastic Ideal as a Model for Empire: The Case of Louis the Pious," *RB* 86 (1976): 235–50; Suzanne Wemple, *Women in Frankish Society* (Philadelphia: University of Pennsylvania Press, 1981), pp. 127–74; J. M. Wallace-Hadrill, *The Frankish Church* (Oxford: Clarendon Press, 1983), pp. 226–92.

20. Jean Chelini, "Les Laïcs dans la société ecclésiastique carolingienne," I Laici nella societas christiana de secoli XI e XII, in SETTIMANE 3 (1965): 23–55; Gerd Tellenbach, *Church, State and Christian Society at the Time of the Investiture Controversy,* trans. R. F. Bennett (New York: Harper, 1959); Ute-Renate Blumenthal, *The Investiture Controversy: Church and Monarchy from the Ninth to the Twelfth Century* (Philadelphia: University of Pennsylvania Press, 1988); I. S. Robinson, *The Papacy, 1073–1198: Continuity and Innovation* (Cambridge: Cambridge University Press), pp. 295–21, 367–41.

21. McKitterick, *Frankish Church; Frankish Kingdoms,* pp. 77–199; Wallace-Hadrill, *Frankish Church,* pp. 189–292.

22. E.g., Anon., *Vita Hludovici pii, MGH SS* 2 607–48, trans. Alan Cabaniss, *Son of Charlemagne: A Contemporary Life of Louis the Pious* (Syracuse: Syracuse University Press, 1961), pp. 44, 60–61, 70, 73, 85; Riché, *World of Charlemagne,* pp. 41–42, 76–81, 152.

23. See *La France de l'an Mil,* ed. Robert Delort (Paris: Editions du Seuil, 1990), pp. 11–23 and passim.

24. Noble, "The Monastic Ideal," *RB* 86 (1976): 235–50.

25. This would include not only monastic orders proper but also clerical and lay evangelical groups who, like monks, derived from the Gospels their particular models of the authentic Christian life. See Gerhard Ladner, *The Idea of Reform: Its Impact on Christian Thought and Action in the Age of the Fathers* (Cambridge: Harvard University Press, 1959); M. D. Chenu, *Nature, Man and Society in the Twelfth Century,* trans. Jerome Taylor and Lester Little (Chicago: University of Chicago Press, 1968); R. I. Moore, *The Birth of Popular Heresy: Documents of Medieval History* (New York: St. Martin's Press, 1975); J. B. Russell, *Dissent and Reform in the Early Middle Ages* (Berkeley: University of California Press, 1965); Edward Peters, ed., *Heresy and Authority in Medieval Europe* (Philadelphia: University of Pennsylvania Press, 1980); Lester K. Little, *Religious Poverty and the Profit Economy* (Ithaca: Cornell University Press, 1978), pp. 97–170; Herbert Grundmann, *Religiöse Bewegungen im Mittelalter: Untersuchungen über die geschichtlichen Zusammenhänge zwischen der Ketzerei, den Bettelorden und der religiösen Frauenbewegung im 12. und 13. Jahrhundert* (Hildesheim: Olms, 1961).

26. Georges Duby, SETTIMANE 3 (1965): 448–61; Frederick Paxton, Bernard Bachrach, Daniel Callahan, Thomas Head, Richard Landes in *HR/RH* 14.3 (1987): 385–421, 447–529. The essays by Frederic Paxton ("History, Historians and the Peace of God"), Daniel Callahan ("The Peace of God and the Cult of the Saints in Aquitaine"), Richard Landes ("Between Aristocracy and Heresy: Popular Participation in the Limousin Peace of God, 994–1033"), and Thomas Head ("The Judgment of God: Andrew of Fleury's Account of the

Peace League of Bourges") have been republished in revised form in *The Peace of God: Social Violence and Religious Response in France around the Year 1000,* ed. Thomas Head and Richard Landes (Ithaca: Cornell University Press, 1992); see also Daniel Callahan, *AN* 89 (1977): 21–43; Richard Landes, *AESC* (1991): 573–59; Duby, *Three Orders,* pp. 21–44.

   27. Noble, *RB* 86 (1976): 235–50.

   28. For example, Jonas of Orlean's treatises on kingship and the laity (in Jonas of Orleans, *A Ninth–Century Political Tract: De Institutione Regis,* trans. R. W. Dyson [Smithtown, N.Y.: Exposition Press, 1983]), Dhuoda's manual for her son William (Dhuoda, *Handbook for William: A Carolingian Woman's Counsel for Her Son,* trans. Carol Neel [Lincoln: University of Nebraska Press, 1991]); the Anonymous Life of Louis the Pious (ed. Cabaniss, *Son of Charlemagne*); Ardo's Life of Benedict of Aniane (Ardo, *The Emperor's Monk: A Contemporary Life of Benedict of Aniane,* trans. Allen Cabaniss [Devon: Stockwell, 1979]); the lives of Wala and Adalhard (*Charlemagne's Cousins: Contemporary Lives of Wala and Adalhard,* trans. Allen Cabaniss [Syracuse: Syracuse University Press, 1967]); *The Annals of St. Bertin,* trans. Janet Nelson (Manchester: Manchester University Press, 1991) (*Annales Bertiniani,* ed. F. Grat, J. Vielliard, and S. Clemencet [Paris, 1964]), and the histories of Nithard and Notker (Nithard, *Historiarum Libri IV,* ed. P. Lauer, *Histoire des fils de Lous le Pieux* [Paris, 1926] English translation by Scholz [1970]; and Notker, *Gesta Caroli Magni,* ed. H. Haefele, *MGH SRG* Nova Series 12 [Berlin: Weidman, 1959], English translation by L. Thorpe, *Two Lives of Charlemagne* [Harmondsworth: Penguin, 1969]).

   29. One can find examples in Odo of Cluny's life of St. Gerald of Aurillac, John of Salerno's life of St. Odo (St. Odo of Cluny, *Life of St. Odo by John of Salerno and Life of St. Gerald of Aurillace by St. Odo,* ed. and trans. Gerard Sitwell [London: Sheed and Ward, 1958]), the miracles of St. Benedict (Aimo, Adrevald et al., *Les miracles de Saint-Benoit,* ed. Eugene de Certain (Société de l'histoire de France) [Paris: Renouard, 1858]), and the chronicles of Richer, Raoul Glaber, and Adhemar de Chabannes (Richer, *Histoire de France, 888–975,* ed. Robert Latouche, 2 vols. [Paris: Champion, 1930, 1937]); Raoul Glaber, *Les cinq livres de ses histoires, 900–1044,* ed. Maurice Prou (Collection des textes ...1) [Paris: Picard, 1886]; Ademar de Chabannes, *Chronique,* ed. Jules Chavonon (Collection des textes ... 20) [Paris: Picard, 1897]).

   30. This article includes a mere sampling of surveyed charters from before 900 to 1050 in Anjou, Poitou, and Touraine, including those of Marmoutier, St. Martin, St. Julian, Cormery, Bourgueil, and Beaumont (women) in the Touraine; St. Florent, Ronceray (women) in Anjou; and St. Cyprian, Trinity (women) and Holy Cross (women) in Poitou.

   31. Constance Bouchard, *Sword, Miter and Cloister: Nobility and the Church in Burgundy, 980–1198* (Ithaca: Cornell University Press, 1987), pp. 45–171; Penelope Johnson, *Equal in Monastic Profession: Religious Women in Medieval France* (Chicago: University of Chicago Press, 1987), pp. 13–61, and *Prayer, Patronage and Power: The Abbey of La Trinité, Vendome, 1032–1187* (New York: New York University Press, 1981); Barbara Rosenwein, *To Be a Neighbor of St. Peter: The*

Social Meaning of Cluny's Property (Ithaca: Cornell University Press, 1989); Stephen White, *Custom, Kinship and Gifts to Saints: The Laudatio in Western France, 1050–1150* (Chapel Hill: University of North Carolina Press, 1988).

32. For example, Andre's Life of Abbot Gauzlin of Fleury (Andreas, Monk of Fleury, *Vie de l'Abbe Gauzlin de Fleury* [Paris: Société de l'édition "Les belles lettres," 1961]) and Helgaud's life of King Robert the Pious (*Abbon, Siege of Paris; Chronique de Flodoard, Chronique de Raoul Glaber, Vie du Roi Robert, par Helgaud, Poème d'Alberon sur le regne de Robert*, ed. M. Guizot [Paris: Briere, 1824]). The major hagiographic collections are listed in the bibliography of Thomas Head, *Hagiography and the Cult of the Saints* (Cambridge: Cambridge University Press, 1990).

33. White, *Custom, Kinship*, pp. 154–76; Rosenwein, *To Be a Neighbor*, pp. 38–48; Frederick Paxton, *Christianizing Death* (Ithaca: Cornell University Press, 1990), pp. 98–102, 134–38; Head, *Hagiography and the Cult of the Saints*, pp. 194–99, 288–89; Jacques Le Goff, *The Birth of Purgatory*, trans. Arthur Goldhammer (Chicago: University of Chicago Press, 1981), pp. 11–12, 41–42, 45–46, 64–68, 81–82, 91–93, 102–7, 122–26; Willibald Jorden, *Das clüniazensische Totengedächniswesen vornehmlich unter den drei ersten Abten Berno, Odo und Aymard, 910–54* (Münster-in-Westfalen: Aschendorff, 1930).

34. Dhondt, *Principautés;* Guillot, *Comte d'Anjou;* R. W. Southern, *Making of the Middle Ages* (New Haven: Yale University Press, 1953), pp. 80–88.

35. Pierre Riché, *Education and Culture in the Barbarian West from the Sixth through the Eighth Century*, trans. John J. Contreni (Columbia: University of South Carolina Press, 1978); M. M. Hildebrandt, *The External School in Carolingian Society* (Leiden: Brill, 1992); John J. Contreni, *Carolingian Learning, Masters and Manuscripts* (Aldershot, Hampshire: Variorum, 1991); *Education, mediévales: L'enfance, l'école, l'Église en Occident, VIe-XVe siècles* (Paris: Institut national de recherche pedagogique, 1991); Christopher Brooke, *Europe in the Central Middle Ages, 962–1154* (London: Longman, 1987), pp. 72–95; Little, *Religious Poverty*, pp. 61–69.

36. Wendy Davies, *Small Worlds: The Village Community in Early Medieval Brittany* (Berkeley: University of California Press, 1988), pp. 183–213; *Cartulary of Redon*, ed. Aurélien de Courson (Paris, 1863); *The Monks of Redon*, ed. and trans. Caroline Brett (Woodbridge, Suffolk: Boydell Press, 1989).

37. There was, of course, some of both. At least two recent studies emphasize how the development of lordship undermined the independent institutions of village life. See Davies, *Small Worlds*, and Jean Pierre Poly and Eric Bournazel, *The Feudal Transformation, 900–1200* (New York: Holmes and Meier, 1991), pp. 9–86. See also Jan Dhondt, *Etude sur la naissance des principautés territoriales en France, IXe au Xe siècle* (Bruges: De Tempel, 1948); Jacques Boussard, "L'Origine des familles seigneuriales dans la région de la Loire moyenne," in *CCM* 5 (1962): 303–32, and "Les destinées de la Neustrie du IXe au Xe siècle," *CCM* 11 (1968): 15–28; Olivier Guillot, *Le Comte d'Anjou et son entourage du XIe siècle* (Paris: Picard, 1972); Georges Duby, *La Société aux XIe et XIIe siècle dans la region mâçonnaise* (Paris: Colin, 1959).

38. John Navone, S.J., *Self-Giving and Sharing: The Trinity and Human*

Fulfillment (Collegeville: Liturgical Press, 1989), pp. 35–44. I am grateful to Sr. Donald Corcoran of Transfiguration Monastery for this reference and insights into Navone's book.

39. Caroline Walker Bynum has challenged the idea that women saints of the high and later Middle Ages experienced conversion in the same way as men, although they may appear to in sources written by men. I examine this question for the early medieval period in my forthcoming book, which deals primarily with laywomen. See Caroline W. Bynum, "Women's Stories, Women's Symbols: A Critique of Victor Turner's Theory of Liminality," in *Fragmentation and Redemption: Essays on Gender and the Human Body in Medieval Religion* (New York: Zone Books, 1992), pp. 27–51.

40. Ardo, "Vita Benedicti," *MGH SS*, XV/1,200–220, chaps. 1.3 and 2.1, trans. Alan Cabaniss, *The Emperor's Monk*, pp. 49–50.

41. Ibid.

42. Ibid.; Friedrich Prinz, *Frühes Mönchtum im Frankenreich, Kultur und Gesellschaft in Gallien, den Rheinlanden und Bayern am Beispiel der monastischen Entwicklung (4.bis 8. Jahrhundert)* (Munich, Vienna: Oldenbourg, 1965).

43. St. Odo of Cluny, "Life of St. Gerald of Aurillac," I.9, trans. Sitwell, p. 103; *PL* 133, c648–49.

44. Ibid., I.5, I.9, I.10, and I.34; Book II.2–6; trans. Sitwell, pp. 97–104, 123–24, 162–67; *PL* 133, c639–704, esp. c645, c647–49, c662–63, c670–74.

45. John of Salerno, "Life of St. Odo of Cluny," Bk. I.9, trans. Gerald Sitwell, p. 10; *PL* 133, c47–48.

46. Barbara Rosenwein, "St. Odo's St. Martin," *JMH* 4 (1978): 317–31.

47. John of Salerno, "Life of St. Odo of Cluny," Bk. I.36, trans. Sitwell, p. 37; *PL* 133, c59.

48. Charles de Grandmaison, ed., *Fragments de chartes du Xe siècle provenant de Saint-Julien de Tours* (Paris: Picard, 1886), III.19–21, XV–XVI.39–43, XXI.57–60; Mary Skinner, "Founders and Reformers of Monasteries in the Touraine, 930–1030," in *Benedictus*, ed. E. Rozanne Elder (Kalamazoo: Cistercian Publications, 1981), pp. 82–83.

49. Joseph Delaville le Roulx, ed. *Notices sur les chartes originales relatives à la Touraine anterieures à l'an mil* (Tours: Rouille-Ladévéze, 1879), pp. 31–38; Michel Dupont, *Monographie du cartulaire de Bourgueil MSAT* 56 (1962):161–64; *PL* 146, 1247–72; Guy Oury, "La reconstruction monastique dans l'ouest: l'abbé Gauzbert de Saint-Julien de Tours," in *RM* 54 (1964):77–84; Skinner, in *Benedictus*, p. 87.

50. "Vita Hervei," Martène, *Thesaurus* 3:1349–50; "Fragmentum statutorum canonicorum," *PL* 138, 1349–50; Jacques Boussard, "Le Trésorier de Saint-Martin de Tours," *RHEF* 47 (1961): 61–81; Guy Oury, "L'Idéal monastique dans la vie canoniale," *RM* 50(1960): 1–29; Oury, *RM* 54 (1964): 120; Skinner, in *Benedictus*, p. 88.

51. "Vita Hervei," Martène, *Thesaurus* 3:1349–50; *GC* 14: 311–17 and Instr. cols. 63, 82; *RHGF,* 10:589, 607; Jean Verdon,"Recherches sur les monastères feminins dans la France du nord aux IXe–XIe siècles," *RM* 59 (1969):62; Mary Skinner, "Benedictine Life for Women in Central France, 850–1100: A Feminist

Revival," in *Distant Echoes: Medieval Religious Women*, I, ed. John Nichols and L. Thomas Shank (Kalamazoo: Cistercian Publications, 1984), p. 91.

52. *CSG* 152, no. 1:217–22; Skinner, in *Distant Echoes*, p. 93; Jean Verdon, in *RM* 59 (1969): 62.

53. *GC* IV, 149 and ms BN coll. Anjou et Touraine, II/1 no. 337; *GC*, I, 153 and BN ms latin, coll. Anjou et Touraine, I, 186; R. W. Southern, *Making of the Middle Ages*, p. 87; L. Halphen, *Le comté d'Anjou au Xe siècle* (Paris: Picard, 1906), pp. 351–52; Duby, *L'An Mil* (Paris: Julliard, 1967), pp. 103–80.

54. It has been argued that women were put into monasteries against their will by their husbands or fathers. In my view, however, most women (and men as well) entered monasteries of their own free choice. Child oblates lacking vocations could leave as adults. See Penelope Johnson, *Equal in Monastic Profession*, pp. 13–34; Jean Verdon, "Le moniales dans la France de l'Ouest au Xe et XIIe siècles," *CCM* 19.3 (1976): 249–52; Skinner, in *Distant Echoes*, pp. 96–97. See also Hugh Feiss, O.S.B., " 'Consecrated to Christ, Nuns of This Church Community': The Benedictines of Notre-Dame de Saintes, 1047–1792," *American Benedictine Review* 45.2 (1994): 283 n36.

55. I use The New Jerusalem Bible (New York: Doubleday, 1985).

56. As in Notker's account of a massacre of Saxons by Louis the Pious' armies. See Einhard and Notker, *Two Lives*, p. 151; Jaffé, *Monachus* II.11.

57. Michel Mollat, *The Poor in the Middle Ages*, trans. Arthur Goldhammer (New Haven: Yale University Press, 1987), pp. 24–53; Little, *Religious Poverty*, pp. 66–69.

58. Paxton, Callahan, Landes, and especially Head in *HR/RH* 14 (1987) or in the *Peace of God*, pp. 21–40, 165–238.

59. Bishop Jonas of Orleans' treatise on kingship includes large sections of his more general treatise on the laity and may first have been published as part of the legislation of the Synod of Paris in 829. See Jonas, *De institutione laicale*, *PL* 106, c121ff; *De institutione regia*, *PL* 106, c279ff; trans. R. W. Dyson, *A Ninth-Century Political Tract*, pp. xi–xiii.

60. Jonas, *Tract*, trans. Dyson, pp. 40–41.

61. Ibid., p. 62.

62. McKitterick, *Frankish Church;* Wallace-Hadrill, *Frankish Church;* Noble in *RB* 86 (1976): 235–50; and Louis' anonymous biographer in *Son of Charlemagne*, ed. Cabannis.

63. Dhuoda, *Handbook for William*, trans. Carol Neel, pp. ix–xxiii; based on P. Riché, ed., *Dhuoda Manual pour mon fils* (Paris: Editions du Cerf, 1975), *SC* 225.

64. Wallace-Hadrill, *Frankish Church*, p. 286.

65. Ibid., p. xxvi, citing Myra Bowers, "Liber manualis," Ph.D dissertation, Catholic University (1977), pp. xxx–xxxviii.

66. Dhouda, *Handbook*, trans. Neel, pp. 53–55.

67. Ibid., p. 97.

68. Odo, "Life of St. Gerald," I.8, trans. Sitwell, pp. 99–100; *PL* 133, c646–47.

69. Ibid., I.9, trans. Sitwell, p. 102; *PL* 133, c647–49.

70. Ibid., I.7–9, 14, 17–24, 26–28, 33, 36, 38, 40, trans. Sitwell, pp. 94–131; *PL* 133, c646–49, 651–59, 661–62, 664–66.

71. Ibid., I.14, trans. Sitwell, p. 108; *PL* 133, c651–52.

72. Paschasius Radbertus, "Life of Wala," I.26, in *Charlemagne's Cousins,* ed. A. Cabannis, pp. 138–41; *PL* 120, c1601–3.

73. BN ms Latin, coll. Anjou et Touraine, I, nos. 132 and 134; E. Martène and C. Chevalier, *Histoire de Marmoutier* I (372–1104) (*MSAT* XXIV) (Tours: Guilland-Verger, 1874).

74. BN ms Latin 12878.

75. *CR* nos. 18, 19. An alod is land or property not held by feudal tenure and thus not subject to any rent to a superior.

76. Charles de Grandmaison, *Chartes S. Julien de Tours,* no. XVI; Guy Oury, "La réconstruction monastique dans l'ouest: l'abbé Gauzbert de Saint-Julien de Tours," *RM* 54 (1964): 69–124.

77. *RHGF* X, 677; P. Tarbé, ed., "Chartes," *Revue retrospective* IX (187) 48–49; J. J. Bourasse, ed., *Cartulaire de Cormery precède de l'histoire de l'abbaye, MSAT* (1861) 6–66; BN ms. Latin, coll. Anjou et Touraine, II/1 no. 10.

78. Mabillon *AB* IV, 108; Lester Little, "Formules monastiques de malédiction aux IXe et Xe siècle," *RM* 58.262 (1975): 377–99. See also Lester Little, *Benedictine Maledictions: Liturgical Cursing in Romanesque France.* The ritual humiliation of the saint's relics showed that they had been dishonored by the count's violation of sanctuary and that their miraculous power had thereby been diminished. "Humiliation" comes from the Latin word "humus," meaning "earth, soil, ground."

79. BN ms Latin coll. Anjou et Touraine, I, no. 228.

80. "Livre noir," ed. P. A. Marchegay, *Archives d'Anjou* (Angers: C. Labussière, 1843–54) I, no. 1.

81. BN ms latin, coll. Anjou et Touraine, II/1, no. 479.

82. Ibid., nos. 318, 450.

83. Bernard Chevalier, "Les restitutions d'église dans le diocèse de Tours du Xe au XIIe siècle," *Études de civilisation médiévale (IXe au XIIe siècles): Mélange offerts á Edmond-Réné Labande* (Poitiers: Centre d'études supérieures de civilisation médiévale, 1974), pp. 129–43; Guillaume Mollat, "La restitution des églises privées au patrimoine ecclésiastique en France du IXe au XIe siècle," *RHDFE* 27 (1948): 408ff.

84. Janet L. Nelson, review of Head and Landes, *The Peace of God,* in *Speculum* 69 (January 1994): 169.

85. Head, *Hagiography and the Cult of Saints,* 131–32. For examples from Touraine, see Sharon Farmer, *Communities of St. Martin* (Ithaca: Cornell University Press, 1991).

86. Susan A. Rabe, *Faith, Art, and Politics at Saint-Riquier* (Philadelphia: University of Pennsylvania Press, 1995), pp. 124–25.

87. Rudolf, Monk of Fulda, "The Life of St. Leoba," trans. C. H. Talbot, in *Medieval Women's Visionary Literature,* ed. Elizabeth Petroff (New York: Oxford University Press, 1986), pp. 107–8; also in *The Anglo-Saxon Missionaries in Germany* (New York: Sheed & Ward, 1954).

88. John of Salerno, "Life of St. Odo," I.8–9, trans. Sitwell, pp. 9–10; *PL* 133, c47–48.

89. "Vita Hervei," Martène, *Thesaurus* 3:1349–50.

90. See the articles by Johnson, Verdon, Skinner, and Feiss cited in note 54 above.

91. Pierre Gasnault and Henri Martin, "Les actes privées de l'abbaye de Saint-Martin de Tours du VIIIe au XIIe siècle," Bibliothèque de l'école de chartes, 112 (1954), pp. 64–65.

92. Chevalier, "Les restitutions d'église," pp. 129–43; Guillaume Mollat, "La réstitution des églises privées au patrimoine ecclésiastique en France du IXe au XIe siècle," *Revue historique de droit français et etranger* 27 (1948): 408ff.

93. Little, *Religious Poverty*, pp. 3–8; Johnson, *Prayer, Patronage and Power*, pp. 69–98; White, *Kinship, Custom.*

94. See note 76 above.

95. Landes and Lobbricon, "The Caroscuro of Heresy," *HR/RH* 14.3 (1987):467–512, 423–44, and *The Peace of God*, pp. 80–103, 184–218; Landes, *AESC* (1991): 573–93.

96. Mabillon *VA* 3.659; John of Salerno, "Life of St. Odo," trans. Sitwell, pp. 85–87; Oury, *RM* 54 (1964): 123.

97. Quoted in Poly and Bournazel, *The Feudal Transformation*, p. 143.

98. Chenu, *Nature, Man and Society*, p. 219.

99. Ibid., pp. 214–15, citing Peter Damian, "Contra clericos regulares proprietarios," VI, *PL* 145, c490.

2. A Call to Active Devotion

1. St. Bernard of Clairvaux similarly held up the possibility of going on crusade as a lay alternative to the monastic pursuit of perfection. See Jean Leclercq, "Saint Bernard's Attitude toward War," *Studies in Medieval Cistercian History* 2, ed. John R. Sommerfeldt, Cistercian Studies Series, no. 24 (Kalamazoo: Cistercian Publications, 1976), pp. 31–32.

2. See F. E. Peters, *Jerusalem: The Holy City in the Eyes of Chroniclers, Visitors, Pilgrims and Prophets from the Days of Abraham to the Beginnings of Modern Times* (Princeton: Princeton University Press, 1995).

3. Jean Dalby Clift and Wallace B. Clift, *The Archetype of Pilgrimage: Outer Action with Inner Meaning* (Mahwah, N.J.: Paulist Press, 1996), p. 10.

4. Ibid., p. 9.

5. Richard R. Niebuhr, "Pilgrims and Pioneers," *Parabola* (Fall 1984), pp. 7, 9; quoted in Clift, *Archetype of Pilgrimage*, pp. 1–2.

6. Clift, *Archetype of Pilgrimage*, pp. 42–61.

7. *The Book of Margery Kempe*, trans. B. A. Windeatt (London: Penguin Books, 1985), I.10, p. 57; I.15, p. 67. Margery always refers to herself in the third person singular, usually as "this creature."

8. Thomas Renna, "Jerusalem in Late Medieval Itineraria," in *Pilgrims and Travelers to the Holy Land*, ed. Bryan F. Le Beau and Menachem Mor, Studies in Jewish Civilization 7 (Omaha: Creighton University Press, 1996), pp. 124–26.

9. Jonathan Sumption, *Pilgrimage: An Image of Mediaeval Religion* (Totowa, N.J.: Rowman and Littlefield, 1975), p. 11.

10. Sumption assumes, moreover, that the majority of pilgrims were poor. The Jerusalem pilgrims who have left accounts, however, came not from the lowest social classes, but from the middle class and the nobility. Surely their lives were less constrained and monotonous than those of the peasantry.

11. Victor and Edith Turner, *Image and Pilgrimage in Christian Culture: Anthropological Perspectives* (New York: Columbia University Press, 1978), p. 2.

12. Turner distinguishes three types of *communitas:* (1) spontaneous and existential, (2) normative, and (3) ideological. The first two of these best describe the types of *communitas* formed during the liminal phase of pilgrimage. The third might well apply to an individual's response to pilgrimage after its completion, as he or she attempts to realize a utopian model. See Victor Turner, "The Center Out There: Pilgrim's Goal," *History of Religions* 12 (1973): 193–94.

13. Felix Fabri, *The Wanderings of Felix Fabri,* in *The Library of the Palestine Pilgrims' Text Society,* trans. Aubrey Stewart (London, 1893; rpt. New York: AMS Press, 1971), vols. 7–10.

14. Pietro Casola, *Canon Pietro Casola's Pilgrimage to Jerusalem in the Year 1494,* ed. and trans. Margaret M. Newett, Historical Series 5 (Manchester: Manchester University Press, 1907).

15. Ibid., p. 300.

16. Ibid., p. 161 n. 1.

17. Birgitta left Rome for Jerusalem in 1372, arriving in Holy Week and leaving in September. Ogier's journey took eighteen months. Margery was gone for about two years.

18. Kempe, *Book,* I.28, pp. 102–3.

19. *The Holy Jerusalem Voyage of Ogier VIII, Seigneur d'Anglure,* ed. and trans. Roland A. Browne (Gainesville: University Presses of Florida, 1975), p. 10.

20. Henri Gilles, *"Lex peregrinorum," Le Pèlerinage,* Cahiers de Fanjeaux 15, 165–75.

21. Casola, *Pilgrimage to Jerusalem,* p. 115.

22. *Lex peregrinorum,* 171–73.

23. Kempe, *Book,* I.26, p. 96.

24. *The Sarum Missal in English,* trans. Frederick E. Warren (London: Mowbray, 1913), 2:166–73.

25. Casola, *Pilgrimage to Jerusalem,* pp. 128–32.

26. Kempe, *Book,* I.28, pp. 102–3.

27. Casola, *Pilgrimage to Jerusalem,* pp. 155, 221.

28. Ibid., pp. 153–54.

29. Ibid., p. 70.

30. Ibid., pp. 198–99, 204–5.

31. Ibid., pp. 181–82, 305–6.

32. Ogier, *Holy Jerusalem Voyage,* pp. 73–74.

33. Casola, *Pilgrimage to Jerusalem,* p. 223, and n. 1. Two other travelers who left accounts of the same voyage called him a Dane, Lorenz Heughlin.

34. Jonathan Riley-Smith, *The Knights of St. John in Jerusalem and Cyrus, c. 1050–1310* (New York: Macmillan-St. Martin's Press, 1967), pp. 332–33. The order of St. John based its existence on caring for and later protecting pilgrims.

35. Ogier, *Holy Jerusalem Voyage,* pp. 71–72.

36. Kempe, *Book,* I.28, p. 103.

37. Aron Andersson, *St. Birgitta and the Holy Land* (Stockholm: The Museum of National Antiquities, 1973), p. 28.

38. Ibid., p. 30.

39. Casola, *Pilgrimage to Jerusalem,* pp. 221–22.

40. Ogier, *Holy Jerusalem Voyage,* p. 23.

41. Ibid., p. 41.

42. Andersson, *St. Birgitta and the Holy Land,* p. 68. Subsequent citations from this source are given parenthetically by page.

43. Casola, *Pilgrimage to Jerusalem,* p. 278.

44. Kempe, *Book,* I.28, p. 104.

45. Andersson, *St. Birgitta and the Holy Land,* pp. 30–32.

46. Kempe, *Book,* I.30, p. 111.

47. Ibid.

48. Kempe, *Book,* I.30, p. 110.

49. Ibid., p. 111.

50. Ogier, *Holy Jerusalem Voyage,* p. 82.

51. Casola, *Pilgrimage to Jerusalem,* p. 345.

52. Ogier, *Holy Jerusalem Voyage,* p. 82.

53. Julia Bolton Holloway, *St. Bride and Her Book: Birgitta of Sweden's Revelations* (Newburyport, Mass.: Focus Texts, 1992), pp. 113–19.

54. Quoted in Andersson, *St. Birgitta and the Holy Land,* p. 8.

55. Quoted in Clift, *Archetype of Pilgrimage,* p. 2.

3. Angela of Foligno

1. Francis of Assisi died in 1226; Clare of Assisi, in 1253. Angela of Foligno was probably professed as a Franciscan tertiary in 1291. She lived through the early stages of the debates over poverty in which her spiritual son, Angelo of Clareno, was a central figure. Her lifetime saw, as well, papal efforts to enclose women religious, to license preachers, to control popular devotion to saints, and to involve lay Christians more deeply in the sacramental life of the Church. See Paul LaChance, Introduction, *Angela of Foligno: Complete Works,* trans. Paul LaChance, Classics of Western Spirituality Series (New York: Paulist Press, 1993), pp. 15–117.

2. See my "Angela of Foligno: Destructuring and Restructuring of Identity," in *Divine Representations: Postmodernism and Spirituality,* ed. Ann W. Astell (New York: Paulist Press, 1994), pp. 47–62.

3. See, for example, the sixteenth-century Umbrian sculpture used to illustrate the cover of the 1993 Paulist Press edition of Angela's *Complete Works.*

4. *Angela of Foligno: Complete Works,* p. 317. Hereafter citations are par-

enthetical by page. For the critical edition of the *Book* in Latin and Italian, see *Il Libro della Beata Angela da Foligno,* ed. Ludger Thier and Abele Calufetti, O.F.M. (Grottaferrata, Rome: Editiones Collegii S. Bonaventurae ad Claras Aquas, 1985).

5. Lawrence Cunningham, *The Meaning of Saints* (San Francisco: Harper and Row, 1980), p. 4.

6. St. Francis, "Admonition I," in *Francis and Clare: The Complete Works,* ed. and trans. Regis Armstrong and Ignatius Brady (New York: Paulist Press, 1982), pp. 25–27.

7. Ibid., p. 70.

8. On the importance of the Franciscan ideal of poverty in its societal context, see Lester K. Little, *Religious Poverty and the Profit Economy in Medieval Europe* (Ithaca: Cornell University Press, 1978).

9. Paul LaChance, *The Mystical Journey of Angela of Foligno* (Toronto: Peregrina, 1990), p. 71.

10. Cunningham, *Meaning of Saints,* p. 65. Angela is recognized as "blessed" in the Roman canon of saints—that is, as qualified for a local cult. The "saint" is canonically defined as being of importance for the universal church.

11. Edith Wyschogrod, *Saints and Postmodernism: Revisioning Moral Philosophy* (Chicago: University of Chicago Press, 1990), p. xxiii.

12. Caroline Walker Bynum, *Holy Feast and Holy Fast: The Religious Significance of Food to Medieval Women* (Berkeley: University of California Press, 1987), p. 236.

13. Ibid. For an interesting discussion of "sacramental strategies," see Jo Ann McNamara, "The Rhetoric of Orthodoxy: Clerical Authority and Female Innovation in the Struggle with Heresy," in *Maps of Flesh and Light: The Religious Experience of Medieval Women Mystics,* ed. Ulrike Wiethaus (Syracuse: Syracuse University Press, 1993), pp. 9–27.

14. Bynum, *Holy Feast,* pp. 144–45. See also Caroline Walker Bynum, *Fragmentation and Redemption: Essays on Gender and the Human Body in Medieval Religion* (New York: Zone Books, 1992), pp. 129–32, 136–38.

15. On the question of authorship and the role of Brother Arnaldo, see Catherine Mooney, "The Authorial Role of Brother A. in the Composition of Angela of Foligno's Revelations," in *Creative Women in Medieval and Early Modern Italy,* ed. E. Ann Matter and John Coakley (Philadelphia: University of Pennsylvania Press, 1994). For a related study, see John Coakley, "Friars as Confidants of Holy Women in Medieval Dominican Hagiography," in *Images of Sainthood in Medieval Europe,* ed. R. Blumenfeld-Kosinski and T. Sell (Ithaca: Cornell University Press, 1991), pp. 222–46.

16. On the meaning of the elevation, see Miri Rubin, *Corpus Christi: The Eucharist in Late Medieval Culture* (Cambridge: Cambridge University Press, 1992), pp. 54–63.

17. See Elizabeth A. Petroff, *Body and Soul: Essays on Medieval Women and Mysticism* (New York: Oxford University Press, 1994).

18. Bynum, *Holy Feast,* p. 144.

19. LaChance, Introduction, in *Complete Works,* p. 88.

20. Bynum, *Holy Feast,* p. 233. For exceptions to this rule, however, see pp. 230–32.

21. Bynum, *Holy Feast,* p. 235.

22. St. Francis highlighted the importance of the institutional church in the person of the ordained ministers, the priests, who could consecrate bread and wine as the body and blood of Jesus Christ: "God inspires me . . . with such great faith in priests. . . . I am determined to reverence, love and honour priests . . . because in this world I cannot see the most high Son of God with my own eyes except for his most holy Body and Blood which they . . . alone administer to others" (*The Testament of St. Francis,* in Marion Habig, ed., *English Omnibus of the Sources for the Life of St. Francis* [Chicago: Franciscan Herald Press, 1973], p. 67).

23. Bynum, *Fragmentation and Redemption,* pp. 136–37. See also Bynum, *Holy Feast,* p. 235.

24. Bynum, *Holy Feast,* p. 229.

25. The first six supplemental steps are a deepening awareness of her own sinfulness, a dissatisfaction with her ordinary life. The first stage of mysticism, as outlined by St. Bonaventure, theologian, mystic and minister general of the Friars Minor, is purgation; the second, illumination; and the third, union. See St. Bonaventure, "The Triple Way," *Mystical Opuscula, The Works of Bonaventure,* vol. I (Paterson: St. Anthony Guild Press, 1960), p. 63. Bonaventure's classic description of the spiritual journey is his *Itinerarium Mentis ad Deum* (The Soul's Journey to God) in which he describes "six . . . steps to pass over to peace through the ecstatic transports of Christian wisdom. The road to this peace is nothing else than a most ardent love of the Crucified. . . . No one can enter through contemplation into the heavenly Jerusalem unless he enters through the blood of the Lamb." See *Bonaventure: The Journey of the Mind to God,* trans. Philotheus Boehner, ed. Stephen Brown (Indianapolis: Hackett, 1993), pp. 1–2. Bonaventure's *Journey* ends: "Let us die and enter into this darkness" (p. 39).

26. Angela probably experienced this third transformation sometime between early 1294 and late summer 1296, but a vision that dates from July 31–August 2, 1300, displays similar features and may record the same experience. See *Complete Works,* pp. 382 n. 118, 401 n. 56, and 402 n. 58. The sixth and seventh steps overlap. There is an oscillation between an awareness of God's presence and God's absence, and Angela uses the topos of darkness to refer both to the experience of being abandoned and of abandonment to the divine presence. On the use of the darkness topos, see LaChance, *The Spiritual Journey,* pp. 242–99, 300–369.

27. LaChance, Introduction, in *Complete Works,* p. 76.

28. Instructions 30 and 32 are the clearest theological statements about the Eucharist in Angela's *Book.* They pose serious questions about editorial interference, however, because the language is much more scholastic and technical than the language of any other part of the *Book.* See pp. 290–99 in *Complete Works.*

29. Aviad M. Kleinberg, *Prophets in Their Own Country* (Chicago: University

of Chicago Press, 1992) approaches the question of "living saints" in the context of the mutual dependence of saints and their followers, an approach which makes clear the implications of stories like Angela's for an ecclesiology which takes seriously the identity of the church as the communion of saints. His discussion of Angela focuses on the relationship between Angela and Brother Arnaldo (pp. 46–50).

30. According to Bynum, the Eucharist was a symbol of "life, birth, and nursing"; the flesh of Jesus "did womanly things" which come together in the Eucharist: "it bled, it bled food, and it gave birth" (*Fragmentation*, pp. 42, 101).

31. André Vauchez, *The Laity in the Middle Ages: Religious Beliefs and Devotional Practices,* ed. Daniel Bornstein, trans. M. J. Schneider (Notre Dame: University of Notre Dame Press, 1993), p. 264.

4. Catherine of Siena

1. Conference held in May 1986 at the University of Florence, organized by Roberto Rusconi. For similar language, see Vittorio Coletti, *Parole dal pulpito: Chiesa e movimenti religiosi tra latino e volgare* (Casale Monferrato: Marietti, 1983).

2. André Vauchez, *The Laity in the Middle Ages: Religious Beliefs and Devotional Practices,* ed. Daniel E. Bornstein, trans. Margery J. Schneider (Notre Dame: University of Notre Dame Press, 1993), pp. xv–xvi.

3. Most recently, see Guy Lobrichon, *La religion des laics en Occident, XIe–XVe siècles* (Paris: Hachette, 1994). Lobrichon is "Persuadé que la 'religion des laics' n'a de realité que dans le compromis et dans la *friction perpétuelle* avec la doctrine voulue et répandue par les ecclésiastiques" (p. 26; emphasis mine). He also speaks of a "corset rassurant" (p. 44) provided to the laity by the medieval clergy.

4. Donald Weinstein and Rudolph M. Bell, *Saints and Society: Christendom, 1000–1700* (Chicago: University of Chicago Press, 1982), p. 204.

5. André Vauchez, "A Twelfth-Century Novelty: The Lay Saints of Urban Italy," in *The Laity in the Middle Ages,* 51–72, and "Mystical Sanctity at the Time of the Avignon Papacy and the Great Schism," 231–42.

6. Guy Lobrichon, *La religion des laics en occident,* p. 187.

7. Caroline Walker Bynum, *Holy Feast and Holy Fast: The Religious Significance of Food to Medieval Women* (Berkeley: University of California Press, 1987).

8. S. Caterina da Siena, *Il Dialogo della divina provvidenza ovvero Libro della divina dottrina,* ed. Giuliana Cavallini (Rome: Edizioni cateriniane, 1980), cited hereafter as *Dialogo.* All translations quoted in this article are my own. The most recent English translation is *The Dialogue,* trans. Suzanne Noffke (New York: Paulist Press, 1980).

9. *Le Lettere di S. Caterina da Siena,* ed. Piero Misciatelli (Florence: Giunti, 1940), 6 vols., cited hereafter as *Lettere.*

10. Richard C. Trexler's *Public Life in Renaissance Florence* (Ithaca: Cornell University Press, 1980) calls Catherine a "holy nun" (p. 349); Shulamith Shahar's *The Fourth Estate: A History of Women in the Middle Ages,* trans. Chaya Galai (1983; London and New York: Routledge, 1990) calls her a "canonness";

Anne Llewllyn Barstow's *Joan of Arc: Heretic, Mystic, Shaman* (Lewiston: Edwin Mellen, 1986) contrasts Catherine's convent life as a nun with Joan's lay status; and Guy Lobrichon's *La religion des laics en occident* calls the Dominican Third Order to which Catherine belonged a "cadre monastique" (p. 176).

11. Raymond of Capua's *vita* of Catherine of Siena, usually called the *Legenda Major*, is published under the title of *De S. Catharina Senensi virgine de poenitentia S. Dominici* in *Acta Sanctorum Aprilis*, vol. 3 (Antwerp, 1675). Cited hereafter as *Legenda*, with the paragraph number. See paragraph 35.

12. *Legenda*, 69.

13. *Legenda*, 74–76.

14. *Legenda*, 71: "Cum enim Sorores illae careant omni clausura, quia quaelibet stat in domo propria, necesse omnino est, quod quaelibet sciat se regere per se ipsam"; 80: "Sancta virgo tria principalia religionis non emiserit vota (quia, ut dictum est, hoc in se status ille non habet)."

15. *Legenda*, 77–79.

16. Letter 219, in *Lettere*, vol. 3, p. 268: "E crescendo in me il fuoco, mirando vedevo nel costato di Cristo intrare 'l popolo cristiano e lo infedele: e io passavo, per desiderio e affetto d'amore, per lo mezzo di loro; ed entravo con loro in Cristo dolce Gesù, accompagnata col padre mio santo Domenico, e Giovanni Singolare con tutti quanti i figliuoli miei. E allora mi dava la croce in collo e l'olivo in mano, quasi come io volessi, e così diceva, che io la portasse all'uno popolo e all'altro. E diceva a me: 'Di' a loro: io vi annunzio gaudio magno'. Allora l'anima mia più s'empiva; annegata era co'veri gustatori della divina Essenzia per unione e affetto d'amore."

17. *Dialogo* 21–27, pp. 49–62.

18. *Dialogo* 23, pp. 51–52.

19. *Dialogo* 24, pp. 55–56: "Si che vedi che tutti v'o messi per lavoratori. Ed ora di nuovo v'invito, perchè il mondo già viene meno, tanto sono multiplicate le spine che anno affocato il seme, in tanto che niuno frutto di grazia vogliono fare. Voglio dunque che siate lavoratori veri, che con molta sollicitudine aitiate a lavorare l'anime nel corpo mistico della santa Chiesa. A questo v'eleggo, perchè Io voglio fare misericordia al mondo, per il quale tu tanto mi prieghi."

20. *Dialogo* 148, p. 422: "Unde acciò che in atto e in affetto usaste la carità... providi di non dare a uno uomo, e a ogni uno a se medesimo, il sapere fare quello che bisogna in tutto alla vita de l'uomo; ma chi n'a uno e chi n'a un'altro, acciò che l'uno abbi materia per suo bisogno di ricorrire a l'altro. Unde tu vedi che l'artefice ricorre al lavoratore e il lavoratore a l'artefice: l'uno a bisogno de l'altro, perchè non sa fare quello, l'uno, che l'altro. Così il cherico e il religioso a bisogno del secolare, e il secolare del religioso; e l'uno non può fare senza l'altro. E così d'ogni altra cosa. E non potevo Io dare a ogni uno tutto? Si bene, ma volsi con providenzia che s'aumiliasse l'uno a l'altro, e costretti fussero di usare l'atto e l'affetto della carità insieme."

21. See my "*Io Catarina*': Ecclesiastical Politics and Oral Culture in the Letters of Catherine of Siena," in *Dear Sister: Medieval Women and the Epistolary Genre*, ed. Karen Cherewatuk and Ulrike Wiethaus (Philadelphia: University of Pennsylvania Press, 1993), pp. 99–102.

22. See for example Letter 207 in *Lettere,* vol. 3, pp. 206–11.

23. Letter 196, in *Lettere,* vol. 3, p. 162: "E io cognosco e so che a tutti in comune lor pare aver male fatto; e poniamoche scusa non abbino nel male adoperare, nondimeno, per le molte pene e cose ingiuste e inique che sostenevano per cagione de'mali pastori e governatori, lor pareva non potere fare altro. Perocchè sentendo il puzzo della vita di molti rettori, e'quali sapete che sono demoni incarnati, vennero in tanto pessimo timore, che fecero come Pilato, il quale per non perdere la signoria, uccise Cristo: e così fecero essi, che per non perdere lo stato, vi hanno perseguitato. Misericordia adunque, padre, v'addimando per loro. . . . rendete pace a noi miseri figliuoli che abbiamo offeso."

24. *Legenda,* 35, 47, 114–17.

25. *Legenda,* 80, 64–65.

26. *Legenda,* 118–22. See also my "St. Catherine of Siena, 'Apostola'," *Church History* 61 (April 1992): 34–46, esp. 44–45.

27. *Legenda,* 239.

28. Lidia Bianchi and Diega Giunta, *Iconografia di S. Caterina da Siena. I. L'immagine* (Rome: Città Nuova Editrice, 1988), esp. 150–51.

5. Margery Kempe

1. Aviad Kleinberg, *Prophets in Their Own Country: Living Saints and the Making of Sainthood in the Later Middle Ages* (Chicago: University of Chicago Press, 1992), pp. 149–50.

2. Margery Kempe, *The Book of Margery Kempe: The Text from the Unique MS. Owned by Colonel W. Butler-Bowden,* ed. Sanford B. Meech with Hope Emily Allen, EETS o.s. 212 (London: Oxford University Press, 1940), I.28.22–28, p. 69. I use this edition throughout, giving book, chapter, line, and page numbers parenthetically. For a modern translation, see *The Book of Margery Kempe,* trans. B. A. Windeatt (New York: Penguin, 1985).

3. De Worde's publication is entitled *A short treatyse of contemplacyon taught by our lord Ihesu cryste, or taken out of the boke of Margerie kempe of Lynn.*

4. The diagnosis of clinical hysteria was first made by H. Thurston, S.J., in his 1936 review of Colonel Butler-Bowden's modernised *Book of Margery Kempe.* For a Freudian approach to Kempe, see Nancy Partner, "Reading the Book of Margery Kempe," *Exemplaria* 3.1 (1991): 29–66.

5. R. W. Chambers, Introduction, *The Book of Margery Kempe,* ed. and trans. W. Butler-Bowden (New York: Devin-Adair, 1944), p. xviii.

6. Sarah Beckwith, "A Very Material Mysticism: The Medieval Mysticism of Margery Kempe," in *Medieval Literature: Criticism, Ideology, and History,* ed. David Aers (New York: St. Martin's Press, 1986), p. 38.

7. Bernard McGinn, *The Presence of God: A History of Western Christian Mysticism* (New York: Crossroad, 1991), vol. 1, p. 30.

8. Ibid., pp. xix, xviii.

9. F. C. Happold, *Mysticism: A Study and Anthology* (Baltimore: Penguin, 1963), p. 100.

10. Clarissa Atkinson, *Mystic and Pilgrim: The Book and World of Margery Kempe* (Ithaca: Cornell University Press, 1983), pp. 40–41.

11. In terming Margery's *Book* "autobiographical," I do not wish, of course, to overlook the complications raised by her dependence on scribes and their part in its authorship. See John C. Hirsch, "Author and Scribe in *The Book of Margery Kempe*," *Medium Aevum* 44 (1975): 145–50.

12. See Atkinson, *Mystic and Pilgrim*, p. 24. Atkinson develops the mirror imagery at some length.

13. The late-medieval *imitatio Christi* gained a rich variety of expressions. It is commonly, but by no means exclusively, associated with the *devotio moderna* promoted by the Brethren of the Common Life, a community with both lay and clerical members that was founded in the Netherlands by Gerard Groote (1340–84). The spirit animating the Brethren gains classic expression in *The Imitation of Christ* by Margery's close contemporary, Thomas à Kempis (1380–1471). Other continental figures who invite comparison with Kempe include Bd. Mary of Oignes, Bd. Dorothea von Montau, St. Bridget of Sweden, St. Frances of Rome, and St. Elizabeth of Hungary. For more information on continental associations with Kempe, see Susan Dickman, "Margery Kempe and the Continental Tradition of the Pious Woman," *The Medieval Mystical Tradition in England: Papers Read at Darlington Hall, July 1984*, ed. Marion Glasscoe, (Exeter: Short Run Press): 150–68; Valerie Lagorio, "*Defensorium Contra Oblectratores:* A 'Discerning' Assessment of Margery Kempe," in *Mysticism: Medieval and Modern*, ed. Valerie Lagorio (Salzburg: University of Salzburg Press), 1986, pp. 29–48; and Ute Stargardt, "The Beguines of Belgium, the Dominican Nuns of Germany, and Margery Kempe," *The Popular Literature of Medieval England* (Knoxville: University of Tennessee Press, 1985), pp. 277–313.

14. Underhill maintains that we should examine the mystic's whole life to determine, by preponderance of evidence, whether one lives the mystic way: "By the superhuman nature of that which these persons accomplish, we can gauge something of the supernormal vitality of which they partake. The things done, the victories gained over circumstances by St. Bernard or St. Joan of Arc, by St. Catharine of Siena, St. Ignatius . . . are hardly to be explained unless [they] had indeed a closer . . . contact than their fellows with that Life 'which is the light of men'" (*Mysticism: A Study in the Nature and Development of Man's Spiritual Consciousness* [New York: Penguin, 1955], p. 414).

15. Janel M. Mueller, "Autobiography of a New 'Creatur': Female Spirituality, Selfhood, and Authorship in *The Book of Margery Kempe*," in *The Female Autograph: Theory and Practice of Autobiography From the Tenth To the Twentieth Century*, ed. Domna C. Stanton (Chicago: University of Chicago Press, 1984), p. 68, n. 5.

16. Karma Lochrie, *Margery Kempe and Translations of the Flesh*, (Philadelphia: University of Pennsylvania Press, 1991). See also Lynn Staley, *Margery Kempe's Dissenting Fictions* (University Park: Pennsylvania State University Press, 1994).

17. For the significance of a symbolic change of clothes, see Dyan H. Elliott, *Spiritual Marriage: Sexual Abstinence in Medieval Wedlock* (Princeton: Princeton University Press, 1993).

18. See Meech and Allen, ed., *The Book of Margery Kempe,* specifically end-notes 116/12 (p. 311) and 124/13 (p. 314), in which Allen observes that the mayor of Leceister's concerns were, in fact, well-founded. The *Albi* or *Bianchi* were a flagellant sect that wrapped themselves head-to-toe in white linen: "gentz vestuz de Blanche Vestûre et soi pretendantz de grande seintetee." They wandered from town to town, and managed to secure a large following of people. Notices warning authorities of this sect had been posted in 1399 by order of Henry IV. See Daniel Bornstein, *The Bianchi of 1399: Popular Devotion in Late Medieval Italy* (Ithaca: Cornell University Press, 1994).

19. Roberta Bux Bosse, "Female Sexual Behavior in the Late Middle Ages: Ideal and Actual," *Fifteenth-Century Studies* 10 (1984): 21. Many scholars assume that the "secret sin" Kempe would not divulge when she was seriously ill after the birth of her first child was sexual in nature.

20. See Nancy Partner, "Reading the Book of Margery Kempe," and Hope Phyllis Weissman, "Margery Kempe in Jerusalem: *Hysterica Compassio* in the Late Middle Ages," in *Interpretation: The Text in Its Context, 700–1600: Essays in Honor of E. Talbot Donaldson* (Norman: Pilgrim Books, 1982), pp. 201–17.

21. Caroline Walker Bynum, *Holy Feast and Holy Fast: The Religious Significance of Food to Medieval Women* (Berkeley: University of California Press, 1987), p. 144.

22. Deborah Sue Ellis, "Margery Kempe and the Virgin's Hot Caudle," *Essays in Arts and Sciences* 15 (1985): 1–11. Ellis notes: "Her very pettiness, neurosis, and illiteracy give her *Book* much of its stylistic value" (p. 1).

23. Denise Despres, "Franciscan Spirituality: Margery Kempe and Visual Meditation," *Mystics Quarterly* 11.1 (1985): 12–18, discusses the influence of Franciscan contemplative techniques on devotional life in England.

24. See especially Mueller, "Autobiography of a New 'Creatur.'"

6. The Pious Infant

1. Although the recognition of miracles was a part of the canonization process, an increasing emphasis was placed upon piety and good works. In addition, the formal canonization process favored postulants for the saint's cause with ties to or influence over the ecclesiastical bureaucracy. Thus candidates for sanctity, both successful and unsuccessful, became increasingly associated with established religious orders and subjected to more rigorous scrutiny before the recognition of divine favor. André Vauchez, *La Sainteté en Occident aux derniers siècles du Moyen Age* (Rome: Ecole Française de Rome, 1981), pp. 25–30. Vauchez traces the origins of pontifical involvement in the canonization process from the papal bull of Pope John XV issued in 993 in the case of Bishop Ulrich of Augsburg. The cult of the saints, however, was of only minor concern to the papacy until the later twelfth century; Innocent III was especially influential in extending papal control of the recognition of sanctity on a widespread scale. The canonization process was not finalized in its present form until the pontificate of Pope Urban VIII (1623–44); at that time, all candidates for canonization who were not martyrs were required to demonstrate doctrinal purity,

heroic virtue, and miraculous intercession after death. Donald Weinstein and Rudolph Bell, *Saints and Society: The Two Worlds of Western Christendom, 1000–1700* (Chicago: University of Chicago Press, 1982), p. 141.

2. Beggars, peasants, and other disenfranchised members of society, as well as children, fall into the category of "marginal" saints whose veneration exemplifies a representation of "universal values" (Gábor Klaniczay, *The Uses of Supernatural Power,* trans. Susan Singerman [Princeton: Princeton University Press, 1990], p. 15). For a more detailed discussion of the marginal qualities of children, see Anna Benvenuti Papi and Elena Giannarelli, "Santi Bambini, Santi da Bambini," in *Bambini Santi: rappresentazioni dell'infanzia e modelli agiographici,* ed. Anna Benvenuti Papi and Elena Giannarelli (Turin: Rosenberg and Sellier, 1991), pp. 7–8. Although the formation of popular cults did not entirely disappear, their number was drastically reduced. The cults of such "popular" saints tended to be extremely limited in appeal, and usually confined to a small area. Such saints, whether male or female, adult or child, shared the characteristic of suffering a horribly violent and undeserved death. See Vauchez, *La Sainteté,* pp. 173–83.

3. The motif of the *puer senex* was not created by the Christians, but rather adapted and applied in hagiographical writings to both child martyrs and to childhood behavior in the lives of adult saints. See Thomas Wiedemann, *Adults and Children in the Roman Empire* (New Haven: Yale University Press, 1989), p. 98. The adaptation of the *puer senex* motif as a hagiographical topos has been seen as a manifestation of the theme of spiritual transcendence over the natural behavior of the age of *pueritia,* and was used in the vitae of many saints over the centuries. See J. A. Burrow, *the Ages of Man: A Study in Medieval Writing and Thought* (Oxford: Oxford University Press, 1988), pp. 94–95.

4. *AASS* Jun. III, 24.

5. These saints are generally martyred princes, such as Kenelm, Wistan, Melor, or Edward, but also include Reginswinde of Lauffen and a servant girl named Tanca. Such children are nearly always of royal or noble blood. D. W. Rollason ("The Cults of Murdered Royal Saints in Anglo-Saxon England," *Anglo-Saxon England* 11 [1982]: 1–22) provides the most comprehensive treatment of English child martyrs, but includes them within a larger group of royal murder victims and fails to attribute special significance to the youth of the child martyrs.

6. In the mid-eleventh century, elements of religious behavior were added to the story of the murder of St. Kenelm. A work entitled "De Infantia Sancti Edmundi," dating from the mid-twelfth century, emphasized the precocious piety of the youthful murder victim. Compositions dating from the pontificate of Innocent III show an even greater concern for religious themes. A vita of St. Wistan dating from the late twelfth or early thirteenth century depicts him as a martyred innocent who had refused to accept the throne at his father's death for religious reasons. See Susan Ridyard, *The Royal Saints of Anglo-Saxon England: A Study of West Saxon and East Anglian Cults* (Cambridge: Cambridge University Press, 1988), pp. 244–45.

7. Saints such as Catherine of Siena and Anthony of Padua supposedly

practiced piety, asceticism, and charity from an early age. For Catherine of Siena, who exhorted her little playmates to flagellate themselves along with her, as well as other examples, see Weinstein and Bell, *Saints and Society*, pp. 38–39. For Anthony of Padua and others, see Michael Goodich, "Childhood and Adolescence among the Thirteenth-Century Saints," *History of Childhood Quarterly* 1 (1978): 287–88.

The motif of the *puer senex* was thus reinstated in the hagiographical tradition, but in a more comprehensive and naturalistic manner than was seen in late antiquity, since examples of behavior in childhood tended to encompass a greater range of instances and experiences than the earlier formulaic invocations of the motif. See Vauchez, *La Sainteté*, pp. 593–95.

8. Peter Abelard, "In Festo SS. Innocentum," *Hymnarius Paraclithensis, Text and Notes*, ed. Joseph Szövérffy (Albany: Classica Folia Editions, 1975), pp. 214–17.

9. Bernard of Clairvaux, "Sermo in nativitate Innocentum," *Opera Omnia, PL* 183, 129–32.

10. Jacobus de Voragine, *Legenda Aurea*, ed. Th. Graesse (Leipzig: Impensis Librariae Arnoldianae, 1850), pp. 62–66.

11. Edward F. Rimbault, "Two Sermons Preached by the Boy Bishop," *The Camden Miscellany*, n.s. 14 (1875): vi–x.

12. Aelred of Rievaulx composed a work on "Jesus at the Age of Twelve." See David Herlihy, "Medieval Childhood," in *Essays on Medieval Civilization*, ed. Bede Karl Lackner and Kenneth Ray Philip (Austin: University of Texas Press, 1978), p. 127. Bernard of Clairvaux used the infant Jesus as an example of the purity of childhood for all faithful Christians to emulate. See *In Conversione S. Pauli Sermo 2, PL* 183, 365.

13. Shulamith Shahar, *Childhood in the Middle Ages* (London: Routledge, 1990), pp. 13–14, 18.

14. Bartholomeus Anglicus described examples of behavior in children which, while unarguably naturalistic, did little to promote the child as a creature of either supreme innocence or superior morality (*De proprietibus rerum* VI. 5–6). Vincent of Beauvais produced a treatise on child care derived from the works of Avicenna, which addressed issues of health and education. Ramon Lull composed the *Doctrina pueril*, which was quickly translated from Catalan into French and Latin for an interested lay audience. These three authors are the most well-known of a tradition dating from the twelfth century. See David Herlihy, "Medieval Childhood," pp. 124–27.

15. The ongoing debate over the ability of children to act in the moral capacity of adults, which had been generally decided in the negative, provided the most significant barrier to the recognition of children as saints in this period. Although many adult saints were reported to have behaved piously as children, virtually no children died after exhibiting such noteworthy behavior. More pragmatic concerns also contributed to the exclusion of children. The ecclesiastical affiliations which had become so important to the promotion of saints during the canonization process were generally not available to children. The practice of monastic oblation had been discouraged by a number of factors,

including the Gregorian reform movement, a growth in population which increased the ranks of adult recruits, and a shift in religious outlook which stressed the importance of free choice in the acceptance of monastic vows. The number of children involved in monastic life declined steadily throughout the eleventh and twelfth centuries, and had virtually disappeared by 1300. See Patricia Quinn, *Better than the Sons of Kings: Boys and Monks in the Early Middle Ages* (New York: Peter Lang, 1989), pp. 195–202. On the other hand, Goodich, *Childhood* (pp. 289–91), sees the continuation of a form of oblation in exposing children to church careers through the agency of an ecclesiastical uncle. Of the thirteenth-century saints whose age at the profession of vocation is known, 25 percent were either oblates or may have been raised in a monastic setting.

16. This does not count the approximately thirty-five alleged victims of Jewish ritual murder venerated as saints from 1144 to the sixteenth century. More will be said about these cases later.

17. This group would also include the legends of earlier child saints which underwent modification in this period to accentuate the pious qualities of the subjects over the circumstances of violent death, and the alleged victims of ritual murder, who were often depicted as being "singled out" by the Jews for their conspicuously pious behavior.

18. *AASS* Jun. I, 237. See also Weinstein and Bell, *Saints and Society,* p. 60.

19. He was joined in his adventures by a monk named Bartholomew, who remained by his side. See Migne, *Dictionnaire Hagiographique,* 2:558.

20. *AASS* Jun. I, 239.

21. Ibid., pp. 247–52, for miracles, canonization, and translation to church built in his honor.

22. Nicholas is by no means the only saint to endure doubts of his sanity. Christina the Astonishing (1150–1224), who flew to the tops of trees and climbed into ovens to escape the odor of human sin, faced similar accusations of insanity by those unconvinced of her holiness. St. Catherine of Siena (1347–80), who began to receive mystical experiences at the age of six, faced accusations of fakery which, however, may have been engendered by her habit of criticizing powerful officials. Public doubt of the sanity of Margery Kempe was at least one significant factor in her failure to achieve sanctity.

23. She was, however, referred to as "puella" rather than "virgo" by Innocent IV, and by the author of her vita; *AASS* Sept. II, pp. 417, 433.

24. Ibid., p. 434.

25. Ibid., p. 440; like St. Francis and his sister, Rose was of bourgeois background, and exhibited a similar repugnance for material possessions. See Vauchez, *La Sainteté,* p. 27.

26. She was said to have predicted the death of Frederick II, and had, at the age of seven, preached against the submission of Gregory IX to Frederick (*AASS,* Sept. II, p. 437).

27. Ibid., p. 434. The canonization process for Rose of Viterbo was instituted soon after her death, in 1252 by Innocent IV. Lists of posthumous miracles were compiled, her vita was composed, and her body examined and found to be miraculously incorrupt. The process was not successfully concluded, how-

ever, until 1457 by Pope Callistus III. See Vauchez, *La Sainteté*, p. 297. Certainly a pivotal ingredient in the official success of her cult, if not its popular appeal, was her affiliation with an established religious order. Her popularity during her lifetime, as well as her posthumous reputation and eventual canonization, was much advanced by the efforts of the Franciscans. The majority of her posthumous cures seems to have been directed at children and women. She favored the latter group with, among other benefits, the restoration of beloved husbands and children to life, and was also evoked in cases of difficult pregnancy (*AASS* Sept. II, pp. 445–76).

28. Ibid., p. 442.

29. Ibid., p. 434: "Quae Virgo tanta omnipotis Dei gratia surfulta, cum in eius pueritia cum aliis puellis se conferret ad fontem cum amfora pro aqua exhaurienda, ut moris est, & uni illarum puellarum amfora, quam portabat, rumperetur & in plurima frusta divideretur, increpata ab eius parentibus, prou puella praefata falso retuleral, quod B. Roas huic casui more puellarum praestiterat occasionem; accesserunt ad locum, ubi amfora rupta erat, & eius frustis & particulis simul reductis, meruit Virgo praefata, ut omnipotens Deus eius potentiam demonstraverit super eam, ut to frusta hinc inde conspersa & divisa, ad proprium locum eorum reducerentur, acsi numquam rupta fuisset. Et sic amfora puellae restituta est integra & sana. . . ."

30. Ibid., p. 434. Effort was also made by the author of the vita to appeal to the tradition of child saints and to the childhood of other saints. Rose was compared in her infancy to John the Baptist, who worshipped Jesus while he was still in the womb, and St. Nicholas, who stood upright in his baptismal font and refused to nurse on fast days. The name of St. Agnes was also invoked.

31. An anonymously authored vita appeared one year and three months after his death, and the process of beatification, attempted four times before its successful completion in 1527, was first begun in 1389. Peter's father, Guy of Luxembourg, died in 1371, and his mother, Mathilda of Châtillon, died in 1373. He was then educated by his aunt, Giovanna of Châtillon. His professional career began at the age of eight, when he was appointed a canon in the cathedral of Paris by the antipope Clement in 1378. Clement seems to have been a strong patron of the child, naming him a canon of Cambrai in 1382. Peter became bishop of Metz in 1384, at the age of fourteen, and in the same year cardinal deacon of the church of St. George in Velabro. At this point, Peter's career stalled, caught in the battle between pope and antipope; this controversy also tainted the first several attempts at beatification in 1389, 1390, 1433, and 1435. In contrast to Rose of Viterbo and other saints with affiliations to mendicant orders, Peter was aligned with the secular clergy, but his cause was promoted by political patronage; papal investigation into claims of Peter's sanctity was solicited in 1389 by Pierre d'Ailly, in the name of Charles VI. Despite numerous investigations, and the odor of sanctity exuded by his corpse, Peter was never formally canonized. See Vauchez, *La Sainteté*, p. 94; *AASS* Jul. I, p. 516.

32. *AASS* Jul. I, pp. 509–10.

33. *Enciclopedia Cattolica* (Vatican City: Ente per l'Eciclopedia Cattolica e per il Libro Cattolico, 1948–54), vol. 3, cols. 587–89.

34. *AASS* Jul. I, pp. 565–628.

35. *AASS* Maii III, pp. 183–84.

36. *Bibliotheca Sanctorum* (Rome: Instituto Giovanni XXIII della Pontificia università lateranense, 1961–70). Also see *AASS*.

37. J. N. D. Kelly, *The Oxford Dictionary of Popes* (Oxford: Oxford University Press, 1986), pp. 296–97. Imelda's sanctity was officially confirmed in 1826, when she was beatified by Pope Leo XII.

38. *AASS* Mar. II, pp. 236–238.

39. See Vauchez, *La Sainteté*, fig. 13, for a fifteenth-century rendition of the young, paralyzed Fina on her deathbed. He places Fina in the category of local saints who were not canonized.

40. *AASS* Mar. II, pp. 235–42.

41. J. P. Migne, *Dictionnaire Hagiographique* (Paris, 1850), vol. 1, 31. His feast day is June 11.

42. *AASS* Sept. III, pp. 309–11.

43. Mattheus Rader, *Bavaria Sancta* (1615), vol. 2, pp. 334–37. An illustration of Agnes in devotion to the Eucharist appears on p. 335. The death of Agnes appeared to contemporaries to be fraught with religious significance. Her desire to escape marriage and remain in the convent, a normal reaction for a child of seven who had known no other life, turned her death into a miracle from God meant to preserve her virginity. The sores on her body were considered by some to be stigmata, although the appearance was described as more like pestilence. When her tomb was opened in 1375, the body was found to be incorrupt. Her beatification was approved in 1705, on the basis of the existing cult.

44. St. Pelagius, who was martyred by the Moslems ca. 925 for refusal to submit to the unnatural demands of Caliph Abd al-Rahman, as well as refusal to renounce Christianity, is the only other example of this claim I have found. Pelagius was immortalized in a roughly contemporary *passio, AASS* Jun. V, pp. 206–14, and in a poem by Hrotswitha of Gandersheim, *Passio Sancti Pelagii*.

45. "Un de ses parents." Migne, *Dictionnaire*, 2:272.

46. She is also known under the variants Reinheldis, Reinlidis, Reinhilde, and Sunte Rendel. *Bibliotheca Sanctorum* 11, 91.

47. Ibid. Perhaps in order to justify the validity of the cult, the legend was enhanced with hagiographical motifs found in other vitae of the region. Archaeological evidence for the cult is based on an epitaph dating from the late thirteenth or early fourteenth century preserved in the parish church of Reisenbeck, diocese of Munster. Because of the uncertain date of the vita, however, the presence or absence of pious behavior in the girl who became worshipped as a saint cannot be determined. Although the legend may only have been retrieved from oral form by the Jesuit M. Strunck in the eighteenth century, excavations at the church in 1809 at the site found no trace of bones, relics, or a tomb.

48. *AASS* Maii I, pp. 164–65.

49. Although perhaps established by popular veneration of the violently murdered child, the cult was undoubtedly promoted by the bishop of Novara,

who took a personal interest in the case and in the remains. According to the legend, the body of the child had become heavier than lead, and could not be moved until the arrival of the bishop. Under his direction, it was placed in a cart, and conducted to Quarona. Miracles followed the translation of the remains, and recognition of the sanctity of the child increased. Her tomb became a popular pilgrimage site, and she was invoked as an aid against epilepsy. In 1409, two chapels were built in her honor at Novarre. Her case was reviewed in 1593 by Clement VIII, and her cult was officially confirmed in 1867 by Pope Pius IX (*AASS* Maii I, pp. 164–65; *Bibliotheca Sanctorum* 10, 76).

50. This statement can be applied to the adult saints who supposedly exhibited such piety in childhood, as well as those who died in childhood. The inclusion of such anecdotes in the *vitae* of adult saints, who were primarily recognized for pious adult behavior, indicates popular interest in such themes.

51. This category would also include those legends of earlier murder victims rewritten in this period to add or emphasize pious behavior on the part of the victim. Such cases were not anomalies in the annals of hagiography for this period; several other cases of innocent death avenged through popular veneration also occurred. Radegund of Augsburg, a servant girl torn apart by wolves in the thirteenth century at whose tomb myriad cures were recognized, was venerated as a holy virgin and linked with devotion to St. Ursula. Margaret of Louvain was killed by robbers along with her employer and his wife, who were innkeepers. Her legend stated that she was vowed to perpetual virginity and had intended to embrace the religious life. See Vauchez, *La Sainteté*, pp. 174–75. St. Belina was a twelfth-century peasant girl of Troyes who died resisting a rape attempt by a local noble and was honored as a virgin martyr (*AASS* Sept. III, p. 259). Although their characters were honored with the reputation of piety in later legends, the elements of their stories more closely conform to the practice of popular veneration of violent death seen with greater frequency in the early medieval period. At most, such legends illustrate the continuing difficulty faced by the medieval papacy on exerting control over popular manifestations of religious impulses.

52. Simon of Trent, the only ritual murder victim to be formally canonized and included in the Roman Martyrology, was only removed from the sphere of popular worship in 1974.

53. Augustus Jessopp and Montague Rhodes James, ed. and trans., *The Life and Miracles of St. William of Norwich, by Thomas of Monmouth* (Cambridge: Cambridge University Press, 1896), pp. 64–65.

54. Ibid., p. 96.

55. Ibid., p. 59.

56. Lourdes, Fatima, Czestokowa, and Medjugorge. Bernadette Soubirous, who lived to the age of thirty-five, was canonized in 1933.

57. Msgr. Joseph Cirricione, "The Venerable Jacinta Marto of Fatima" (Rockford, Ill.: TAN Books and Publishers, 1992), pp. 44–45.

58. The cult of Maria Goretti, easily comprehensible in medieval terms, is frequently puzzling to modern American Catholics. At the conference at which this paper was first given, a female discussant at one session expressed

outrage over the canonization of Maria. "What kind of role model is she?" she asked. This question brings to mind an incident related by a female student in one of my classes on popular religion at Ithaca College. The student, who had attended an all-female Catholic high school in southeastern Pennsylvania, told me that, on the day of the senior prom, the principal announced on the PA system that all the students should pray to St. Maria Goretti. "But," the student said, "they never told us why."

7. Elizabeth Leseur

1. Peter Brown, *The Cult of the Saints: Its Rise and Function in Latin Christianity* (Chicago: University of Chicago Press, 1983); Pierre Delooz, *Sociologie et Canonisations* (Liège: Faculte de droit, 1969); Michael P. Goodich, *Vita Perfecta: The Ideal of Sainthood in the Thirteenth Century,* Monographien zur Geschichte des Mittelalters 25 (Stuttgart: Hiersemann, 1982); André Vauchez, *La Sainteté en Occident aux derniers siècles du moyen âge d'aprés les procés de canonisation et les documents hagiographiques,* Bibliothèque des études fançaises d'Athènes et de Rome 241 (Rome: École Française de Rome, 1981); Donald Weinstein and Rudolph M. Bell, *Saints and Society: The Two Worlds of Western Christendom, 1000–1700* (Chicago: University of Chicago Press, 1982); and Stephen Wilson, ed., *Saints and Their Cults: Studies in Religious Sociology, Folklore and History* (Cambridge: Cambridge University Press, 1983) represent the scholarly historians on this subject. Among the theologians are: Lawrence Cunningham, *The Meaning of the Saints* (San Francisco: Harper and Row, 1981); Christian Duquoc and Casiano Floristan, eds., *Models of Holiness,* Concilium 129 (New York: Seabury Press, 1979); Karl Rahner, "The Church of the Saints," *Theology in the Spiritual Life, Theological Investigations* 3 (Baltimore: Helicon, 1960).

2. Kenneth L. Woodward cites these statistics: "Between the year 1000 and the end of 1987, popes held 303 canonizations, including group causes. Of these saints, only 56 were laymen and 20 were laywomen. Moreover, of the 63 lay saints whose state of life is known for certain, more than half never married. And most of these lay saints were martyred, either individually or as members of a group" (*Making Saints: How the Catholic Church Determines Who Becomes a Saint, Who Doesn't and Why* [New York: Simon and Schuster, 1990], p. 336).

3. Cunningham, *Meaning of the Saints,* p. 19.

4. She is included in Hilda Graef, *Mystics of Our Times* (New York: Hanover House, 1962), pp. 107–26.

5. Felix petitioned Rome to begin the process of beatification in 1936. According to Verbillon, all went well with the cause until 1941, but then, perhaps because of the war, the bishop of Besancon failed to call a hearing of witnesses at Jougne. In 1950 Felix died. An attempt was made in June 1955 to reopen the process, but that occurred only much later, in 1990. See June Verbillon, "The Silent Apostolate of Elizabeth Leseur," *Cross and Crown* 11 (1959): 43.

6. Elizabeth Leseur, *A Wife's Story: The Journal of Elizabeth Leseur with an*

Introduction by Her Husband, trans. V. M. (New York: Benziger, 1919), p. 43. Subsequent citations are parenthetical by abbreviated title (*Journal*) and page.

7. A full-length study is devoted to this theme: A. M. Rulla, *La communione de santi nel pensiero di Elisabetta Leseur* (Paris, 1935).

8. Elisabeth Leseur, *Lettres sur la souffrance* (Paris: Gigord, 1919), p. 157; translation mine. Subsequent citations are parenthetical by abbreviated title and page.

9. Quoted by Felix Leseur in his introduction to *A Wife's Story,* p. 27.

10. *The Dialogues of Catherine of Siena* are full of this theme; e.g., "The sufferings you endure will, through the power of charity, suffice to win both atonement and reward for you and for others" (trans. Suzanne Noffke, Classics of Western Spirituality [Mahwah: Paulist Press, 1980], p. 30).

11. For support for this view, see Joanne Wolski Conn, *Spirituality and Personal Maturity* (Mahwah: Paulist Press, 1989), chap. 3 and p. 115.

12. Wendy Wright summarizes the pattern advocated by de Sales: "The devout wife of the courtier will move modestly attired among garish finery, attend dances and theatre without attachment to the frivolity and licentiousness that sometimes accompany these diversions, fast on prescribed days but otherwise eat moderately of foods set before her, pray fervently but only as often and as long as the discharge of her familial duties recommends, cultivate friendships that are based on mutual religious aspirations and practice the unobtrusive virtues of meekness, temperance, integrity and humility" (in Wendy Wright and Joseph Powers, ed., *Francis de Sales, Jane de Chantal: Letters of Spiritual Direction,* Classics of Western Spirituality [Mahwah: Paulist Press, 1988], p. 56). See Francis de Sales, *Introduction to the Devout Life,* trans. John Ryan (Garden City: Image Books, 1966), p. 44, and Part III.

13. "A Little Treatise on the Life of a Christian Woman, Composed by Elizabeth Leseur for Her Niece Marie on the Occasion of Her First Communion" and "A Little Treatise on the Christian Life Written by Elizabeth Leseur for Her Nephew, André D—— at His First Communion," included in *The Spiritual Life: A Collection of Short Treatises on the Inner Life by Elizabeth Leseur,* trans. A. M. Buchanan (London: Burnes, Oates, Washbourne, 1922). André was her godson. Before her death in 1905, Elizabeth's sister Juliette asked Elizabeth to accept in her stead the responsibility of being godmother for Marie.

14. See *Journal,* pp. 111–20.

15. *My Spirit Rejoices: The Diary of a Christian Soul in an Age of Unbelief* (Manchester, N.H.: Sophia Institute Press, 1996). I quote from the Press's Christmas catalogue, 1997. The back cover of the book declares, "Here you'll discover a path to holiness mapped—and then walked with quiet grace—by a good woman in circumstances like your own."

16. "Decree on the Apostolate of the Laity," in *The Documents of Vatican II,* ed. Walter M. Abbott, S.J., and Msgr. Joseph Gallagher (Baltimore: The America Press, 1966), I.2, pp. 491–92.

17. It is regrettable that key witnesses to Elizabeth's sanctity were not called to give testimony during their lifetimes. See Weinstein and Bell, *Saints*

and Society, as well as Woodward, *Making Saints,* p. 118, for reasons why the politics of canonization have seldom favored the laity.

8. Gertraud von Bullion

1. John Stratton Hawley, Introduction, in *Saints and Virtues,* ed. John S. Hawley (Berkeley: University of California Press, 1987), p. xviii. Gertraud's ancestors include Bd. Ida of Boulogne (†1113), the mother of the crusader king of Jerusalem, Godfrey of Bouillon, and Don Fernando de Bullones, better known as St. Anthony of Padua (†1231). Gertraud's family had a special devotion to their "cousin," St. Anthony; Gertraud decorated his altar in the parish church; and she was buried on his feastday, June 13, in 1930. Founded on October 18, 1914, Schoenstatt, too, aspires to be a "family of saints." Karl Leisner (†1945), a member of Schoenstatt and a young martyr-priest of Dachau, was beatified in 1996. Other Schoenstatters are currently being considered for beatification—notably Joseph Engling (†1918), Gertraud von Bullion (†1930), Father Franz Reinisch (†1941), Sister Maria Emilie Engel (†1955), Brother Mario Hiriat (†1964), John Pozzobon (†1985), and Father Joseph Kentenich (†1968), the founder of Schoenstatt. Here and throughout I use the English spelling of "Schönstatt."

2. See Margret Simon, "Gertraud of Bullion: Instrument of a New Beginning," in *Gertraud of Bullion: The Celebration of her 100th Birthday,* trans. Jean Frisk, privately published for the Schoenstatt movement (Waukesha, 1992), p. 11.

3. Quoted by G. Birkle in "Gertraud of Bullion: Seed For New Life," trans. Maria Kleimeyer, in *100th Birthday,* p. 18.

4. Gertraud von Bullion, *Aus ihren Briefen und Schriften* (Neuwied: Neuwieder Verlagsgesellschaft mbH, 1981), p. 466: "Mutter, wenn ich eine Heilige werden soll, so gib, daß neimand es merkt und ich es am allerwenigsten." Hereafter I cite parenthetically by page from this edition. The translations are mine.

5. Dogmatic Constitution on the Church *(Lumen Gentium),* in *The Documents of Vatican II,* ed. Walter M. Abbott, S.J., and Joseph Gallagher (Baltimore: The America Press, 1966), chap. 4, sec. 31, pp. 57–58; emphasis mine.

6. Decree on the Apostolate of the Laity, in *Documents,* chap. 1 sec. 2, p. 492; chap. 2 sec. 7, p. 498. The emphasis again is mine.

7. John D. Gerken, S.J., *Toward a Theology of the Layman* (New York: Herder and Herder, 1963), p. 98.

8. Ibid., p. 102. Gerken argues for a Christian existential ethic and the morally obligatory nature of a vocation, once it has been recognized.

9. C. A. Schleck, "Vocations," in *The New Catholic Encyclopedia* (Washington, D.C.: Catholic University of America, 1967).

10. Karl Rahner, S.J., "Notes on the Lay Apostolate," in *Theological Investigations* 2, trans. Karl-H. and Boniface Kruger (Baltimore: Helicon, 1967), pp. 319–52, esp. p. 336.

11. Ibid., pp. 340, 323.

12. Ibid., p. 340.

13. The Decree on the Apostolate of the Laity points to Mary as "the perfect example" of the lay apostolate: "While leading on earth a life common to all men, one filled with family concerns and labors, she was always intimately united with her Son and cooperated in the work of the Savior in a manner altogether special" (chap. 1, sec. 4, p. 495).

14. The belief that Mary has "descended" into the shrine, "taken possession" of it, and acts from it in response to the explicit invitation and serious striving of her children is part of the so-called "Schoenstatt secret." This "local attachment" to the original shrine in Germany's Rhine Valley near Coblenz has extended itself historically through the multiplication of replica shrines throughout the world, the growth of Schoenstatt centers on six continents, the dedication of home shrines (in a concrete realization of the "domestic Church"), and the visits of the Pilgrim MTA to millions of homes through the International Schoenstatt Rosary Campaign.

15. For information about the life of Gertraud von Bullion, I am indebted to Nikolaus Lauer's biography of her, *Serviam: Antwort der Liebe* (Schönstatt: Schönstatt-Verlag, 1932; repr. 1991). I thank Margret Simon of the Schönstatt-Frauenbund for her generous assistance in my research.

16. Mary Ward (†1646) is often ranked with St. Vincent de Paul as a promoter of the lay apostolate. Her innovative foundation was suppressed during her lifetime and received official papal approval only in 1877.

17. Quoted in Lauer, *Serviam*, p. 20. Translation mine.

18. Schoenstatt had been founded only shortly before, on October 18, 1914, when Father Kentenich and a group of boys who were students at the Pallottine minor seminary near Vallendar/Coblenz made a "Covenant of Love" with the Mother of God in a small shrine that served as a meeting place for the Marian Sodality. They invited Mary to transform the shrine into a place of pilgrimage where she herself would be "present" and apostolically active through the distribution of graces. To show the sincerity of their invitation, they pledged their practical striving for holiness and their willingness to be used by her as instruments for the renewal of the world in Christ. This pledge was fulfilled in an often heroic way on the battlefields of World War I. There the ideals of Schoenstatt spread through the ranks of the soldiers and army nurses. When Hitler later rose to power, Schoenstatt was a well-known movement of renewal within the church in Germany, and the Gestapo singled out its leaders for persecution and arrest. During Father Kentenich's imprisonment in the concentration camp at Dachau, the movement became international.

19. ". . . nicht Eigenbrötelei, sondern Gerhorsam war einer Gnadenanregung gegenüber, die große persönliche Opfer von Ihnen verlangte." Father Kentenich's letter to Gertraud and his remarks about her life are included in *Aus ihren Briefen*, pp. 10–13. The entire letter, from which I quote here and immediately hereafter, is found on p. 10. Father Kentenich was thirty-five years old when Gertraud first wrote to him; she, twenty-six.

20. Father Kentenich defined the personal idea philosophically in Platonic terms as *idea praeexistens in mente divina*. By it he meant that a particular

"thought" of God stands behind the creation of every individual, who is brought into existence as an original, unique reflection of Christ the Logos, "through whom all things were made" (cf. John 1:3). The individual can, to a certain extent, come to recognize this ideal image of himself or herself and actively cooperate in actualizing it through conformity to God's wish and will in daily life. In psychological terms, this means directing the predominant passions of the affective soul-life toward the achievement of a "favorite thought" that expresses (albeit imperfectly) the core of the personality in its fundamental orientation toward God.

21. This shift in emphasis from doing to being is in accord with the basic Thomistic principle oft quoted by Father Kentenich: "The order of being determines the order of acting." Karl Rahner, S.J., has expressed the same thought in these words: "Since the structure of a being is the objective and given norm of its operation, it therefore belongs to the moral obligation of man to be and become by free choice that individual that he is" (*Gefahren im heutigen Katholizismus* [Einielden: Benziger, 1950], p. 20; quoted in Gerken, *Toward a Theology,* p. 108).

9. Raissa and Jacques Maritain

1. Raissa Maritain, *Raissa's Journal,* presented by Jacques Maritain, trans. Antonia White (Albany: Magi Books, 1974), pp. 79–80 (cited hereafter as *Journal*), and *We Have Been Friends Together* and *Adventures in Grace: The Memoirs of Raissa Maritain,* trans. Julie Kernan (Garden City: Image Books, Doubleday, 1961), p. 120 (cited hereafter as *Memoirs*).

2. Jacques Maritain, *Notebooks,* trans. Joseph W. Evans (Albany: Magi Books, 1984), p. 129.

3. Cf. Jacques and Raissa Maritain, *Prayer and Intelligence,* trans. Algar Thorold (New York: Sheed and Ward, 1943), pp. 3–4. Cited hereafter as *Prayer.*

4. All the books they had read stressed the importance of having a spiritual director. Cf. *Notebooks,* p. 68; *Memoirs,* p. 175.

5. *Webster's New International Dictionary of the English Language.* 2d ed., unabridged, vol. 1 (Springfield: Merriam-Webster, 1974), p. 574, col. 3. The adjective "passive" is unfortunate, suggesting as it does a state of passivity, of inactivity or idleness. But, in fact, Dom Butler says that the "perfect" contemplatives, who experience the higher mystic states and extraordinary contemplation, are those who "in the midst of business *can keep the mind in singleness and fixed on God*" (*Western Mysticism,* p. 134; quoted in Kenneth E. Kirk, *The Vision of God* (New York: Harper Torchbooks, 1966), p. 580. Cf. *Journal,* pp. 358–59.

6. The *Peasant of the Garonne* (New York: Holt, Rhinehart, and Winston, 1968), p. 220. Translation by Michael Cuddihy and Elizabeth Hughes of *Le Paysan de la Garonne: Un vieux laïe s'interroge à propos du temps présent* (Desclée De Brouwer, 1966). Cited hereafter as *Peasant.*

7. There are those who would limit infused contemplation to the few who are given such extraordinary graces; others do not see the latter as essential to it. Cf. James Arraj, *Mysticism, Metaphysics and Maritain* (Chiloquin, Ore.:

Inner Growth Books, 1993), pp. 140–41. However, it is an issue with which any book on mystical theology is forced to deal; the literature on it is enormous. Cf. Kirk, *Vision of God,* cited in n. 5 above.

8. Translated, respectively, by Marshall Suther (New York: Philosophical Library, 1955) and Joseph W. Evans (New York: Kenedy, 1960); the latter cited hereafter as *Liturgy.*

9. *Notes on the Lord's Prayer,* arranged and edited by Jacques Maritain. Trans. from the French (New York: Kenedy, 1964), p. 13. Hereafter cited as *Notes.*

10. *Peasant,* pp. 197–98; Cf. Kirk, *Vision of God,* pp. 517–34.

11. In *Notebooks,* p. 247, n. 1, Jacques states, "The book is by the two of us, but it was Raissa who wrote this page."

12. Cf. *Notebooks,* p. 247; *Journal,* p. 366; *Liturgy,* pp. 33–35. Quoting from the last-mentioned book, Jacques in *Peasant* describes the second group as perhaps being able to only recite rosaries—any attempt at wordless prayer merely giving them a headache or making them sleepy. Cf. p. 231.

13. For an English translation, see *The Fruits of Contemplation* (St. Louis: Herder, 1953).

14. Cassian, IX, 31 (Cf. *Dictionnaire de Spiritualité,* article on contemplation, cols. 1924 and 1926).

15. In *Guidelines for Mystical Prayer* (Denville, N.J.: Dimension Books, 1978), Ruth Burrows makes a similar distinction, naming the arid form "light out" and the consoling form "light on." I am grateful to Dr. Janet Ruffing, R.S.M., for calling my attention to this book.

16. These are: "(1) meditation becomes unfeasible; (2) the soul has no desire to fix the imagination on any particular object, interior or exterior; (3) the soul is pleased to find itself alone with God, fixing its affectionate attention on him" (n. 107). Cf. R. P. Garrigou-Lagrange, *Perfection Chrétienne et Contemplation* 2, pp. 421–22.

17. Maritain speaks of it as taking place "in the depths of the supra-conscious of the spirit" (*Peasant,* p. 230). On the supra-conscious of the spirit, cf. *Mysticism,* pp. 86ff.

18. *Sum. theol.* I–II, 68, 5.

19. In *Liturgy,* Jacques and Raissa insist that although open contemplation seems always linked to high perfection, it does not follow that one whose contemplation is masked is less perfect (p. 46). But in *Peasant* (p. 231), Jacques speaks of Wisdom, Understanding, and Knowledge as "the highest gifts." St. Thomas also ranks them, in *Sum. theol.* I–II, 68, 6, as "more excellent"—though he includes counsel also in this group—which seems to imply that open contemplation *is* "higher" than the masked form. Hence, with respect to the latter, a certain lack of clarity persists. In *Mysticism,* James Arraj comments that, at the time Maritain was writing *Peasant,* he was "like a scout who had gone exploring in an uncharted land and left indications of some of the important landmarks without having the energy and opportunity, because of his great age, to cover the terrain in detail" (p. 90).

20. The French is *amour fou.* Both types of love are disinterested, i.e., love-for-the-good-itself-of-the-beloved; both involve the gift of self. But in friendship

the emphasis is on giving what one *has*—which may go so far as the giving of one's life—whereas in love, one gives what one *is* (*Notebooks*, p. 220).

21. For a beautifully written and very moving account of a young couple's mad, boundless love for each other and its transformation, see Sheldon Vanauken, *A Severe Mercy* (San Francisco: Harper, 1980).

22. Jacques defines this as "a state in which human life and human conduct are ordinarily aided by the invisible and very secret *inspiration* of God" (*Notebooks*, p. 230, n. 1).

23. Jacques adds (*Notebooks*, p. 249, n. 1), p. 249, n.1, "that certain spouses can decide on such a renunciation by reason of a particular and entirely personal call . . . is an altogether different question." Raissa and Jacques did so decide, vowing chastity in 1912. Concerning this, Raissa writes: "We decided to turn our lives more definitely towards the work of contemplation and to sacrifice to this quest many of those things and hopes that are normal in the life of the world" (*Memoirs*, p. 339). Jacques is more explicit: "It was after taking long counsel . . . that by mutual agreement we decided to renounce a thing which in marriage fulfills not only a deep need of the human being—both of body and of spirit—but is lawful and good in itself, and at the same time we renounced the hope of being survived by sons and daughters. . . . It implied no scorn for nature, but in our course towards the absolute . . . we wanted to clear the way completely for our search for contemplation and union with God, and for this precious pearl to sell other goods of great value in themselves." Quoted by Julie Kernan in *Our Friend Jacques Maritain* (Garden City: Doubleday, 1975), pp. 46–47. Cf. Judith Suther, *Raissa Maritain, Pilgrim, Poet, Exile* (New York: Fordham University Press, 1990) p. 30; p. 37, n. 1.

24. Jacques specifies this as "family duties and vocational duties, Mass on Sundays, cooperation in some apostolic work, the desire to help one's neighbor as much as possible, and a few moments of vocal prayer at home" (*Peasant*, p. 233).

25. *Peasant*, p. 236.

26. He observes, perceptively, that women are, today, even more burdened than men. Due to the absence of domestic help, they are enslaved to the mechanical gadgets which "enable" them to manage without such help (*Peasant*, p. 239).

10. Dorothy Day

1. See Richard Kieckhefer, "Imitators of Christ: Sainthood in the Christian Tradition," in *Sainthood: Its Manifestations in World Religions*, ed. Richard Kieckhefer and George D. Bond (Berkeley: University of California Press, 1988), esp. pp. 12–17. Jesuit theologian Karl Rahner has complicated this basic dichotomy from a juridical and theological perspective by arguing that laypeople living evangelical poverty and/or engaged full-time in charitable works and parish ministries do so, not as laypersons per se, but rather as "extensions" of the hierarchy and as participants in the official hierarchical apostolate. See his "Notes on the Lay Apostolate," in *Theological Investigations* 2,

trans. Karl-H. and Boniface Kruger (Baltimore: Helicon, 1967), pp. 319–52. Rahner's attempt to clarify the "apostolate of the laity" effectively redefines it more narrowly than most would accept.

2. Edith Wyschogrod, *Saints and Postmodernism: Revisioning Moral Philosophy* (Chicago: The University of Chicago Press, 1990), p. 255.

3. For a discussion of the relative evaluation of the cataphatic and apophatic ways, see Peter Pellegrin's essay on Margery Kempe in this same volume.

4. See Daniel Di Domizio, "The Prophetic Spirituality of the Catholic Worker," in *Revolution of the Heart: Essays on the Catholic Worker,* ed. Patrick G. Coy (Philadelphia: New Society Publishers, 1988), pp. 217–38; Mel Piehl, *Breaking Bread: The Catholic Worker and the Origin of Catholic Radicalism in America* (Philadelphia: Temple University Press, 1982).

5. Wyschogrod emphasizes that "the saintly desire for the Other is excessive and wild. In traditional Christian theological language, the saint desires not only the welfare of the Other, the cessation of another's suffering, but also the Other's beatitude" (*Saints and Postmodernism,* p. 255). Wyschogrod defines sainthood in a way that includes theists "like Dorothy Day and Mother Teresa," but also "saints" outside of "specifiable theological and institutional frameworks" (pp. 34–35).

6. John A. Coleman, S.J., "Conclusion: After Sainthood?" in *Saints and Virtues,* ed. John Stratton Hawley (Berkeley: University of California Press, 1987), p. 223. Coleman argues that "for modern hagiography and perhaps uncanonizable saints we must turn either to . . . fictional characters [such as we find in the works of Graham Greene, Iris Murdock, Flannery O'Connor and Ignazio Stone] or to uncanonized saints such as Dorothy Day, Thomas Merton, Dag Hammarskjöld, Simone Weil, Dietrich Bonhoeffer, or Etty Hillesum."

7. Wyschogrod, *Saints and Postmodernism,* p. 152.

8. For information about Dorothy Day's life, I rely mainly on *The Long Loneliness: An Autobiography* (San Francisco: Harper and Row, 1952), which includes an introduction by Daniel Berrigan. Subsequent quotations from this work are cited parenthetically by title *(LL)* and page. For other accounts of Day's life, see William Miller, *A Harsh and Dreadful Love* (New York: Liveright, 1973); *Dorothy Day: A Biography* (San Francisco: Harper and Row, 1983). The early history of the Catholic Worker movement is most fully treated in Dorothy Day, *House of Hospitality* (New York: Sheed and Ward, 1939).

9. Dorothy Day, *From Union Square to Rome* (Silver Spring, Md.: Preservation of the Faith Press, 1938), pp. 19–20. See also *The Long Loneliness,* p. 20.

10. Dorothy Day, *The Eleventh Virgin* (New York: Albert and Charles Beni, 1924), pp. 8–10; also referred to in Day, *Union Square,* pp. 18–24; *The Long Loneliness,* pp. 19–22.

11. Day, *From Union Square,* pp. 98–108.

12. Ibid., p. 121.

13. Ibid., p. 122. See also Day, *The Long Loneliness,* pp. 132–33.

14. This double baptism—Episcopalian and Catholic—sounds strange to Catholics in the post–Vatican II church, which recognizes the validity of Christian baptism in other denominations.

15. See Dorothy Day, "Maurin's Program," *Catholic Worker* (June–July 1933): 4, and Peter Maurin, "Early Essays," *Catholic Worker* (June–July 1933): 1; "To the Bishops of the U.S.: A Plea for Houses of Hospitality," *Catholic Worker* (October 1933): 1.

16. Day, *House of Hospitality,* p. 241: "When we succeed in persuading our readers to take the homeless into their homes, having a Christ-room in the house as St. Jerome said, then we will be known as Christians because of the way we love one another. We should have hospices in all the poor parishes. We should have coffee lines to take care of the transients; we should have the help we give sweetened by mutual forebearance and Christian charity. But we need more Christian homes where the poor are sheltered and cared for."

17. See Dorothy Day, "Room for Christ," *Catholic Worker* 12 (December 1945): 2; Jean Danielou, S.J., "Toward a Theology of Hospitality," *Catholic Worker* 18 (June 1952): 4.

18. Dorothy Day, "Notes by the Way," *Catholic Worker* 12 (December 1945): 1. For a development of the theme of voluntary poverty, see Day, "The Scandal of Mercy," *Commonweal* 51 (1949): 99–102.

19. Day, *House of Hospitality,* p. 155.

20. See Wyschogrod's treatment of the saint's body as a *sensorium* in *Saints and Postmodernism,* pp. 14–19.

21. Dorothy Day, "Room for Christ," *Catholic Worker* 12 (January 1946): 2.

22. Ibid. See also Dorothy Day, "Poverty Is the Face of Christ," *Catholic Worker* 18 (December 1952): 6.

23. Dorothy Day, "On Pilgrimage," *Catholic Worker* 15 (May 1948): 3; "The Council and the Mass," *Catholic Worker* 29 (September 1962): 2; and "They Knew Him in the Breaking of the Bread," *Catholic Worker* 4 (February 1937): 1. See also Bridget O'Shea Merriman, O.S.F., *Searching for Christ: The Spirituality of Dorothy Day* (Notre Dame: The University of Notre Dame Press, 1994), esp. p. 98.

24. Day, *House of Hospitality,* pp. 78–79. For further discussion of the short-age of rations, see *Long Loneliness,* p. 216, and *House of Hospitality,* p. 158.

25. Wyschogrod, *Saints and Postmodernism,* p. 256.

26. Ibid., p. 13.

27. Jon Sobrino, "Political Holiness: A Profile," in *Martyrdom Today,* trans. Dinah Livingstone, *Concilium,* vol. 163, ed. Johannes-Baptist Metz and Edward Schillebeeckx (New York: Seabury Press, 1983), pp. 18–23.

28. Cf. Wyschogrod's somewhat different discussion of "political saints" like Nelson Mandela, wherein she raises the question of whether genuine saint-hood is possible in a "political sphere already contaminated by relations of power" and dependent on violence (*Saints and Postmodernism,* pp. 150–55).

29. Wyschogrod, *Saints and Postmodernism,* p. 256.

11. Chiara Lubich

1. Chiara Lubich, "A Collective Way," *Living City* 24.4 (April 1985): 2.

2. Ibid., p. 3. Lubich refers specifically to *The Imitation of Christ,* book I, chapter 20, where à Kempis observes, "As often as I have been among men I have returned less a man."

3. Lubich, *Meditations* (New York: New City Press, 1986), p. 9.

4. See Lubich's address upon receiving the Italian Catholic Publishers' Guild Author of the Year Award in Milan; published in translation as "The Key Ideas of a Collective Spirituality," *Living City* 34.6 (June 1995): 13–19.

5. Ibid., p. 17. Lubich quotes from Karl Rahner, "Elementi di spiritualita nella Chiesa del futuro," in *Problemi e prospettive di spiritualita,* ed. T. Goffi and B. Secondin (Brescia, 1983), pp. 440–41.

6. Edwin Robertson, *Chiara* (Ireland: Christian Journals, 1978), pp. 10–11.

7. Lubich, *May They All Be One: Origins and Life of the Focolare Movement* (New York: New City Press, 1984), p. 31.

8. Ibid.

9. Lubich, "Un po' di Storia," manuscript, p. 7. I thank Adele Colella for help in translating this and other sources from the Italian.

10. Lubich, *May They All Be One,* p. 33.

11. Ibid.

12. Ibid., p. 32.

13. Lubich, "Letter to 'Carissimo Fratello in Gesu'," May 11, 1948; quoted in Judith M. Povilus, *United in His Name: Jesus in the Midst in the Experience and Thought of Chiara Lubich* (New York: New City Press, 1992), p. 51.

14. Lubich, "Recording at Grottaferrata, Italy," March 21, 1964; quoted in Povilus, *United in His Name,* p. 52.

15. Lubich, *May They All Be One,* p. 52.

16. See Lubich, *Unity and Jesus Forsaken* (New York: New City Press, 1985).

17. Lubich, *May They All Be One,* p. 68.

18. Lubich, "Letter to 'Carissime Sorelline'," January 2, 1945; quoted in Povilus, *United in His Name,* p. 72.

19. For a useful treatment of the general tradition, see Richard Kieckhefer, "Imitators of Christ: Sainthood in the Christian Tradition," in *Sainthood: Its Manifestations in World Religions,* ed. Richard Kieckhefer and George D. Bond (Berkeley: University of California Press, 1988), pp. 1–42.

20. *Bulletin of the Pontifical Council for the Laity,* no. 26 (1979): 79.

21. Lubich, *The Word of Life* (New York: New City Press, 1975), p. 89. Here Lubich echoes St. Paul: "This is the will of God, your sanctification" (1 Thess. 4:3).

22. Ibid., p. 88.

23. Ibid., p. 90.

24. Francis de Sales, *Treatise on the Love of God,* VIII, 7.

25. Lubich, *May They All Be One,* p. 37.

26. Ibid., p. 38.

27. Ibid., p. 40.

28. *Bulletin of the Pontifical Council for the Laity,* p. 81.

29. Lubich, *May They All Be One,* p. 35.

30. Klaus Hemerle, "Quale Profilo del Laico," *GENS* 18.1 (January 1988): 7.

31. Lubich, "A Collective Way," p. 4.

32. Quoted in Lubich, *Unity and Jesus Forsaken,* pp. 11–12. Jesus Cervera, O.C.D., is professor of spiritual theology at the Teresianum in Rome.

33. Ibid., p. 12. Lubich always insists that the individual's way to sanctity is never exclusively individual, because any charism within the church belongs to the church and thus necessarily has a collective dimension.

34. *Bulletin of the Pontifical Council for the Laity,* p. 79.

35. Lubich, *Meditations,* p. 9.

36. Quoted in Donald W. Mitchell, *Spirituality and Emptiness: The Dynamics of Spiritual Life in Buddhism and Christianity* (New York: Paulist Press, 1991), p. 32. See also my "Buddhist and Christian Postmodern Spiritualities," in *Divine Representations: Spirituality and Postmodernism,* ed. Ann W. Astell (New York: Paulist Press, 1994).

37. See *Bulletin of the Pontifical Council for the Laity,* p. 79.

38. Lubich, "Talk to the Synod of Bishops on the Vocation and Mission of the Laity," October 13, 1987; published in English as "Spiritualities and Movements," *Living City* 27.1 (January 1988): 4.

39. Lubich, "Talk at the Basilica of St. Mary Major in Rome, Italy," November 30, 1987, transcription, p. 2.

40. Ibid., p. 5.

41. Ibid.

42. Ibid., p. 8.

43. Lubich, "Spiritualities and Movements," p. 5.

44. Lubich, "Questions and Answers to the Volunteers and Extern Married Focolarini," February 25, 1981, at Castel Gandolfo, Italy, transcription, p. 5.

45. Lubich, "Is Holiness Compatible with Advancing One's Career?" *Living City,* 29. 6/7 (June/July 1990): 3.

46. Lubich, "Questions and Answers," p. 4.

47. Ibid., pp. 10, 11.

48. Lubich, "Is Holiness Compatible with Advancing One's Career?" p. 3.

49. Lubich, "Spiritualities and Movements," p. 5.

50. Lubich, "Questions and Answers," p. 15.

51. Ibid., p. 18. Here Lubich has in mind such Pauline passages as "Whatever you do, do everything for the glory of God" (1 Cor. 10:31).

52. Lubich, "Is Holiness Compatible with Advancing One's Career?" p. 3.

53. Lubich, "Questions and Answers," p. 18.

54. Lubich, "Talk to the Superior Generals," May 29, 1987, at Frascati, Italy, transcription, p. 14.

55. Lubich, "Conference Call to Her Communities," December 11, 1986, from Rocca di Pappa, Italy, transcription, p. 1.

56. Lubich, "Talk at the Basilica of St. Mary Major," p. 11.

57. Ibid, p. 12.

58. See Lubich, *Unity and Jesus Forsaken.*

59. Lubich, "Talk to the Superior Generals," pp. 4–5.

60. Lubich, *Meditations,* p. 9.

CONTRIBUTORS

ANN W. ASTELL received her Ph.D. from the University of Wisconsin-Madison in 1987. A medievalist, she is professor of English at Purdue University. Her publications include *The Song of Songs in the Middle Ages* (1990), *Job, Boethius, and Epic Truth* (1994), *Chaucer and the Universe of Learning* (1996), and *Political Allegory in Late-Medieval England* (1999), all from Cornell University Press, as well as an edited collection of essays, *Divine Representations: Postmodernism and Spirituality* (Mahwah, N.J.: Paulist Press, 1994).

MARY WALSH MEANY is associate professor and former chair of religious studies at Siena College. Her research has focused on Franciscan spirituality, the *Vita Christi* tradition, and various women mystics, especially Catherine of Siena, Julian of Norwich, and Angela of Foligno.

DONALD W. MITCHELL is professor of Asian and comparative philosophy in the Department of Philosophy at Purdue University and director of the Religious Studies Program there. He is on the executive board of the Society for Buddhist-Christian Studies and is associate editor of its journal, *Buddhist-Christian Studies.* Mitchell received his Ph.D. from the University of Hawaii. He is author of *Spirituality and Emptiness: The Dynamics of Spiritual Life in Buddhism and Christianity* (Mahwah, N.J.: Paulist Press, 1991), as well as numerous articles, and the coeditor of *The Gethsemane Encounter: A Dialogue on the Spiritual Life by Buddhist and Christian Monastics* (New York: Continuum, 1997).

ASTRID O'BRIEN is associate professor in the philosophy program at Fordham University-Lincoln Center. Her scholarly interests lie in medieval philosophy, especially the philosophy of Thomas Aquinas, and in spirituality; she has published articles in both areas. She is currently seeking access to the family records and journals of Lucie-Christine, a married mystic of the nineteenth century, in order to write her biography.

PETER J. PELLEGRIN received his Ph.D. in 1999 from the University of Southwestern Louisiana. His dissertation, "'Þis Creatur': Margery

Kempe's Pursuit of Spiritual Virginity," empahsizes the *imitatio Mariae* in *The Book of Margery Kempe.*

JANET RUFFING, R.S.M., is an associate professor of spirituality and spiritual direction in the Graduate School of Religion and Religious Education at Fordham University. A member of the Sisters of Mercy of the Americas, she received her Ph.D. in Christian Spirituality in 1986 from the Graduate Theological Union, Berkeley, California. A founding member of the coordinating council of Spiritual Directors International, Ruffing is the author of *Uncovering Stories of Faith: Spiritual Direction and Narrative* (Mahwah, N.J.: Paulist Press, 1989). She is presently editing a collection on "Mysticism and Social Transformation."

KAREN SCOTT received her Ph.D. from the University of California-Berkeley in 1989 and is presently associate professor of history at DePaul University. She has published six major articles on St. Catherine of Siena and is now completing a book-length study of the saint in her ecclesial context.

MARY S. SKINNER received a Ph.D. in history from Syracuse University in 1977 and a master's degree in theological studies from the Weston School of Theology in 1989. Currently a faculty member at SUNY-Empire State College in Rochester and Corning, she is finishing a book-length study of historical women's spirituality.

KRISTINE T. UTTERBACK is associate professor of history at the University of Wyoming. Her publications include *Pastoral Care and Administration of Souls in Mid-Fourteenth-Century Barcelona: Excercising the Art of Arts* (Lewiston, N.Y.: Edwin Mellen, 1993). She is presently completing a book on medieval women's pilgrimage and spirituality, called "On the Road to God: Medieval Women and Pilgrimage, 1000–1500."

PATRICIA MARY VINJE received her Ph.D. in historical theology and spirituality from Marquette University in 1982. Her revised dissertation, *An Understanding of Love According to the Anchoress Julian of Norwich,* was published by the University of Salzburg in 1983. Her book, *Praying with Catherine of Siena,* was published in English (1990) and Korean (1996) by St. Mary's Press. She is at work on a book-length study of the history and theology of consecrated virgins and hermits.

PATRICIA HEALY WASYLIW is associate professor of history at Ithaca College. She completed her Ph.D. in 1993 at SUNY-Binghamton, with a dissertation entitled "Martyrdom, Magic and Murder: Child Saints and Their Cults in Medieval Europe."

Index

World War II, 22–23, 175, 225 n.18

Wright, Wendy, 223 n.12

Wyschogrod, Edith, 22, 64, 161–62, 171–72, 197 n.67, 229 n.5, 230 nn.20, 28

Z

Zdislava of Bohemia, Blessed, 12

Zeppenfeld, Alois, 135

Zita, Saint, 11